omrade or Brother?

Comrade or Brother?

A History of the British Labour Movement 1789–1951

Mary Davis

Pluto Press

LONDON • BOULDER, COLORADO

First published 1993 by Pluto Press
345 Archway Road, London N6 5AA
and 5500 Central Avenue
Boulder, Colorado 80301, USA

British Library Cataloguing in Publication Data
A catalogue record for this book is available from
the British Library

ISBN 0 7453 0760 4 hbk
ISBN 0 7453 0761 2 pbk

Designed and Produced for Pluto Press by
Chase Production Services, Chipping Norton.
Typeset from author's disks by
Stanford Desktop Publishing Services, Milton Keynes.
Printed in the EC by T J Press, Padstow

To my mother, Celia Davis (née Yampolsky) for the past and the present and for the rich heritage bequeathed to me by the once large Yampolsky family – Jewish immigrants to Bethnal Green from Tsarist Russia.

To my children, Joseph and Esther, for the joy of the present and the hope of the future.

Contents

Acknowledgements

It is not the lot of women authors to be able to thank their wives or their typists for all the support given to them during the process of writing. For us meals still have to be cooked, clothes washed and the myriad unacknowledged mothering and household tasks, not to mention paid work outside the home, still have to carry on as normal. Writing has to fit in around it all, 'with one hand tied behind us' (Hannah Mitchell). The period in which this book has been written has been an especially difficult time for me personally and it sometimes felt as though both hands were tied behind me. I can only hope that this is not reflected in the book.

Nonetheless, I have received great moral support and encouragement from my friends, comrades, sisters, colleagues and students – some of whom fit all these categories. I am grateful to South Bank University for the highly prized and long fought for sabbatical term (although I asked for a year!) without which this book would have taken even more years to complete. I am grateful to the London Road Computer Centre staff at South Bank, in particular Maurice Morgan, for help and advice. South Bank and the trade union movement provides the much cherished facility for me to come into contact with a unique group of students who provide us in the Centre for Trade Union Studies with the opportunity and challenge of teaching and learning from them. I am particularly indebted to the past and present students on the Certificate in Labour and Trade Union Studies course for their constant inspiration without which this book would have been less likely. Despite the criticisms that pepper this book, I am also grateful to the TUC education department for funding the Labour History study circle and the later evening class, the participants in which have read, commented on and criticised this book in draft form for over two years. My colleague Paul Philo knew better than I that without such external discipline I would probably have drifted into some other project and left this, after an initial burst of enthusiasm, unfinished.

Apart from my students, several people from different walks of life whose opinions I value greatly have read and commented on the draft.

I am particulary grateful to John Foster of Paisley University for his rigorous and painstaking scrutiny. He was the first to have read it, and this coupled with the fact of his own reputation as a labour historian (and communist) made his opinion more important than his modesty would like me to reveal. My colleague and sister historian Kate Hudson at South Bank also read the draft and made very helpful comments. The manuscript was also read by two of my sisters on the TUC Women's Committee – Terry Marsland (MSF) and Judy McKnight (NUCPS, now General Secretary of NAPO) – the latter providing me with useful information on women in the Civil Service. My thanks also to Stella Dadzie, the author and educator, for her time and trouble. I am especially grateful to Andrew Rothstein, a foundation member of the Communist Party of Great Britain, whose sharp mind, memory and experience of many of the twentieth-century events chronicled here have provided a living link with the past. I am honoured that Andrew, now in his 90s, and a comrade who played a key role in many past battles, devoted such care and attention to my manuscript.

I have not agreed with everything that people have said, but where I have, the substance has been incorporated in the text. It is standard practice to absolve anyone but the author from mistakes and errors of judgement. I hope there are not too many of these, but they are mine alone.

Specialist and academic libraries are usually acknowledged by authors. Whilst I too gratefully acknowledge such help, I also wish to pay tribute to the generally unacknowledged and underfunded local library service. My local library, the Marcus Garvey library in Tottenham, has been more helpful than it knows in my research for this book. It has a rich collection of books on the black (and women's) movement and serves Tottenham well.

Final thanks to David Northmore for compiling the index.

Mary Davis
July 1993

Introduction

This book has been a long time in the making, although the practical possibility of actually writing it is comparatively recent. Certainly the kind of study of the labour movement attempted within these pages is long overdue – a strange statement perhaps given the huge growth of labour history as an academic discipline over the last 20 years. The literature on this subject is, by now, immense, so can another general history especially in light of the trend towards increasing specialisation be sustained? The reader will obviously be the final judge, but it would seem appropriate here to explain my aim in making this attempt and in so doing perhaps substantiate the claim for yet another book. My purpose in writing it is three-fold.

The vast majority of the work on the history of the British labour movement has been written by and for academics. This is certainly not a criticism – much pioneering work has been accomplished and our knowledge of the subject has deepened beyond 'the great events' and the 'great leaders'. Nonetheless the more painstaking the search to reconstruct historical reality, the less accessible the fruit of that research has often proved to be. Maybe this shouldn't matter too much: does good history writing need to be accessible to an audience beyond the dreaming spires of academia? After all, serious scholarship is one thing, popular historical chronicling quite another. However this somewhat artificial distinction is much less easy to make when dealing with the subject of labour history. There are two main reasons for this. First, the inheritors of that history are very much alive and well in the active labour movement in Britain today. Secondly, as anyone who has been involved in trade union education will know, the history of the movement is altogether lacking in the otherwise excellent courses provided by the TUC and affiliated unions. The main focus in these 'student centred' courses is the workplace and the building of effective trade union organisation. The courses are concerned with current realities and acquiring the necessary skills to deal with them. Learning about, let alone reflecting upon, the origins and historical development of the movement is not part of the scheme of things. And yet, shop stewards and activists at all levels frequently express a desire to acquire this kind of knowledge – the evidence for which is shown in the popularity of the relatively few courses run for trade unionists (usually in the evening) on this subject. Having myself taught one such course for the past eight years and witnessesd the tremendous and unflagging enthusiasm of the students, I can give personal testimony to this observation.

It is hardly surprising that labour history should be such a popular subject for labour movement activists. All oppressed and exploited groups have the right to reclaim their past – none more so than the working class itself. The inheritors of the struggle for working-class rights and trade union freedoms are predisposed to want to know something of their past. If the labour movement itself fails to impart such information, then it will either filter through in a distorted form or remain unknown. Indeed it remains a criticism of the British labour movement that it neglects its own history save for the occasional celebratory or commemorative foray. Hence my first purpose, an accessible history for today's activists.

Having perceived the need for workers to know something of their own history and organisation, the problem raised earlier about accessible secondary source material is at once apparent. However, accessibility is not the only criterion. A general historical account of the labour movement written as a narrative, sympathetic or otherwise, would not fit the bill. What is required is something that would, within the framework of an account of the development of the labour movement, provide a stimulus for assessing certain key themes and issues, many of which have current relevance for activists today. In other words, what is needed is something analytical, which stimulates thought and discussion, but is at the same time partisan from a working-class standpoint. Why partisan? Most people are, historians included. We all have opinions and outlooks which shape our view of the world, and in the case of historians this influences their view of the past no matter how objective their work appears to be. Such a process is overt or covert depending on whether the 'outlook' of the writer conforms to the predominant norm of his/her own society – the further away from the norm the more overtly biased or partisan the writer is said to be. To the extent that the prevailing outlook in our society is one which values individualism and market forces, then the present writer is overtly partisan in that her outlook is founded on values which are entirely contrary to the norm. It is perhaps as well to be open about one's standpoint right from the outset. As a labour movement activist whose theoretical (and hence practical) per-spectives are still, unfashionably, informed by Marxism, I see the labour movement as a vehicle which not only expresses working-class aspirations, but also struggles to achieve them. This entails winning reforms in this society, but also recognising the extent to which the power of capital through its control of the means of production and the state continues to prevent the ultimate goal of the working class – namely the ending of exploitation. Such a goal is not always consciously expressed – whenever it has been, class struggle is at its sharpest and consensus politics most seriously threatened, often with devastating results. Rival ideologies lie at the very heart of such a struggle and are as contentious today, within the labour movement and outside it, as they have ever been. To declare my own partisanship within this battle of ideas is not therefore simply a matter of nailing my colours to the mast in the interpretation of long forgotten battles. It is part of the process of encouraging debate and discussion around the key ideological questions about which there has been much debate in the past and which still have a relevance in determining the future of the labour movement of today.

Hence a second purpose in the writing of this book is revealed, namely to revive the spirit of debate, using the vehicle of labour history, among the activists of today. In so doing it is to be hoped that much of my interpretation will be questioned and criticised: the past does not belong to me, it belongs to us all – my intention is to allow a wider audience to reclaim it in an active way.

There is also a third purpose in writing this history. Like many other feminists and anti-racists I have long been concerned about the historical and prevalent image of the working class as all white and all male. If we define the working class as those who neither own nor control the means of production and hence have to sell their labour power for a wage, then clearly women and black people are intergral elements. It also follows that they should, therefore, be integral elements within the labour movement, as indeed they are and always have been. However a persistent gender-blind and colour-blind approach has obscured this fact. It is further obscured because of the understandable tendency to write the history of the movement in terms of those who rose to prominence within it, and of course women and black people rarely did (and still don't). A general work of this kind cannot pretend properly to redress this imbalance since far more research needs to be done especially in the field of black workers' participation. Much more work has been done on the history of women workers and trade unions. But herein lies a problem. Redressing the balance in relation to women is not simply a matter of disproving the myths by discovering hitherto forgotten women leaders, because this in itself obscures the fact that in the main the movement was and is led by men. On the other hand most of the evidence we have indicates that women were not only present and active but encountered insuperable obstacles, male attitudes being chief amongst these. The tendency recently to write accounts of women's organisation separate from the 'main movement' does not force us to understand these obstacles and the frequent battles against them within their proper context. Hence my aim is to integrate what we know about women workers historically (and the even smaller amount we know about black workers) into a general labour movement history. This is not merely an antiquarian nicety but essential for understanding the development of the movement including one of its chief weaknesses.

Finally, a word about method and organisation. There is no particulary good reason for starting in 1789 and ending in 1951 i.e the French Revolution and the end of the third Labour government, although the decades themselves have some significance. The first marks the onset of industrialisation and the second witnesses the adjustment to the neo-colonialist era. To go much beyond the 1950s runs dangerously close to the area of current affairs! Nonetheless, my teaching experience shows that students are more interested in the recent past, and hence there is a fuller treatment of events post-1880 which help to establish a closer link with the present. The book is divided into three parts, all of which correspond to a new stage in the development of capitalism and hence to some extent to a new stage within the labour movement too. The first chapter in each of these parts has the same title, 'Economic and Political Background'. The aim of this is to enable the general reader who may have no knowledge at all of the period under discussion to place the labour movement within an economic and political context. The history of the movement abstracted from society is, to me, incomprehensible. It is also important to understand changes in the occupational structure since this had (and still has) a significant bearing on trade union organisation. The place that women occupied within the labour market will also be looked at in this context. The following chapters within each part will then trace the main development of the labour movement, with further reading suggested at the end of each.

Because this is a general work covering such a vast period no pretence is made to original research, although some primary sources, particularly memoirs, speeches and autobiographies, have been used where appropriate. It is a work of interpretation which draws heavily on the mass of secondary sources, good, bad and indifferent. I have not attempted to acknowledge this in the customary academic fashion via footnotes, but instead have indicated the sources used (where possible these include contemporary novels) at the end of each chapter.

General works that have been consulted throughout are listed in the bibliography at the end of the book. I have interrupted the flow of the text only to attribute direct quotations. The specialist scholar, therefore, will find this book less useful than the inquiring shop steward or labour movement activist for whom it is intended and whose possible lack of knowledge of the subject has not, I hope, been confused with lack of intelligence.

The preparation of this book has been assisted throughout by a novel process of 'active writing' in which a microcosm of the target readership in the form of a Labour History Study Circle/evening class, funded by the TUC, have met monthly at the Centre for Trade Union Studies, South Bank University, to discuss and criticise these chapters hot off the word processor. It would thus be tempting to blame the students for inadequacies in the finished product, and reserve the praise for my own efforts. Books cannot be written by committees so I must take full responsibility, but in doing so I hope that the class has learned as much as I have from the exercise and I thank them for indulging me with the privilege of foisting my work and ideas upon them.

Part 1

1789–1850: Industrialisation – Crisis and Struggle

1 Economic and Political Background 1789–1850

Britain in 1850 would have been unrecognisable in every way to an adult who had fallen into a deep sleep in 1780 and awoken 70 years later. Of course great changes occur in every society even within a shorter historical time span, but the changes in this period were so far-reaching that the term 'industrial revolution' commonly used to describe them hardly does justice to their magnitude. The changes were not sudden; neither were they confined to industry. During this 70-year period Britain was transformed from a predominantly agrarian and rural society into one whose wealth was based on industrial production and whose population was increasingly located in fast expanding towns, some of which had been mere villages 70 years before.

The changes that could be seen with the naked eye were less significant than their underlying causes. Beneath the surface the balance of wealth creation and distribution was undergoing a radical change, the obvious (though not immediately visible) sign of which was a change in the class structure of Britain. This was not a matter of tinkering about at the edges, but as hindsight shows turned out to be the most fundamental change in Britain's class structure and class relations since the decline of serfdom. Bourgeois and proletarian came to replace peasant and lord as the dominant classes in society. This in its turn was reflected in political changes which finally enabled the new industrial capitalists, the new wealth creators, to emerge triumphant over the aristocracy. But in a peculiar British compromise, the values of both sections of the old and new ruling class managed to find a consensus which ensured a degree of political stability not found in other European countries.

The Development of Capitalism

The term 'industrial revolution' also masks the true character of this era. It was one in which the capitalist mode of production assumed absolute dominance, a feat which could not have been possible without industrialisation but which nonetheless was not *caused* by it. Likewise the industrial revolution did not bring about the use of machinery. Its

9

significance lies in the fact that its discoveries enabled a new source of motive power (first water and then steam) to be harnessed to the already existing and new machinery. This in turn meant that full-scale *mass* commodity production became possible. The era of modern capitalist industry had begun.

The First Phase – Merchant Capital
Capitalism was not a sudden creation of the late eighteenth century. There were two distinct but linked phases in the history of capitalist production. The first phase, merchant capital together with capitalist agriculture emerged triumphant in the seventeenth century following its long battle with feudalism. Its success was represented politically by the victory of the parliamentary side (as represented by Cromwell and the Roundheads) over the old-guard feudal aristocrats (as represented by Charles I and the Cavaliers) in the English Civil War. This first phase of 'immature' commodity production was characterised by the fact that the instruments of production themselves were sufficiently 'simple' to permit their ownership by individual producers. Domestic production was controlled at first by the guilds but later by richer craftsmen or by merchants who had accumulated capital through overseas trade. The establishment of the great livery companies in the sixteenth and seventeenth centuries is a reflection of this. These companies acquired legal monopolies of their respective trades, whilst the huge trade companies, like the East India company, had legal monopolies of overseas trade within their areas of operation. Such monopoly privileges were protected by the state, which during much of the seventeenth and eighteenth centuries operated on the basis of mercantilist economic theory. Mercantilism held that the source of a nation's wealth lay not in its productive capacity but in its trading strength. Hence the acquisition of favourable trade balances was the goal of the economy. Such a goal could be achieved only through economic regulation by the state. Consequently a panoply of legislation known collectively as the Navigation Laws and the Old Colonial System, in addition to the granting of monopoly rights, was obligingly enacted and policed by the state. This might seem paradoxical given that English society including the state was dominated by the landowners who were preoccupied with protecting their own interests.

However, from the seventeenth century onwards there was an interdependent harmony between the merchants and the landowners – the former had the means and the money, the latter had the political power.

The potential conflict between them was mitigated by the fact that the decay of feudalism enabled the richer merchants to invest their vast wealth into the land itself and hence to renew the 'vitality' of an otherwise decaying and parasitic landowning clique. It was this fresh injection of wealth into agriculture and the establishment of capitalist relations of production which enabled it by the early eighteenth century to become highly productive – in short to undergo what is commonly termed an 'agrarian revolution', enabling England not only to become self-sufficient in food but an exporter of grain. This in turn had an important impact in stimulating and sustaining an expansion in population, the significance of which was apparent later. Much of this was accomplished with a great deal of political upheaval to which the battles of the seventeenth century bear testimony. Nonetheless the harmony could last only while the means of production itself remained at its 'immature' phase and hence required no great amount of new capital investment to maintain high profit. All that was required during this phase was state protection and monopoly rights for the few to ensure that there was no competition from 'interlopers'. So, although merchant capital was linked to commodity production, such production could and did remain at a very basic level in the home country, supplemented as it was by exploitation of Britain's colonies (the oldest of which was Ireland).

Initially these colonies were simply plundered, but later in the seventeenth century they also became important markets for English goods. This meant that they were themselves allowed to develop some production provided that this was strictly in accordance with the needs of the English, and that any trade in the goods so produced was expropriated and controlled by England. This included of course the lucrative slave trade which in itself permitted the development of the even more lucrative sugar, tobacco and cotton trades in the West Indies and later in the southern states of America (the latter also being English colonies). The trade in human beings was not confined at first to black people, but because the west coast of Africa provided such an abundance of human commodities (quite literally), the triangular trade (in which slaves were taken from Africa and transported in vile conditions to America or the West Indies) assumed great importance. It was hugely profitable in itself, but its significance was greater than providing greedy merchants with super-profits. Slavery provided, without knowing it, the bridge between merchant and industrial capital in Britain. It satisfied the former while providing the latter with the raw material of future wealth – raw cotton.

The Second Phase – Industrial Capital

The possibility of developing the means of production to enable capitalism to proceed to its fully industrial phase was in a sense linked to the very success of mercantilism. Vast stores of accumulated capital lay in readiness for productive investment in no matter what, but on the other hand the lucrative opportunies for industrial investment developed in opposition to mercantilism. A new class of producers slowly developed outside the protected circles of the landowning/mercantile oligarchy. Such a development was not to be wondered at; its realisation was dependent on a number of factors among which the technical inventions of the late eighteenth century acted as a spur. Most schoolchildren learn about Kay's flying shuttle, Hargreave's spinning-jenny and other inventions (the most important of which was the steam engine), which revolutionised the means of production. The practical utilisation of such technology became possible only when the conditions were ripe, and these conditions were bequeathed by the success of merchant capital. For example, for industrial production to develop it is necessary to have a growing proportion of the population engaged solely in manufacture. This is possible only if society can produce enough surplus food first to stimulate and sustain a growth in population and secondly to feed its non-agricultural workforce. Herein lies the significance of the agrarian revolution mentioned earlier, and the enclosure movement to which it was linked. It is quite wrong to suppose that enclosures drove people off the land and forced them into the towns – the so-called enforced proletarianisation thesis. Whilst it is true that enclosures did alter the system of land ownership in favour of ever larger estates, it had the effect, certainly in the short term, of increasing the demand for agricultural labour. The fact that the population continued to grow throughout the eighteenth century also meant the growth of the domestic market for manufactured goods. In addition favourable conditions were in place through the existence of developed markets overseas, a reasonable system of transport and a developed commercial infrastructure including a banking system through which the capital accumulated from this first phase of trade and production could be redirected to any more profitable enterprise when the opportunity arose.

The Cotton Industry

The first industry to be fully prepared for such a challenge was the cotton industry. First spinning (using the labour of women and children) and then weaving were fully mechanised and gradually relocated in large factories near a source of motive power to drive the new machines. It was, however, slavery which made the whole development possible in the first place. Raw cotton is not grown in Britain. It is a wholly imported raw material from the plantations of the West Indies and North America – such plantations were worked entirely by the labour of slaves.

At first water power was used to drive the machines which processed the raw cotton. Thus the early factories were located near fast-flowing streams (hence the use of the term cotton 'mill') but later, after the discovery of the steam engine, the mills were moved to be within easy reach of coal – the new energy source. South Lancashire provided an ideal site for the cotton industry, not only because of its coalfield but also because of its canal link with Liverpool from whence the imported raw cotton entered and the manufactured product could be exported. The technology of steam power allied to other inventions was applied later to other branches of the textile industry (woollen cloth and linen), and later still to such industries as iron and steel production. Cotton paved the way.

The pre-conditions for industrial development were laid in previous centuries of capitalist development. It was mass production, not capitalism, which was the new discovery. The question remains as to why the transition from its first to its later stage turned out to be an almighty upheaval socially, politically and ideologically. This second phase of capitalist development required not only an improvement in the means of production but also a major change in the relations of production. Such change could not be 'accommodated' within the existing system; it presented a direct challenge to it. In short it challenged the landed and merchant oligarchy which had ruled Britain in the preceding centuries. The challenge might have been a revolutionary one, as it was in other European countries, but for the fact that the landed aristocracy in Britain displayed an infinite capacity to adapt and compromise. The aristocracy already displayed such capacity in the post-feudal era by the transformation of agrarian class relations and its compromise with merchant capital to the mutual benefit of both. Rich merchants had bought their way into political power by themselves becoming landowners. In this sense the compromise was not so painful for the aristocracy, which by this time had thrown off all its feudal relics and was fully capitalised.

The term 'aristocracy' is thus slightly confusing, but is used to distinguish ennobled landowning capitalists from their merchant, commercial or industrial counterparts. Furthermore the use of the terms implies, as it should, a continuity with a very old landed class, which in Britain more than in any other European country retained its estates almost intact for centuries. The reason for this was the strict enforcement of property laws, in particular primogeniture, and settlement and entail. These were the rules whereby property (in the form of land) had to be passed intact to the eldest son. Three very important consequences flowed, unwittingly, from this: first, the land was preserved in large estates and hence was amenable to techniques which would increase its yield and change its production relations: secondly it meant that a peasantry hardly existed in Britain; and thirdly it meant that those who had money could not buy land but formed instead dynastic or commercial alliances with those who owned it. The fact that Britain by the mid eighteenth century remained a country whose main source of wealth was the land masks the reality of the penetration of capital into agricultural production and the interrelationship between agrarian, commercial and merchant capital.

Industrial capital, however, posed a much more far-reaching challenge to the old system. The new factory owners were not interested in the slightest in buying their way into the landed aristocracy. They were busy transforming Britain into a country whose predominant source of wealth was industrial rather than agricultural production. They were ready to challenge the old order root and branch if it obstructed their relentless puruit of surplus value.

Politics and Ideology

The entrepreneurs who pioneered the process of industrialisation did not emerge from the charmed circles of the existing ruling class. Rather, they were more likely to have been small masters or richer artisans keen to exploit a good thing when they saw it. The new technology did not require a vast capital outlay in the early stages, and anyway most enterprises were fairly small scale, at least at the start. The main obstacles in the path of this phase of capital development lay in the fact that the entire economic and political system was geared to preserving monopoly privileges for the old order. The right to vote and to be elected was restricted in the main to those who owned land and swore loyalty to the state religion, the Church of England. The right to overseas trade was strictly controlled by the great trading companies and was encumbered by a bewildering array of import and export duties. The House of Commons and the two main parties within it, Whig and Tory, existed to preserve such privileges against not only the 'swinish mulitude' but also the new threat of these industrial parvenu interlopers. Small wonder then that the new class of entrepreneurs appeared so radical at the end of the eighteenth century in their opposition to the 'great corruption' of church and state.

The new industrialists had their own (non-conformist) religion, and their own economic and political theories to guide them. Adam Smith, Ricardo, Mill and Bentham were their ideological mentors. The new 'science' of classical political economy, founded by Smith, was developed in opposition to mercantilism. The notions of *laissez-faire*, free trade and freedom for the operation of the market mechanism were in sharp contrast to the established traditions of protectionism and state intervention. Smith and his school even opposed Britain's existing colonial policy, supporting American independence on the grounds that if America remained a British colony its economy would remain stagnant and would hence be a less useful market for British manufactured goods.

Although by 1783 the British government was forced to recognise the fact of American independence, the needs of the growing new business community were hardly noticed, let alone catered for. Contemporary observers of whatever political persuasion were not sure how to assess the as yet small-scale changes in the economy. In any case the long war with France from 1793 to 1815 and the attempts to defeat British radicalism (itself inspired by the French revolution) were the sole concern of public policy. During these years, however, textile and armaments manufacturers did very nicely. By 1815, with most of Europe in a state of economic collapse and the American market ready to buy as much as Britain could produce now that the French wartime economic blockade was over, great new opportunities existed for the take-off of mass production techniques using the new technology.

The post-war government appeared impervious to such developments. Under Lord Liverpool the Tories continued to act in the interests of their class. The symbol of protectionist policies was the Corn Law of 1815 – a piece of legislation based more on dogma than on reason. A set-piece battle loomed between the unenfranchised owners of the 'new money' and the ruling-class representatives of 'old wealth'. By 1822, however, it was clear that the moment of crisis had passed – the ruling-class had seen the danger and were prepared to compromise. Surprisingly enough it was the Tories who took the initiative. They were the party most responsible for changing Britain's economic policy to accommodate the needs of the industrialists, while the Whigs, when in power, initiated the corresponding political reforms. Together both were enough to buy off the 'captains of industry' and hence to ensure a fusion of the old and the new, avoiding the political and social upheavals which rocked the thrones of most other European countries in 1830 and 1848. The secret unlocked by the British ruling-class in the first half of the nineteenth century was to detach any opposition from the force the rulers feared most – the working people. A victory for the masses would entail a lasting defeat for the existing order; far better, then, to head off such a threat by a voluntary change of attitude from above.

The old Toryism was incapable of perceiving the need for such concession. Toryism in general was rescued by such men as Huskisson (president of the Board of Trade), Peel (Home Secretary), Canning (Foreign Secretary) and others, all of whom came to prominence in the reshuffle of 1822. In an attempt to forestall political reform they appeased the manufacturing interest, at least temporarily, by initiating moves in the direction of freeing trade. The Navigation Laws were modified to permit foreign countries to trade directly with British colonies, many import duties were reduced, and even the Corn Laws were modified. None of this went far enough. It merely whetted the appetite of an increasingly prosperous and confident bourgeoisie for more reform which, at the very minimum, included the right to vote.

The Reform Act of 1832 was the culmination of years of political struggle during which the bourgeoisie were quite happy to make common cause with the working class. When, eventually, a reluctant Whig government led by Lord Grey was forced to give way the resulting political settlement was just sufficient to break the dangerous unity of the third estate. The act fulfilled Grey's stated aim of providing a measure which would 'afford sure grounds of resistance to further innovation'. It would appear on first reflection that the Reform Act changed little. It added only 217,000 voters to the electoral roll and had minimal effect on the composition of the House of Commons. Prime Ministers and their cabinets continued to be drawn in the main from the ranks of the aristocracy throughout the nineteenth century.

On the surface, therefore, everything remained the same. Britain was still ruled by aristocrats. However, from 1832 onwards the old order could maintain its tenuous existence only provided it reflected the interests of the class which really owned Britain's wealth – the owners of the new means of production, the bourgeoisie. The political history of Britain until 1867 reflects the gradual adaptation of policy in the light of the new compromise. A certain degree of governmental instability ensued as the main political parties struggled to find new identities which conserved their old interests while at the same time acknowledging what was new. This led ultimately to a split in the Tory Party in 1846 when its leader, Peel, finally accepted the logic of this gradual conversion to free trade (as witnessed in his budgets of 1842 and 1845) by repealing the Corn Laws – the last symbol of the old protectionist system.

The change in government policy on this and many other matters was not simply the product of the intellectual wisdom of Whig and Tory leaders. Rather, it was a response to the unrelenting pressure of the business community that no government after 1832 could afford to ignore. The Whigs under Melbourne went a long way to satisfying the political demands of the bourgeoisie with such measures as the Poor Law Amendment Act, the Municipal Corporations Act and a host of others. The Tories, under pressure from such middle-class organisations as the Anti Corn Law League, went a long way to satisfying the economic demands of the business interest. Neither party, however, needed to be pressurised into fulfilling the objective that all men of property, old and new, shared in common, namely the protection of their property rights against the force of the common enemy – the real creators of their wealth – the working people.

Thus it was that by the middle of the nineteenth century Britain's foreign and domestic policy was subordinated to the needs of the bour-geoisie. Free trade and *laissez-faire* were triumphant, leaving the way clear for Britain as the first industrial nation to exercise an unrivalled dominance over world trade. Britain had become the workshop of the world, her wealth solidly based on the pre-eminence of her textile, engi-neering and ship-building industries. The only threat to such prosperous stability resided in the increasingly better organised and class conscious labour movement which during these years posed a continual problem for the ruling class. Such a threat was fuelled by the appalling hardship that industrial capital in its early years (characterised by repeated booms and slumps) inflicted on its workforce. Where possible, resistance was met with repression, but sometimes concession was the only way to prevent the ultimate of all horrors – social revolution.

By 1850 the language of class was commonplace; it was clear that the stark relations of production based on the ownership of capital on the one hand and the sale of labour power on the other formed the dominant feature of the economy to which all else was reduced. There had been some doubt about this at the end of the eighteenth century when many had regarded the industrial changes as a mere blip on the economic landscape and the myth of the golden age of the English rural idyll was invoked as the alternative to the 'dark satanic mills'. Even if the mass of the population didn't work in such hell holes, the fact was that capitalist relations of production undermined the independent artisan of whatever trade. Hence, although it was possible to perceive distinctions among 'the working people' relating to trade, skill and degree of control over the work process, there was a growing perception that the relationship between capital and labour, whatever form it took, was based on exploitation.

The Workforce

The occupational structure of the workforce, linked with its geographical location, had changed beyond recognition by 1850. Precision is difficult since reliable evidence is hard to come by. The first of what came to be a regular census every ten years was taken in 1801. For the time before that, useful though fragmentary information has been compiled using a variety of chiefly local sources, parish registers and some tax returns. Until 1837, when civil registration of births, deaths and marriages became a legal requirement, census evidence was unreliable and this unreliability was compounded by a lack of skill on the part of the unsupervised census enumerators. Methods improved after 1841 and it is only from then that, despite many other limitations, the census becomes the chief primary source of information on population trends.

The four censuses between 1801 and 1831 (inclusive) provide valuable information on the size of the male and female population and give crude information on broad occupational categories (agriculture, trade, manufacture and handicraft), but they tell us little about women's work. The enumerators kept a simple tally which, apart from the deficiency of the kind of information sought, was prone to inevitable recording inaccuracies. In 1841 the tally method was replaced by a system more akin to today's methods by which each head of household was required to complete a questionnaire from which the enumerators compiled their statistics, but again there was hardly any classification of occupation.

Demographic historians have thus had to make their own estimates of the structure of the labour force in the first half of the nineteenth century using a variety of primary sources, chief among them being returns by factory inspectors. These show that from 1835 onwards in the textile industry (cotton and woollen factories), Britain's largest industry, women employees outnumbered men and continued to do so throughout the century and beyond. Out of a population of roughly 16 million in 1841 the textile industry employed around half a million people, making it second only to agriculture as an employer of labour. Women accounted for some 56 per cent of this total. Despite their predominance in this first factory-based industry, women were not to be found in the new up and coming industries like engineering, iron and steel production and railway building. But given that such industries occupied only a minority of the workforce anyway, even as late as 1861, it would clearly be erroneous to assume that women's exclusion from them has any bearing on the total numbers of women employed. Despite the lack of reliable and detailed information, it would be safe to assume that women continued to work, as they always had, in their traditionally accepted spheres. We know that domestic service was the biggest single employer of female labour. We know much less about the numbers of women engaged in dressmaking, millinery and the like – all workshop or even home-working occupations which escaped notice because as offshoots of women's domestic roles they were so taken for granted. The small numbers of women who worked in less traditional areas like chain making in the West Midlands or as 'pit brow lassies' (at the suface of coal mines) have attracted more attention precisely because they were atypical. The same can be said of the much larger number of women who worked in textile factories. They excited a great deal of controversy even at the time because their presence brought women's labour out into the open in a way that the more traditional and 'unseen' occupations did not.

Further Reading

Ashton, T.S., *An Economic History of England – the 18th Century* (Methuen, 1966).

Deane, Phyllis, *The First Industrial Revolution* (Cambridge University Press, 1965).

Chambers, J.D. and Mingay, G.E., *The Agricultural Revolution 1750-1880* (Batsford, 1966).

Dobb, M., *Studies in the Development of Capitalism* (Routledge, 1947).

Flinn, M.W., *Origins of the Industrial Revolution* (Longman, 1966).

Hill, C., *Reformation to Industrial Revolution* (Pelican, 1969).

Pinchbeck, Ivy., *Women Workers and the Industrial Revolution* (Cass, 1969, first published 1930).

Wrigley, E.A. (ed.), *An Introduction to English Historical Demography* (Weidenfeld & Nicolson, 1966).

2   The Impact of the French Revolution 1789–1815

The magnitude of the huge changes wrought by industrialisation were hardly understood at the beginning of the process. A factory proletariat had barely come into existence at the turn of the eighteenth century and the modern language of class and class struggle was almost unknown. Nevertheless, the economic effects of industrialisation and the political effects of the American War of Independence and the French Revolution inspired new thinking and the formation of new, independent and radical forms of organisation of working people. With a frightened eye on France the government met British radicalism with harsh repression. All forms of protest, however mild, were deemed to constitute a serious threat to the existing order.

The French Revolution

The French Revolution of 1789 can be compared in its impact worldwide only to the Russian Revolution of 1917. It did not merely shatter the old order in France but its ideology (encapsulated in its slogan 'liberty, equality, fraternity') inspired the downtrodden of many other countries inside and outside Europe to follow suit.

In England ruling-class reaction to events in France were less predictable than elsewhere. England was the only country in Europe to have undergone a revolution to free itself from the yoke of feudalism and absolute monarchy. If the French were about to do likewise while preserving property rights, albeit in an altered form, then even Pitt (Tory Prime Minister 1783–1801, 1804–06) was prepared to give it a cautious welcome at the outset, especially since a section of the aristocracy in France had fired the opening shots in the opposition to Louis XVI. The newly rich entrepreneurs in Britain who had money but no political rights gave the revolution a more enthusiastic welcome, identifying with the well-to-do section of the third estate. However, both these groups in England modified their views when it became apparent that the masses in France had demands of their own and that for a short time, until

1794, under the leadership of Robespierre, they occupied centre stage. This left only the working people of Britain to continue to support and identify with the more far-reaching aims of the real revolutionaries in France. Coming at the beginning of a major process of economic transition in Britain, the French Revolution had a more widespread political effect here than the American War of Independence of the previous decade even though the latter had prepared much of the ideological ground for the subsequent eruptions in Europe.

There was a long radical tradition in Britain which had reached its zenith at the time of the English revolution of 1640 and subsequent civil war. There are many parallels to be drawn between this revolution and the one in France over 100 years later, not the least being a popular democratic strain representing the interests of those without property. This was expressed in England by the Levellers and the Diggers and in France by the Jacobins. In both countries popular radicalism was ultimately defeated, resulting in the triumph of a new oligarchy, which in both cases represented a compromise between landed and commercial property. This compromise in England, misleadingly named the Glorious Revolution, was achieved in 1688. However, it was not until 1789 that once again a truly independent and democratic popular radical movement came to the fore on a scale far greater than the movement generated to support the American struggle against British colonial domination 13 years previously.

Tom Paine and Mary Wollstonecraft

The essence of the popular democratic ideal in Britain was to be found in the writings of Thomas Paine, and in practical terms in the work of the Corresponding Societies. Paine's most famous book *The Rights of Man* was published in 1791 in reply to Edmund Burke's *Reflections on the Revolution in France*. The latter was a diatribe against the revolution, condemning the masses who participated in it as the 'swinish multitude'. Burke's argument was based on the traditionally accepted premise that political rights were founded on the ownership of property – those who had none were 'blessed' only with duties. This was the natural order of things, and to tamper with the natural order would lead only to anarchy. Paine's book not only defended the cause of the revolution against its most outspoken conservative critic, but also argued that French principles of equality could and should be applied to this country. Based on these, principles in Part Two of the book (published as a separate 6d pamphlet and said to have been 'in almost every hand'), he drew up a practical social and political programme for far-reaching reform that was radical even by today's standards.

Paine's radicalism, however, must not be be confused with socialism – the latter being a much later development in the history of political thought. Paine did not attack property rights as such; his main target was the landed aristocracy and the hereditary principle. In this his appeal was as much to the unenfranchised traders and manufacturers as to the propertyless masses. Nonetheless, *The Rights of Man* showed that political democracy was not an abstraction, it was based on a revolutionary notion that all men are born naturally equal and that the purpose of government is to make natural rights effective. Governments that fail to do this must be opposed. 'Government', he asserted, 'is nothing more than a natural association' to be based on equal representation, not on privilege, monarchical or otherwise. Such views, combined with the social programme, captured the essence of the democratic ideal and ensured that his book became a universal textbook for the working-class movement for many decades. Within three years it had sold over 200,000 copies.

Although Paine's programme included the almost unheard of demand for maternity benefits it did not have much else to say specifically about women, despite the fact that women played an important role in the French Revolution. However, in the heightened ferment of radical ideas and class understanding that ensued in the coming decades there was, for the first time, the glimmerings of an awareness of the appalling injustices suffered by the 'unseen' half of the human race. One of the main arguments running throughout this book will be that the question of women's rights becomes a public issue for the working-class movement as a whole only at moments of great social and political upheaval generated by mass movements inspired, in turn, by ideologies that challenge the existing order root and branch. This was one such moment. Inspired by the revolution and its foundation in the doctrine of reason and natural rights, Mary Wollstonecraft, an impoverished 'gentlewoman' published in 1792 her pioneering work *A Vindication of the Rights of Women*. The book is dedicated to Talleyrand (a member of the French Constituent Assembly charged with writing a new constitution) to whom she writes an open letter. She asks him to:

> Consider ... whether, when men contend for their freedom, and be allowed to judge for themselves respecting their own happiness, it be not inconsistent and unjust to subjugate women ... Who made man

the exclusive judge, if woman partake with him of the gift of reason? (Wollstonecraft, *Vindication of the Rights of Women* 1792, p. 11)

'Tyrants are all eager to crush reason', she says, but then goes on to challenge him with acting in a similar manner when 'you *force* all women, by denying them civil and political rights, to remain immured in their familes groping in the dark'. Women, she asserts, 'may be convenient slaves, but slavery will have its constant effect, degrading the master and the abject dependent'. So runs the central argument of the book, the remainder of which is a refutation of all the dogma used to justify women's subjugation. Its challenge still remains largely unanswered.

In her unfinished novel 'Maria, or the Wrongs of Women', Mary Wollstonecraft showed that she was aware of the link between women's oppression and class exploitation, and that both were given spurious legitimacy by organised religion, in this case Methodism. Had she simply confined herself to championing the cause of the few educated and articulate women it is unlikely that she would have met with such furious opposition, and be dubbed 'a hyena in petticoats'. It is also evident that some among the (male) radical intelligensia supported her views and followed William Godwin's attack on the conventional family form in which women were forever doomed to a life of submission. In the wake of the fierce anti-Jacobinism that followed Britain's declaration of war on France, such advanced radical views were countered with the main ideological weapon in the armoury of the establishment, that of an evangelical Christian religious revival. Not only was religion an antidote to revolution but it was also the means by which women could be restored to their proper place at the centre of family life.

The Corresponding Societies

Thus it was that Paine and Wollstonecraft provided much of the ideological inspiration for English radicalism, though it is undoubtedly true that the former was more widely read than the latter. Their ideas clearly influenced the fledgling radical movement during this period. The most important of the radical organisations were the Corresponding Societies, formed in almost every major (and sometimes minor) English and Scottish town during 1792. The largest, although not the first, was the London Corresponding Society (LCS), the founder and secretary of which was a shoemaker, Thomas Hardy. It became the centre of a loose federation of similar bodies existing nationwide (literally 'corresponding' with each other), the main aims of which were to campaign for social reform and political democracy (including manhood suffrage) along the lines of Paine's programme as outlined in Part Two of his *Rights of Man*.

Some have claimed that the LCS was the first working-class political organisation to have been formed in Britain. Others (e.g. E.P. Thompson in *The Making of the English Working Class*), say that the description 'popular radical' is more accurate. The uniqueness of the organisation is not dependent on the truth of either one of these descriptions. What makes the Corresponding Societies so important, aside from the fear which they engendered in the ruling class, is the fact that they were truly independent organisations, formed by and for working people. The term 'working people', as opposed to 'working class', more accurately expresses the fluidity of class relations existing at this time of rapid economic change. The membership of the Corresponding Societies reflected this, composed as it was of artisans – small masters and journeymen, shopkeepers, clerks. A conscious decision was made to base the LCS on the 'lower orders'. This was done by making the organisation as open as possible, as enshrined in one of the rules which said that the number of members should be 'unlimited', and also by keeping the subscription rates low (1d per week). This might not seem particularly noteworthy by twentieth-century standards, but it was an important departure in the eighteenth century when politics and political organisations were the exclusive domain of rich and powerful interest groups plotting in secret.

Repression

In 1793 Britain went to war with France – a war which lasted until 1815 with the final defeat of Napoleon at Waterloo. This meant that the activities of the Corresponding Societies were deemed to be not only seditious but also treasonable. Paine escaped to France to avoid certain arrest. While he was there he was elected as a deputy for Pas de Calais to the convention. In Britain the radicals were harried by state and more 'unofficial' agencies. The latter consisted of so-called Church and King mobs who were left free (and freely encouraged) to abuse and attack the followers of Paine and to rampage through the streets burning his effigy. State persecution started by banning the works of Paine followed by the trials and transportation of leading Scottish radicals like Thomas Muir. An attempt in 1794 to convict seven leading members of the LCS, including Hardy, backfired on the government when the jury acquitted the men.

Despite persecution and infiltration by government agents, membership of the societies continued to grow at least until 1795. The defeat of the Jacobins in France in 1794, ending as it did the period of revolutionary advance, and combined with the fact of the war itself, enabled the government to capitalise on anti-French feeling and launch the harshest weapon in its repressive anti-radical armoury. This took the form of the Two Acts in 1795 – the Treasonable Practices Act and the Seditious Meetings Act. The former redefined treason to include words as well as deeds, while the latter so narrowed the right of assembly as to make political meetings impossible. This was coupled with the growth and more efficient organisation of the repressive apparatus of the state, as seen by the import of German mercenaries and the housing of the troops in barracks in order to separate them from the radical influences of the civilian population. The effect, as intended, was to drive the Corresponding Societies underground. By 1797 the LCS had collapsed.

The apparent success of government repression and war fever in smothering the Corresponding Societies was not enough to douse the spirit of rebellion, which now took new forms. Most threatening to the English government in view of the war with France were the naval mutinies at Nore and Spithead in 1797, and the Irish Rising of 1798. The latter was led by the Society of United Irishmen, an organisation formed in 1791 (a year before the LCS) that was inspired by Jacobin ideas, and that united catholic and protestant in its ranks. Indeed its leader, Wolf Tone, was a protestant lawyer. He and others saw in the French war a chance to rid Ireland from English control. To this end Tone went to France to plan for a French invasion to coincide with a rising of the Irish people. Three attempts were made between 1796 and 1797, but by the time the French finally arrived in August 1798 it was too late. (The French delay was caused by the change in foreign policy initiated by their new leader, Napoleon Bonaparte.) The Irish leaders had all been arrested (due in the main to the work of the government informer, Thomas Reynolds), but anyway the most favourable opportunity – the time of the English naval mutinies the previous year – had been missed.

Trade Unionism

Such events inspired terror among the propertied classes and resulted in further repression. However, the economic effects of the war and the more profound and destabilising effects of industrialisation ensured that protest was never far from the surface. Much of this protest took the form of industrial action or 'combination' of one form or another at the point of production. This, of course, implies the existence of trade union organisation.

There has been much debate among historians as to the origins of trade unionism. The traditional view, propounded by the first historians of the trade union movement in this country, Sidney and Beatrice Webb (*A History of Trade Unionism*, 1894), is based on the Webbs' definition of a trade union as 'a continuous association of wage earners'. With this in mind, they can therefore find no evidence of trade union existence prior to the eighteenth century. Whilst the Webbs do not make the mistake (made by many of their disciples) of assuming that trade unionism was a by-product of industrialisation, their original definition fails to take account of the continuous struggle between labour and capital even during the period of handicraft production.

An understanding of capitalist relations of production during the mercantile period has led some modern historians to see the guild system in a new light as they connect it to the increasing evidence being found to substantiate the existence of struggle waged at the point of production in earlier centuries. There were almost 400 labour disputes in the eighteenth century. Most of these did not involve 'continuous associations' but nevertheless they were concerned with such 'trade union' issues as wages and hours of work. It is nonetheless undeniable that more permanent forms of organisation to defend the economic interests of workers originated at a time when the 'changing conditions of industry ... reduced to an infinitesimal chance the journeyman's prospect of becoming a small master' (Webb, 1894, p. 1). In other words the changes in the means of production meant that an artisan (i.e. a worker who owned his/her own tools) could no longer expect to rise in the world.

Thus it was that by 1789 there was a well-established tradition of workplace organisation to defend wages and living standards. Many of the trade societies formed among the artisans were non-political. They had national structures (for example among shoemakers, brushmakers, tailors and hatters) which facilitated the common practice of 'tramping' (an organised system of finding work in other parts of the country) and sufficient organisation to maintain members in times of sickness or unemployment. The immense dislocation caused by industrialisation, exacerbated by 22 years of warfare and huge rises in food prices, gave an added impetus to workplace combination and trade organisation. This took varied forms, not all of them consistent with the Webbs' definition of trade unionism, or of the more moderate operations of some of the trade societies. In these conditions the post-1790 industrial organisation of workers amounted to a considerable threat to the propertied classes resulting in drastic state repression which itself was fuelled by the constant fear of the spread of revoltion this side of the Channel.

It is simply not possible to chronicle the many examples of protest in almost every craft or trade. Most of it was highly localised and often took the form of 'collective bargaining by riot' or of machine breaking, later known as Luddism. Luddism was not simply a protest against new technology. Many of those who participated in it, like the framework knitters, were already using complex machinery, usually the property of the employer but used on the workers' own premises. The machines were broken as a means of coercing employers into awarding pay rises, particularly during periods when, as during the Napoleonic war, food prices were especially high. (Machine breaking in Yorkshire, the subject of Charlotte Bronte's novel *Shirley*, is set in the winter of 1811–12.) In comparison with this form of machine wrecking, its use as a protest against the new steam-driven technology was surprisingly limited. It was exaggerated at the time and has been used since to heap abuse on 'backward looking' workers who oppose 'progress'. Farm labourers destroyed threshing machines in some areas in the 1830s (sometimes known as the Last Labourers' Revolt). There was protest against the introduction of the power loom in the 1820s and in Lancashire spinning-jennies over a certain size were wrecked in 1778–80. The anti-technology aspect of machine wrecking was, however, far less significant than its earlier use as a weapon in the collective bargaining process.

Understandably workers were reluctant to leave written accounts of these secretly planned operations, so most of them, including the more conventional strike activity, remain shrouded in mystery. It was all illegal. However, we know the activity was widespread because employers petitioned parliament to do something about it. They complained that the existing laws against combination and conspiracy were not drastic enough. The master millwrights of London demanded a short Act of Parliament to solve the problem once and for all. Parliament obliged in 1799 by passing, in great haste, the notorious Combination Acts.

The Combination Acts were not simply more of the same repressive dose. This was a draconian measure which banned every kind of combination or meeting leading to combination and made offenders liable to summary conviction by two magistrates. In addition offenders (contrary to the principles of English law) were obliged to give evidence against themselves. The whole procedure was designed to avoid the delays in sentencing that were necessitated under the old laws of conspiracy. While the Acts banned all combinations they were used primarily against workplace combinations.

Although the law remained in existence for 25 years it did not succeed in eradicating trade unionism or, indeed, industrial strife. The fact that so many unions 'appeared' when the law was repealed in 1824 is proof of this. It is very difficult to get precise information about such unions existing in a period of illegality. Naturally enough they were not keen to leave written records, nor to announce their existence as trade unions. More often than not they still called themselves friendly societies since such bodies could maintain a legal existence. The 1794 Friendly Societies Act made a legal distinction between trade unions and friendly societies. The latter were benefit organisations providing some kind of insurance cover to dues-paying members who fell on hard times caused by sickness, injury or old age. However, it is very likely that many friendly societies did far more, and performed much more of a trade union function. There was a big increase in the number of friendly societies during the last quarter of the eighteenth century, and at least a quarter of them did not register with the Registrar for fear that their account books would be officially scrutinised. The increase was concentrated in those areas in which the process of industrialisation was causing maximimum upheaval. Many of these unions/friendly societies were small, short lived and locally based.

Women in the Early Labour Movement

Some of the unions formed in these years, especially among textile workers, involved women; the Manchester Spinners' Society, for example, formed in 1795, was predominantly female. This little remarked upon fact reveals something very important about early trade union history, namely that it was not, as it came later to be, a purely male-dominated affair. In fact, given that the first branch of the cotton industry to be mechanised was spinning, that women were the spinners and that the mill owners showed a decided preference for female labour initially, it would not be too wild to assume that women might have been among the pioneers of the trade union movement. Difficulties in finding reliable information about early trade unions and political organisations operating in a period of semi or total illegality are hugely magnified when it comes to knowing, let alone assessing, the role of women. The hypothesis that women, as the first factory workers, might also have been the pioneers of modern trade unionism cannot be adequately tested without painstaking local research beyond the scope of this book. Lack of evidence, however, is no reason for doubting the importance of attempting to find it, especially when it touches upon such a crucial gap in our understanding of the development of the labour movement and the place of women within it.

By 1815 it appeared that although there had been nearly two decades of popular protest there was little that was tangible or permanent to show for it. The Corresponding Societies, Luddism, trade unionism and the movement for Irish freedom had all been beaten or supressed – the 'old corruption' of church, state and the landed/mercantile oligarchy was still, as ever, firmly in the saddle. Despite this, however, the ideas nourishing radicalism and trade unionism were vibrant. Repressive legislation, war hysteria and economic hardship all played their part in checking the organisational form, though not the spirit, of revolt. The post-war period witnessed the reinvigoration and revival of both.

Further Reading

Bronte, Charlotte, *Shirley* (first published 1849; contains fictionalised account of change in the woollen industry and Luddist response).

Claeys, G., *Thomas Paine – Social and Political Thought* (Unwin Hyman, 1989).

Munby, L. (ed.), *The Luddites and Other Essays* (Katanka, 1972).

Rule, J. (ed.), *British Trade Unionism 1780–1850* (Longman, 1988).

Thompson, E.P., *The Making of the English Working Class* (Gollancz, 1963).

Wollstonecraft, Mary, *Vindication of the Rights of Women* (Everyman, 1929, first published 1790)

3   Post-war Radicalism 1815–36

The Treaty of Vienna, signed by the five great powers in 1815, marked the end of the French revolutionary and Napoleonic wars. France was defeated. The revolution was over. Everywhere in Europe kings, princes and aristocrats reclaimed their privileges. Britain, the most consistent partner in the anti-French coalition, was a victor power and emerged stronger than ever. Nonetheless a powerful opposition movement developed in the post-war period. Although solidly based among artisans in particular, the movement attracted support from a broad alliance which until 1832 cut across class boundaries. The very fluidity of the class structure, reflecting as it did the still transitional nature of class relations at this time of ongoing industrial change and economic instability, was in turn reflected in new forms of protest. This protest was inspired by a welter of political ideologies most of which defy characterisation in the parlance of modern socialist or labourist politics. Old traditions of protest were revived and new ones were invented. As thinkers and activists on the left struggled to comprehend the immense changes of which they were part they produced a rich intellectual legacy (much of which has unfortunately been forgotten) which within the beginnings of a socialist framework, encompassed an analysis of the family and the subjugation of women.

The Old Regime

The old order in Britain, unlike Europe, had not been overthrown. It was business as usual, with the same Tory government pursuing the same narrow and partisan policies in the interests of the landed aristocracy. For the opposition, too, it was business as usual. The radicalism of the previous period, having suffered a temporary setback, re-emerged in the post-war years with a much wider base and a much broader appeal. Its target was the Tory government, which in the years between 1815 and 1822 earned itself the dubious reputation of being the most reactionary administration of the nineteenth century.

Britain in 1815 was the usual playground for the rich and powerful, with the Prince Regent setting the tone for wild extravagance. The contrast between the indulgences of the royal entourage and the lives of the mass of people was all the more marked given the post-war escalation in the cost of living. Food prices remained high and the upward trend was accentuated by the government's decision to tax items of common consumption like tea and sugar. This was a cold-blooded move to shift the burden of taxation on to those who could afford it least – a fact made more obvious by a simultaneous decision to abolish the more equitable income tax that had been introduced briefly during the war. In addition the post-war recession led to unemployment and savage wage cuts in many industries, exacerbating the dislocation and misery caused by the process of industrialisation.

The Radicalism of the Intelligensia

For about five years after the Vienna treaty the government was seriously troubled by a torrent of popular radical revolt assailing it from diverse and sometimes unexpected quarters. Whilst the causes of protest were not hard to find, its widespread nature is somewhat surprising given that, unlike the war years, there was no coherent national organising focus other than a few small and relatively obscure sects. Individuals rather than organisations acquired a mass following. Names like Burdett, Cobbett, Hunt and Cartwright were better known and remembered than organisations like the Society of Spencean Philanthropists. The written word, whether periodical, political tract or poem, exercised a powerful appeal, especially when illustrated by a cartoon.

This was the golden age of political caricature and satirical writing. The considerable talent of such artists and writers as Hone, Cruikshank and Gilray were so successfully put to the service of the radical movement that the government actually resorted to replying in kind, unleashing an amazing pamphlet war. The best example of this was Hone's 'Political House that Jack Built', a radical lampoon of the clergy, government and monarchy. It was illustrated by Cruikshank and sold in tens of thousands. 'The Constitutional House that Jack Built' was the 'official' pro-government response – a parody of a parody. The sheer intellectual onslaught of the supporters of radical reform could not be matched by government scribes. The poets Shelley, Wordsworth, Byron and Coleridge were all overtly politically active in the radical cause in this period, a fact often glossed over in the selection and interpretation of their works that has subsequently found its way into the canons of English literature. Coleridge and Wordsworth changed their views in later life. Byron died young, in the battle to free Greece from its domination by the Ottoman Empire. Shelley also died at an early age, but it is unlikely that he would have moved to the right politically. His politics went beyond radicalism and towards socialism as an honest reading of *Queen Mab* indicates. Shelley was also committed to women's liberation. His poetry was an inspiration to later feminists like Charlotte Despard, Millicent Fawcett and the Pankhursts, all of whom paid him fulsome tribute. Unlike most male poets before or since, the issue of women's liberation features strongly in Shelley's verse and is central to his vision of a new social order. One frequently quoted line from 'The Revolt of Islam' expresses this link succinctly: 'Can man be free if woman be a slave?'. Shelley was undoubtedly influenced by Mary Wollstonecraft. He married the child of her union with William Godwin (also named Mary), the child the mother never lived to see since she died giving birth. Support for women's liberation and opposition to the conventional family form provided a link between pre- and post- (Napoleonic) war radical thought in that, uniquely, new forms of non-oppressive personal social relations were a major plank in the deliberations of both.

The Radical Revolt 1815–22

An intellectual revolt on its own could have been contained. The real threat to the government lay in the protest of 'the people all tatter'd and torn' (Hone) which surfaced with force on several occasions during these years. Such events as the Derbyshire Rising, the Pentridge Rising, the March of the Blanketeers, the Spa Fields meeting and the huge demonstration in St. Peter's Field, Manchester (Peterloo) all serve to indicate the breadth, diversity and widespread geographical scale of the demand for economic and political reform. There was little ideological conformity – handloom weavers protested against the loss of their livelihoods caused by the introduction of the power loom; William Cobbett, the popular writer and editor of *Twopenny Trash*, looked back nostalgically to the days of pre-industrial England, while the Spenceans (followers of Thomas Spence), the most socialistic in outlook, campaigned for the England to be declared 'the people's common farm'.

Such evidence as exists shows that women played an important part in the radical movement. Female Reform Societies were formed in many Lancashire towns following the example of Alice Kitchin who set up the first one in Blackburn, probably in 1818. These Female Reform

Societies mustered large contingents to send to the Peterloo meeting at which many women as well as men bore the brunt of the violence of the yeomanry.

The more 'respectable' middle-class elements organised in the Hampden Clubs (named after John Hampden who, together with Francis Pym, was a leader of the parliamentary cause in the seventeenth century) and attempted to exert peaceful pressure for reform as an antidote to the more violent protests of the masses. Such violence undoubtedly did occur, as at Spa Fields in London in 1816, but mostly it was greatly over-exaggerated and sometimes directly inspired by government *agents provocateurs*, as in Derbyshire in 1817 and in the Cato Street conspiracy of 1820, in an effort to discredit the radical cause.

But however much the government tried to fool others it could not fool itself to the extent of the popular protest, hence its recourse to draconian repressive measures and state-inspired violence like the massacre of peaceful protesters at Peterloo in 1819. (This outrage caused Shelley to write one of the best ever poems of political protest, 'The Mask of Anarchy'). Habeas corpus (the right not to be imprisoned without a trial) was suspended in 1816 and efforts were made to eliminate the radical press by the introduction in 1819 of the notorious stamp duty (a fourpenny tax on all cheap pamphlets and newspapers). This was dubbed a 'tax on knowledge' and inaugurated the 'war of the unstamped press'. The Gagging Act of 1817 forbade all meetings.

The Anti-slavery Movement and the Black Radicals

By the end of the eighteenth century there was considerable opposition to the slave trade for both economic and humanitarian reasons. It was the radicals, however (like John Thelwall of the London Corresponding Society), who linked the struggle against slavery with the fight against a corrupt ruling class at home. In the post-1815 period opposition to the slave trade was a powerful and popular force within the radical movement. When a proposal was made at the Congress of Vienna in 1815 to renew the rights of French slave traders a massive petition containing over one and a half *million* signatures was handed to parliament. The majority of the signatories were working people.

By 1815 there were upwards of 10,000 black people living in Britain. From their ranks sprang two prominent radical leaders, both members of the most left wing of the radical groups, the Spenceans. One of these, Robert Wedderburn, the son of a slave, was jailed for two years for his political activities, and the other, William Davidson, was hanged and beheaded for his part in the Cato Street conspiracy of 1820. (This was a plot to blow up the cabinet which was infiltrated and probably inspired by *agents provocateurs*.)

Owenism and Co-operation

Robert Owen is the personification of the ideological confusion that characterised radical reformers in the opening decades of the nineteenth century. He distanced himself and was thus sometimes unpopular with the mainstream of the post-1815 radical movement. Owen was a paradox. As a wealthy and successful mill owner he was a product of the industrial revolution. As a thinker he was the product of eighteenth-century rationalism but was also later influenced by the writings of French Utopian socialists, in particular Fourier. He was a social reformer and as such his work falls into three distinct phases – only the last one of which brought him into direct contact with the labour movement.

Owen's theory that man's character is created for and not by him led him to take a direct and practical interest in social reform and education for the masses. He attempted to put his ideas into practice in his own factory at New Lanark and then appealed to the rich and powerful to follow his example. He made direct personal approaches to the Prince Regent, to Sidmouth, to the Duke of Wellington and even to some of the crowned heads of Europe to become agents of social change. Such appeals to reason in an attempt to transcend class interest fell, unsurprisingly, on deaf ears. This then led him to go it alone – to create his own model society by establishing model co-operative communities in America and Britain. All of these communties were short lived. The failure of these experiments led him and his followers to see the necessity of fighting from within – first through more practical forms of co-operation and then through trade unionism.

Owen is often hailed as the father of the co-operative movement. This is not strictly true, especially if we acknowledge that the modern movement is based on consumer co-operatives. Consumer co-operatives (many of them short lived) grew rapidly in the 1820s while Owen was in America. These co-operative shops were often closely connected with the trade union movement. William Lovett, one of the founders of the London Co-operative Society, wrote in 1824:

> When Mr. Owen first came over from America (1829) he looked somewhat coolly on those 'trading associations' and very candidly declared that mere buying and selling formed no part of his 'grand

co-operative scheme'; but when he found that great numbers among them were disposed to entertain his views, he took them more in favour, and ultimately took an active part among them. (*Life and Struggles of William Lovett*, 1876, 1967)

Owen was more disposed towards producer co-ops. He initiated an interesting experiment in the practical application of the labour theory of value by establishing a 'labour exchange' in 1832 in premises in Grays Inn Road, London. An exchange of labour literally took place in the form of labour notes being issued for items produced by individuals. These labour notes could then be exchanged for articles of an equivalent value. Value was determined by the cost of materials and labour time necessary for production. Success was brief as the amount of 'comparatively useless articles ... preponderated over the useful' (Lovett) and the value of the labour notes depreciated.

Communitarianism (the establishment of model communities run along socialist lines in which all property was held in common) and co-operation were just two examples in the 1820s of the efforts of radical thinkers to find solutions for the oppressed in a rapidly changing society, the workings of which they had not as yet fully understood. The failure of these experiments led to an awareness of the need for a much more direct form of workers' organisation – trade unionism. Owen recognised this and played a leading part in attempts at general unionism in the early 1830s.

The worsening of living standards during the long-term economic crisis of the 1830s and 1840s gave greater urgency to a more practical way of fighting back. Industrialisation was as yet incomplete. Cotton still dominated the economy and yet cotton goods fell in price. Employers adopted the classic remedy of cutting wages, with devastating results given that there was no fall in price of the basic necessities of life.

Trade Unionism

It is difficult to separate political and trade union activity in the first half of the nineteenth century. Unions themselves were highly political organisations bearing little resemblance to their modern inheritors. That they appeared as organisationally separate is due to the fact that radical political organisation was all but extinguished by 1820 by repressive legislation and state brutality. Trade unions continued the radical tradition through different organisational forms, but with one important difference, namely that they, rather than the radical clubs, were the vehicles for the development of a specifically working-class (often anti-capitalist) consciousness. This can be seen in the twin developments within trade unionism in these years.

One such development was the steady progress of trade union organisation within individual trades, which also involved the attempt to weld the various small trade clubs into some kind of unified (in some cases national) organisation. Secondly there were attempts to form general unions of all workers irrespective of trade. These two initiatives were not in conflict – often the leaders of the former were involved in the latter. John Doherty, leader of the cotton spinners, is the most obvious example. Men like Doherty, William Benbow (a Lancashire shoemaker), Owen and many others looked on trade unionism not just as a means for protecting and improving workers' living standards but also as a vehicle for changing the entire political and economic order of society. In order to achieve this Benbow popularised the strategy of the 'national holiday' (a general strike). In essence he and others were beginning to appreciate, well before Marx revealed it more precisely, that political power, being based on economic wealth, could be dislodged by workers only at the point of production. The inescapable logic of this argument inevitably produced a potentially very revolutionary variant of trade unionism, jettisoned in the second half of the nineteenth century.

Before the depression of the 1830s there was a short period of relative economic stability during the 1820s with something approaching a boom in the middle years of the decade. In these conditions the newly remodelled Tory government was persuaded by men like Francis Place that trade unions were not the dangerous beasts they had seemed during the war years. Francis Place had been a trade unionist, a member of the Breech Makers' Society, who had become a successful master tailor. By 1824 he served as the Radical MP for Westminster (a constituency which despite the corruption and exclusiveness of the voting system was one of the few boroughs that had a relatively large electorate) and in this capacity was one of the very few in parliament with any first-hand knowledge or experience of workers' organisations. His views by this time were fairly 'safe', which probably explains why the government was prepared to listen to him. Thus, in 1824 the Combination Act was repealed. Place's argument was that the legalising of trade unions would serve to *discourage* them. He and other political economists like him believed that wages were ruled by the law of the market, and that allowing workers the freedom to combine would teach them how futile it was to wage a war that was impossible to win. Workers obviously did not share Place's view, as witnessed by the immense increase in union activity including strike action following repeal of the act. The fact that so many seemed suddenly to appear came as a surprise only to those who thought that the Combination Acts had actually abolished unions rather than driving them underground.

The government was so worried by this development that it rushed through the 1825 Trade Union Act. Its purpose, very much like that of contemporary legislation, was to reduce the effectiveness of trade unions by making it difficult to organise strikes without falling foul of the law. The clauses forbidding 'molestation' or 'obstruction' in order to persuade workers to 'abstain' from work gave judges such wide powers of interpretation that even peaceful picketing could be criminalised.

Nonetheless trade unions themselves remained legal. There is evidence of considerable organisation among spinners, potters, shoemakers, brushmakers, shipwrights and even among domestic servants. (A short-lived Union of Maidservants was formed in Edinburgh in 1825.) The factory-based cotton spinning industry was probably the best organised in trade union terms. At first the associations of male spinners were locally based with many local strikes, but intermittent attempts were made to establish federations with the aim of equalising piece rates. John Doherty, secretary of the Manchester cotton spinners, led a successful attempt to achieve unity resulting in the formation of the Grand General Union of Cotton Spinners in 1829. This, though it lasted for only a brief time, was the springboard for further attempts at general unionism.

Today we associate the attempt to form 'one big union' for all workers of all trades with syndicalism, which as a theory was a much later development. Whatever label we attach to attempts to form general unions of all trades in the early nineteenth century there is no escaping the fact that they were all founded on the premise that the industrial might of the working class could be used to change the political system. Three attempts were made to unite workers in this way. One was as early as 1818 with the formation of the Philanthropic Hercules. The next was initiated by Doherty in 1829 (surviving until 1831) – the National Association for the Protection of Labour. Finally, and perhaps the most famous, there was the Grand National Consolidated Trades Union (GNCTU), 1833–4.

The attempts by the state and employers to crush the GNCTU is well known, culminating as it did in 1834 with the transportation of the Tolpuddle Martyrs. (These were six agricultural labourers from the village of Tolpuddle in Dorsetshire who, having joined the GNCTU, were accused and found guilty in a show trial of 'administering illegal oaths'. This ancient piece of legislation was dredged up as the means of defeating trade unionism, given its now legal status, in an attempt to discourage others. There was a mass campaign to prevent the sentences being carried out, which although unsuccessful in its immediate aim succeeded in pressuring the government to commute the sentences of the six.)

It is probable, however, that internal divisions within the GNCTU would have caused its eventual demise. Although Owen occupied an influential position within the union he was in constant disgreement with two of its other more militant and class-conscious leaders, J.E. Smith and James Morrison. The withdrawal of the GNCTU's largest affiliate, the Tailors' Union, following its strike in April 1834 in which the employers cleverly exploited sexual divisions in the industry, was another major factor contributing to the collapse of the umbrella organisation.

Women, Socialism and Trade Unionism

The feminist ideas of Mary Wollstonecraft had a greater influence on the radical and trade union movement of the post-war period than during her own lifetime. (She died from complications arising from the birth of her daughter in 1797.) Owen actively supported the ideas of women's emancipation, and the communitarianism of the 1820s sought to give practical expression to new and non-oppressive ways of living. However, it was not until the 1830s that such ideas emerged in a more popular form from the comparatively tiny intellectual glasshouse in which they had been nurtured. Women themselves played an active role campaigning for sexual equality and publicly promoting socialism as the only means for its achievement. This period is unique in the extent to which male leaders of the labour movement were open and supportive of such initiatives.

Such women as Anna Wheeler, Fanny Wright, Eliza Macauley, Emma Martin, Eliza Sharples and Frances Morrison were all prepared to transgress social convention in campaigning against sexual oppression and class exploitation. Frances Morrison was married to James Morrison, the editor of the GNCTU newspaper the *Pioneer*. This not only had a regular women's page (initially entitled a 'page for the ladies' which changed its name, following protests, to 'women's page'), but also contained editorials jointly written by the Morrisons in which the demand for equal pay for work of equal value was raised, probably for the very first time. Other issues covered in the women's page of the *Pioneer* and elsewhere in the paper have a similar contemporary ring to them – drunken husbands, women's responsibility for housework, male hostility to women in the trade union movement, the sexual division of labour, and much more.

The GNCTU had a large female membership and women were encouraged to organise in separate 'lodges of industrious females' (women's branches). This policy reflected and served the purposes of two antagonistic trends in the labour movement. On one hand the traditional, and probably majority, view was that women in an era of technological change were a threat to men's jobs and pay rates, and that trade unionism existed to protect the existing situation. Given the prevalence of the sexual division of labour within and between industries it made sense, according to this argument, to maintain separate spheres for women in trade unions too. On the other hand there was a dawning recognition that sexual divisions were in the interest of the employer and that the way to overcome the super-exploitation of women was through trade union organisation. Given that no women were in the leadership of sexually mixed unions, Morrison and others in the GNCTU thought that separate women's organisation would encourage more women to become self-mobilising, thereby lessening their reliance on men.

The Reform of Parliament

All radicals, whatever else divided them, had been united for decades in their opposition to the corrupt aristocratic club which passed itself off as the legitimate government of the British Isles. Out of a population of around 14 million in 1831 (in England and Wales) only about 400,000 men had the vote. There was no uniform electoral law applying to the whole country, but in general (saving some anomalous exceptions in the borough franchise) only wealthy landowners could vote and be elected. Even in the odd seat where this general rule did not apply corruption was so rife that votes were easily bought and sold. Apart from the size and composition of the electorate, the most glaring anomaly lay in the distribution of the 558 House of Commons seats which, by the 1830s bore almost no relation to where people actually lived. Populous industrial towns like Manchester, Birmingham, Leeds and Sheffield were entirely unrepresented. Seventy per cent of MPs were returned from the southern counties of England – Cornwall returned 42! Gatton in Wiltshire returned two MPs – it had only one voter. Old Sarum, an uninhabited hill in the same county, enjoyed a similar privilege of double representation. The phrase 'rotten borough' (in widespread use at the time) is a good description of these and many other similar examples of the deformed parliamentary system which, according to the Duke of Wellington, 'was beyond the wit of man to consider ... more perfect'.

The vast majority of the population, rich and poor, were unenfranchised but had more 'wit' than Wellington. The existing reform societies were given a huge boost by two coincidental events in 1830. One was the death of the king (George IV) which by convention, brought about a general election. The other was news of the revolution in France resulting in the downfall of the hated Charles X. A wave of revolt spread over Europe, Britain included. The reform societies were organised mainly on class lines. The middle-class joined the political unions, and the various working-class groups eventually cohered around the National Union of the Working Classes formed in 1830.

The 1830 election produced the first Whig government for almost half a century. Grey, the new Prime Minister described himself as an 'aristocrat both by position and nature ... with a predilection for old institutions'. Nonetheless, such was the nature of the forces for reform outside parliament that even Grey was forced to see the writing on the wall. He therefore produced a reform bill which would, he hoped, 'afford sure grounds of resistance to further innovation'. Even this modest measure took two years to get through the mother of parliaments, and even then only because the strength of the mass movement was powerful enough to create a near-revolutionary situation.

The shock troops and the backbone of this movement were the workers. Well organised and often armed, they struck fear into the owners of property including their erstwhile middle-class allies organised in the political unions. In 1831 when the House of Lords rejected the Bill, revolutionary outbreaks occurred in many towns including Bath, Derby, Worcester and Nottingham. In Merthyr, the scene of serious 'disturbances', the red flag was raised for the first time in Britain as a symbol of revolt. Bristol was actually taken over for some days by the rebels. Learning the European lesson of a failure to compomise, a frightened British establishment was forced, in June 1832, to pass the Reform Bill.

The compromise was just enough to split the reform movement. It satisfied only the industrialists, around 217,000 of whom were enfranchised – the only additions to the electoral register. Many of the more heinous abuses in the borough franchise and the distribution of seats were cleared up. The Reform Act gave nothing to the working class who had made the whole thing possible. For them the Act was the 'great betrayal', and was popularly referred to as such in the years to come.

Their masters in the factories now joined the aristocracy as their political masters in Westminster. The goal of the workers' movement was, and remained, adult (male) suffrage.

Even before the fight for parliamentary reform regrouped with greater clarity, it was clear that the movement was strong enough to force its own will on the new system. A device known as 'exclusive dealing' was used to elect radical MPs in areas like Oldham where the movement was very strong. A list of electors was published along with their voting preferences and those who refused to support the radical candidates (in Oldham's case Cobbett and Fielden) were boycotted by the unenfranchised working class. Boycotting took the form of refusal to buy the products or patronise the shops of Tory or Whig voters. A handbill issued in Oldham in the 1832 election spelled out this novel strategy:

> The enemies of reform are everywhere alarmed at the non electors adopting exclusive dealing. The nation and your enemies know the immense power of the working class ... Therefore, workingmen, if you wish well to yourselves, lay out your money with those electors of Oldham who support ... Fielden and Cobbett ... The electors' franchise is a trust to be used for your benefit, and not a right to be used against you. (Quoted in Foster, *Class Struggle and the Industrial Revolution*, 1977)

After 1832 the lessons learned by the activists about the connection between economic and political power were more obvious than hitherto. Before the Reform Act the industrialists who exploited labour economically could nonetheless pose as the workers' friend politically. Excluded from political power themselves, the bourgeoisie were as vehement in their condemnation of the aristocracy as any working-class radical. Indeed they could also be very radical themselves. In broad terms 1832 changed all this. The strangely contradictory role of the industrialists was ended, even if, owing to the fluidity of the class structure and the prevalence for many years to come of many very small-scale capitalists, there still remained some blurring of the edges. From now on political protest remained largely the preserve of the working class in organisations free from middle-class leadership.

The fact that women remained totally unenfranchised was relatively unremarked at the time, given the exclusion of the vast majority of the population. However, women remained an integral part of most movements of political and ecomomic protest at least until mid century when the nature of such protest began to assume a decidedly less revolutionary character. Meanwhile the 'great betrayal' inspired rather than dampened the labour movement and ensured that in the coming two decades, with the absence of middle-class radicalism, it became more class conscious than ever before.

Further Reading

Butt, J. (ed.), *Robert Owen: Prince of Cotton Spinners* (David & Charles, 1971).

Cole, G.D.H., *Attempts at General Union 1818–1834* (Macmillan, 1953).

Foot, P., *Red Shelley* (Bookmarks, 1984).

Foster, J., *Class Struggle and the Industrial Revolution* (Methuen, University Paperback, 1977).

Frow, R. and E., *Political Women 1800–1850* (Pluto Press, 1989).

Kirby, R.G. and Musson, A.E., *The Voice of the People: John Doherty 1798–1854* (Manchester University Press, 1975).

Lovett, W., *Life and Struggles of William Lovett* (Macgibbon & Kee, 1967, first published 1876).

Rickwood, E. (ed), *Radical Squibs and Loyal Ripostes: Radical Pamphlets by William Hone and Loyal Counterblasts Illustrated by George Cruikshank* (Adams and Dart, 1971).

Stedman-Jones, G., *Languages of Class* (CUP, 1983).

Taylor, Barbara, *Eve and the New Jerusalem* (Virago, 1983)

4   The Age of Chartism

The temporary demise of the trade union movement after Tolpuddle and the 'great betrayal' of 1832 had the effect of focusing activity more sharply on other issues. Two campaigns in particular attracted a mass working-class following in the 1820s and 1830s. One was to reduce the hours of work in the factories and improve working conditions generally; the other was to oppose the hated Poor Law Amendment Act of 1834. From 1836 onward these campaigns, along with other more long-standing elements of workers' organisation, coalesced into one mighty all-embracing movement – Chartism.

Living Standards

The issues of poor relief and factory reform were not new ones for the labour movement. How could they be? The latter was a direct product of the process of industrialisation and the former was sharply accentuated by it. There is continuing debate among economic historians about the 'standard of living question'. Put simply, the protagonists (known as the optimists and the pessimists) argue about whether industrialisation in the years up to (roughly) the mid nineteenth century had the effect of raising (optimist) or lowering (pessimist) working-class living standards. Without here examining the masses of conflicting evidence, suffice it to say that almost all *contemporary* observers, whatever their political allegiance, were convinced that the hardship of the masses was acute. Victorian novelists like Dickens, Mrs. Gaskell and even Disraeli (in *Sybil*) wrote about the condition of the urban working-class in stark, even horrifying, terms as did contemporary observers like Friedrich Engels (in his *Condition of the Working Class in England in 1844*). Numerous government enquiries (known as 'Blue Books') attested to urban squalor producing alarming mortality rates and health defects. Reports of factory commissioners (after 1833) also provide evidence of the extent of child labour, horrifyingly long working hours and abysmal working conditions. Their reports do not, of course, cover the even worse conditions of employment outside the jurisdiction of the very limited factory legislation. In 1842 the official government inquiry headed by Edwin Chadwick published its *Report on the Sanitary Condition of the Labouring Population of Great Britain*. It, too, made dismal reading and even spurred the government into limited public health reform.

Factory Reform

Most historians of the factory reform movement date its genesis from the 1830s. It is certainly true that the movement was very active after that date, but this happened only because it was able to build on the solid foundations that had been laid 20 years earlier. There are two reasons why more attention is paid to the later rather than the earlier period. One is that the factory system had, by the 1830s extended to other branches of textile manufacture, in particular to one of the oldest industries, woollen cloth. Secondly, the movement had acquired some powerful support from diverse and unexpected quarters outside the ranks of the working-class. Two names illustrate this diversity. One was Richard Oastler, a Tory of the old school who had never come to terms with industrialisation and the new social order to which it gave rise. He wrote a series of letters in 1830 for the *Leeds Mercury* denouncing what he called 'Yorkshire slavery' – a damning indictment of conditions in the worsted mills of Bradford. The other was a cotton mill owner and an MP, John Fielden. Important though men like these were to the cause of factory reform, their contribution, which because of their class position attracted much publicity, was minimal in comparison to that of the much less celebrated but far deeper and more consistent mass campaigns led and waged by working men and women whose very lives were threatened by the inhuman exploitation to which they were subjected in the early factories.

The first signs of the movement for factory reform are to be found as early as 1814 among the cotton spinners of Manchester who formed what was known as a 'short time committee'. Although these and other similarly named committees were closely allied to the cotton trade unions, they existed independently of them and hence carried on their campaign for shorter working hours at times when their unions may have been temporarily broken. This campaign spread throughout the factory districts, led and organised by working men and women long before Oastler's or Fielden's appearance on the scene. Putting the record straight on this point is necessary not just for the sake of historical accuracy. It is also important because it helps to counter the widespread belief (still prevalent) that the workers are their own worst enemies and the hardship they suffer is brought about by their own greed and stupidity. Child labour, so this argument runs, existed only because avaricious parents wanted the extra income brought in by their offspring. In this fashion the key role played by the workers themselves, through their trade unions, in enforcing factory legislation is also obscured. Until 1833 the absence of a factory inspectorate meant that the only means of enforcing the very limited extant factory legislation was by means of the 'common informer'. Such individuals were invariably trade union officers or representatives who, of course, had first-hand experience of the widespread abuses perpetrated by the factory owners. The 1833 Factory Act ended this system by establishing inspectors to police the new legislation which dealt in the main with limiting the hours of women and children. It was the owners themselves who found a way to circumvent this by enforcing a relay system, a kind of double shift. Most factories were, in any case hardly ever checked, and it was this and the flouting of the law which gave rise to the general demand of the short time committees for a ten-hour day for all which was finally partially implemented in 1844.

Blaming the workers for what was in essence the stupendous greed of their masters does little justice to the fact that they were the initiators of reform. The same argument would have us believe that infant mortality was widespread in the factory districts because mothers went out to work, leaving their babies with old women or young children who gave them 'mother's little comforter' (laudanum) and sops in the absence of any safe substitute for breast milk. The alarmingly high rates of infant mortality in the factory districts attracted a great deal of attention in the 1820s and 1830s, but no practical help was given to working mothers whose labour was so attractive to the mill owners. The absence of any kind of childcare provision, let alone maternity leave, meant that women often gave birth on the factory floor and returned to work within days of their 'confinement'. It was easier for Victorian moralists to blame mothers than to tackle the problem. To have done so would have meant publicly acknowledging that women played a role outside the home – a fact which the factory system had brought out into the open for perhaps the first time, exposing the huge contradictions in the prevalent ideology of the sanctity of home, hearth and family. Within this construct the idealised notions of feminity and 'women's place' sat uncomfortably with the now publicly exposed reality of the lot of working-class women.

The Poor Law

Until 1834 the system of poor relief in Britain was based on principles established 300 years earlier during the reign of Elizabeth I. There had been many changes in the form and adminstration of poor relief during this long period but essentially the principles established in 1601 remained. These were that society had a duty to provide work for the able-bodied poor and to provide subsistence for those who, through age or infirmity, could not work. It all sounds very humane, but in practice it wasn't. This was because the finance and implementation of any scheme based on these principles fell to the smallest administrative unit of society – the parish. In order to fulfil its commitments the parish had to levy a special poor rate the amount of which depended on the scale of the problem. There was thus, in the absence of any state responsibilty, a direct local material incentive in devising various stratagems either to play down or to hide poverty in order to reduce the poor rate. Chief among the devices used were the laws forbidding vagrancy and defining 'settlement'. The aim was to ensure that the poor of one parish could not become a burden to the overseers of the poor in another parish.

By the end of the eighteenth century it was evident that the system was not only stretched to its limit but was inoperable as it stood. The steady rise in population and the effects of enclosures (in removing the rights to common land which had acted as a traditional bulwark against low agricultural wages) forced some to realise that the causes of the resulting widespread poverty were to be found in low wages and high food prices. The only way to alleviate this without depopulating the agricultural areas was to use the poor rate to provide some form of supplementary allowance.

Many different schemes embodying this principle of 'outdoor relief' were tried. The most famous was the Speenhamland system first introduced in Berkshire in 1795 and spreading later to many southern counties. Under this system deficient wages were supplemented on a sliding scale based on the price of bread and taking into account the number of dependants supported by each applicant. The relief obtained through this and other similar systems was certainly neither generous nor inspired by humanitarian or altruistic motives. However, in contrast to what was to come any form of outdoor relief seemed kind.

The political economists of the industrial era developed a new social philosophy echoes of which are to be found in the 'two nation' Toryism of today. For them the only way to help the nation's poor was to increase the nation's capital – a job to be left to the wealth creators (the capitalists). Within the framework of classical political economy, the theories of over-population expounded by Thomas Malthus, and of utilitarianism developed by Jeremy Bentham, were the foundation of a massive attack on the old poor law culminating in the 1834 Report of the Royal Commission on the Poor Law.

Imbued with the ideological dogma of Malthus and Bentham, the commissioners set out to prove that the effect of subsidising wages was to make the working-class demoralised and lazy by encouraging, to quote the report of the commission, 'a bounty on indolence and vice'. They also tried to prove that the system caused population growth since the 'child benefit' element encouraged the poor to 'breed recklessly'. Many other similarly unproven (and unprovable) excuses were given by the commissioners as reasons for ditching the old system. Underlying all the dogma the real concern of the critics of the old poor law was its mounting cost – a cost borne by the wealth creators who had better things to do with their money than subsidise the poor.

So, given the impossibility of denying the existence of poverty, what was the alternative to 'outdoor relief'? The Poor Law Amendment Act of 1834, based on the recommendations of the commissioners, offered a simple solution resting upon the limited aim of relieving only the 'deserving poor' rather than poverty itself. The Act abolished all forms of outdoor relief and instead sanctioned only 'indoor relief' administered through a network of workhouses under the control of central government. Those applying for help would be deemed to be deserving if they passed the workhouse test which was based on the principle of 'less eligibility'. This meant that if anyone was granted relief 'his situation on the whole shall not be made really or apparently so eligible as the situation of the independent labourer of the lowest class'. In other words, workhouses were to be made as horrible as possible in order to deter the poor in favour of the utterly destitute. The choice for the poor was stark – the workhouse or starve.

The regime of the workhouse was intolerably harsh, almost penal. Families were separated, food was sparse, accommodation dismal, and all but the very sick were forced into hard and unrewarding work. The undeserving poor who failed the workhouse test had, according to this utilitarian philosophy, only themselves to blame for their situation. They were left to their own devices and the whims of private charity. Poverty, if it could not be cured by 'self help', was to be punished. The spectre of the workhouse haunted the poor for the next 100 years and helps explain the fear and shame of the very admission of poverty.

It was easy enough to pass a law like this, but not so easy to implement it. Opposition was on a scale never before witnessed on any other issue. When the commissioners turned their attention, in 1837, to implementing the Act in the north the opposition was so strong and so widespread that they were forced in some cases to give up entirely. Over a quarter of a million people joined a demonstration near Bradford in 1837. Over the whole of the West Riding and especially in Huddersfield the implementation of the Act was delayed. This was also the case in the factory districts of Lancashire. The short time committees were used as the basis of opposition, however, the later involvement of the Chartists frightened off some of the 'respectable' support for opposition from Tories like Disraeli and *The Times* which had initially opposed the New Poor Law.

The government's timing was bad. It was attempting to introduce the law during a time of severe trade depression when many workers had been laid off or were on short time. Any form of indoor relief (let alone the awful workhouse) was inappropriate in these circumstances – a temporary problem did not require a permanent 'solution'. Even some employers could see this – they didn't want their labour force to be lost permanently to the workhouse. The opposition remained strong until the mid 1840s, by which time the government was forced to give way and allow outdoor relief to continue in the north even though workhouses were finally built.

Chartism

To describe Chartism simply as a political movement based on the demands contained in a six-point charter is both correct and misleading. The charter itself, launched in 1838 by members of the London Working Men's Association, was not the product of new or original thinking. It contained the standard radical demands that had been articulated in one form or another for the past 40 years. Thus this simple description of Chartism gives us no clue as to its real significance.

So, wherein lies the significance of Chartism? First it would not be an exaggeration to say that it was the single most important working-class political movement of the nineteenth century. Its mass support was clearly visible in the presentation of three 'monster' petitions to parliament in 1839, 1842 and 1848, each containing literally millions of signatures. From this mass support came the formation of the first ever working-class political party – the National Charter Association, founded in 1840. Secondly, although Chartism was the culmination and highest point of a long radical tradition, it also represented something qualitatively new.

Its most class-conscious elements were gravitating away from radicalism and towards socialism. Guided by such theoreticians as Bronterre O'Brien (the 'schoolmaster of Chartism') and later George Julian Harney and Ernest Jones (both were closely associated with Karl Marx and Friederich Engels who were resident in Britain as political exiles from their native Germany), an important 'left' trend within Chartism which later became the leadership made connections between political oppression and economic exploitation.

Despite its divisions and tactical errors, Chartism posed an enormous threat to the established order precisely because at times it was able to weld together class consciousness with political consciousness, and to articulate this potent mixture. Even more than this, it managed, in the early years at least, to form alliances with small property owners in a huge anti-government alliance the uniqueness of which lay in the fact that it was led by class-conscious workers.

The defeat of Chartism in the 1850s represented a massive defeat for the working-class movement and ushered in a new phase in the history of the British labour movement. Chartism was both a positive and a negative turning point in this history: its existence promised much; its eclipse turned those promises into far-off dreams, still unfulfilled.

Chartism cannot be said to have failed. After all, it existed as a movement capable of mobilising mass support for over 14 years. The more important question is why it did not fulfil its potential. To explain this involves looking beyond the conventionally labelled divisions between the so-called 'moral force' and 'physical force' wings of Chartism and instead analysing the social composition on which its different political perspectives rested. The fact that Chartism was a uniquely working-class movement is not sufficient explanation of its social composition. The working class was still in the process of formation and could not, therefore, be considered as a homogenous entity. The elements comprising Chartism in the early stages were wide ranging, reflecting social diversity. The demands of the charter were broad enough to win support from factory workers, from artisans (skilled workers who owned their own tools), from workers like the handloom weavers whose hand skills were rendered obsolete by industrialisation, from women workers and from black and Irish workers. There was even support early on from lower middle-class radicals – shopkeepers, professional people or owners of small workshops.

The charter provided a means by which a fragile unity could be built, but such unity could not weather the turbulent storms of the revolutionary insurgence of 1839. In that year, after parliament had rejected the first petition, the delegates to the Chartist Convention gave confused messages as to the next stage in the campaign. They first accepted and then rejected a call for a general rising, and planned for strike activity instead. Nonetheless, armed risings did take place, the most notable of which was in Newport under the leadership of the former mayor of the town, John Frost. There were outbreaks in other towns, too, but given the forcible dispersal of the convention, there was no central co-ordination and each individual revolt was supressed by the military. Mass arrests followed and many of the Chartist leaders were subsequently imprisoned.

By 1840 when the insurrectionary mood had subsided and the movement regrouped, the more 'respectable' elements, notably the middle-class faction around the Birmingham banker Joseph Attwood, and an artisan group led by William Lovett, had dropped out altogether. This could have led to greater ideological clarity and unity of the remaining forces had there been a more profound understanding of the key importance of the struggles of the factory workers. However, the militancy of the industrial struggle took the leadership of the National Charter Association (formed in 1840 as a political party organisation) by surprise. This was clearly seen in 1842 when the hesitancy and divisions among the Chartist leaders resulted in a tragic lost opportunity.

The General Strike of 1842

1842 was the year in which the first ever general strike took place. The momentous events of August and September of that year are usually referred to by historians disparagingly as the 'Plug Riots'. The implication behind such a description is that the episode was the work of half-starved, half-crazed, desperate workers who spontaneously travelled the length and breadth of the country pulling out the plugs of the steam boilers that operated the machinery, forcing other mindless workers to walk out and join them. Such a description bears no relation to the facts. The strike was well planned and organised by the trade unions, and involved nearly half a million workers throughout Britain. It spread from its nucleus at the heart of the cotton industry in Lancashire and involved workers in almost every other major trade. Whilst it is true that the immediate cause of the strike was the proposal of the cotton manufac-turers to cut wages by 25 per cent because of the severe trade depression, the strike was also highly political in character, involving the demand for the charter as its central aim. At countless meetings the strikers passed resolutions declaring that they would not return to work 'until the People's Charter is the law of the land'.

The signs were good. The political and industrial wings of the movement had come together and the mood was militant. Sales of the Chartist newspaper the *Northern Star* were high, and over three million signatures were collected on the second Chartist petition presented to parliament in 1842. So, what went wrong? The main problem was one of central leadership and direction. The strikers had their own leaders, almost all of whom were Chartists, and some, like Richard Pilling (leader of the Ashton weavers) and Alexander Hutchinson (general secretary of the smiths' union and editor of the *Trades Journal*) were socialists. However, although various trade conferences were called during the course of the strike, and despite much meticulous local planning, there was little in the way of central co-ordination given the absence of a nationally organised trade union movement.

So why didn't the National Charter Association fill the breach – after all, the strike was for the charter? The Chartist leadership was not only taken by surprise by the strike, it was also divided in its attitude towards it. It expressed support in general terms, especially as time went on, however, plotting a strategy was much more difficult, especially as it became clear that some of the Chartist leaders including Hill (editor of the *Northern Star*) and at times Feargus O'Connor (the paper's owner) viewed the strike as an employer-inspired diversion from the fight for the charter. Given O'Connor's idiosyncratic politics it is not all that surprising that he vacillated. More surprising was Harney's inexplicable outright opposition to the strike in view of his left-wing credentials. In short, the Chartist leadership at this stage was at best incapable of grasping the full significance of this truly momentous display of working-class power and at worst unable to give it the central direction it needed so badly. Thus it was that by September, after numerous bloody confrontations with the troops and more than 1,500 arrests, the strike was finally broken.

There is little doubt as to the significance with which the strike was viewed by the forces of law and order. It was a critical and unique moment in which both the economic *and* political power of capital was threatened. Lord Abinger, the judge at the mass show trial of those charged with sedition for their participation in the strike, expressed the establishment view succinctly:

> The establishment of the Charter would become an odious tyranny devoted to democratic principles, and elected by persons a vast majority of whom have no property and depend on manual labour ... The first thing such an assembly would do would be to aim at

the destruction of property. (Quoted in M. Jenkins, *The General Strike of 1842*, 1980)

The Chartist Land Plan

The defeat of 1842 had very important consequences for the future of Chartism. O'Connor sought to revive the movement by taking it in a new and, as it turned out, unproductive direction. He turned his back on the temporarily defeated factory workers and instead sought to base Chartism's support on the permanently defeated pre-industrial hand trades like the handloom weavers.

Given that the future direction of industrial Britain held little for such workers, O'Connor (echoing William Cobbett almost 30 years earlier) conjured for them dreams of the past – of a 'golden age' of rural Britain untainted by factories and grimy towns, where sturdy peasant proprietors retained their independence. The fact that such a time had never existed did not lessen its romantic appeal and hence the attraction of the proposal to recreate something like it in the form of the Chartist Land Plan's vision of model rural communities. This was a grand scheme of O'Connor's, launched in 1843, in which workers were invited to take shares. Its objects as stated in the *Northern Star* were:

> to purchase land on which to locate its members, in order to demonstrate to the working-classes of the kingdom, firstly, the value of the land as a means of making them independent of the grinding capitalist; and, secondly to show them the necessity of securing the speedy enactment of the People's Charter ...

Land was bought and several settlements started on this basis with lots being drawn to determine which of the shareholders would be given a house and a smallholding. The pages of the *Northern Star* bear witness to the enormous amount of effort and energy consumed by this Utopian scheme – all to no avail since the whole enterprise failed miserably within a few years.

Socialism and Internationalism

Whilst O'Connor was preoccupied with his dreams of peasant proprietorship, the political leadership of Chartism gravitated in an increasingly socialist direction under the influence of Harney. He was the effective editor of the *Northern Star* from 1843 onwards and exercised even greater control of the paper when its offices moved to London the following year. London at this time was the centre for European revolutionary exiles forced to flee from their own countries in the wake of the failure of the revolutions of 1830 and the subsequent imposition of reactionary regimes. Marx and Engels were at the centre of the network of émigrés, and Harney not only made their acquaintance and moved in their circles but in 1845 helped to form the Society of Fraternal Democrats. This was an organisation of representatives of the socialist and workers' movements of European countries that aimed to give practical meaning to the principles of proletarian internationalism. It is widely regarded as the forerunner and indeed the prototype of the First International. Harney ensured that its activities, along with reports of the struggles of workers in other countries, received wide coverage in the *Northern Star*.

Thus it was that in the mid 1840s the leadership of the Chartist movement, whilst not completey united, was increasingly socialist in orientation. Positive though this was, it was too late. The special conditions that had facilitated such wide working-class unity around the charter were by now passing and were only fleetingly resurrected in 1847–8. The new leadership had little appeal to those groups that had already defected, and the Land Plan absorbed the interest of the declining hand trades. Skilled workers, after the defeat of 1842, turned increasingly to trade unionism of a more sectional type. Within the most important and the most militant industry, cotton textiles, the employers had begun to recognise trade unions and to establish a system of collective bargaining. This meant that the best-organised and potentially most dangerous section of workers could obtain concessions through legal and peaceable means, provided they mended their ways and divorced themselves from the old traditions. Hence Chartism's base of support was much narrower, resting as it now did on unskilled workers and politically advanced artisans and others.

1848

The government had learned much from working-class upheavals of previous decades and had taken steps to prepare itself for fresh outbursts. This preparation was clearly to be seen during the third and final revival of Chartism in 1847–8. Coinciding as it did with the international slump of 1847, the revival was given an immense boost by the news of the revolution in France in 1848. The fact that Britain was one of the very few European states whose government remained intact in that year was due in part to its successful mobilisation of troops and special constables (consisting of property owners and even of some better paid skilled workers), a force that threatened to massacre the huge demonstration massed in Kennington Common on 10 April 1848. The demonstrators had planned to march to Westminster to present the third Chartist petition which contained almost two million signatures. In the event caution and fear (in particular of O'Connor) prevailed. The demonstration was dispersed and a small deputation was sent to parliament instead.

The government followed its 'victory' with a wave of repression and mass arrests of Chartist leaders, including William Cuffay, a black man, the son of a slave. Cuffay was a tailor and had emerged as one of the most prominent leaders of London Chartism. He was the main organiser of the Kennington Common meeting and vehemently opposed the decision to disband it. He was later put on trial for 'levying war against the Queen' and sentenced to transportation for life to Van Diemen's Land (now Tasmania). If historians have failed to acknowledge that a respected Chartist leader was black, contemporary observers did not. *The Times* described him as 'half a "nigger"'. A more sympathetic account in *Reynold's Political Instructor* said of him that he was 'loved by his own order' and that he was a 'scion of Afric's oppressed race'.

After 1848

Chartism was not defeated in 1848 but it never again became the national mass movement that it once had been. This was due partly to bitter internal divisions which finally resulted in a complete break between the socialists (led by Harney and Ernest Jones), and O'Connor and his followers who favoured an alliance with the middle-class National Parliamentary and Financial Reform Association (a body which advocated a rate payers' franchise). The split was complete by 1850, with the socialists now in control. Harney launched a new paper, the *Red Republican* which stated in its first issue that Chartism had 'progressed from the idea of simple political reform to the idea of social revolution'. In the same year the *Red Republican* carried the first English translation of *The Manifesto of the Communist Party* written in 1848 in German by Marx and Engels.

Internal divisions and government repression, however, are not sufficient reasons to explain the inability of Chartism to sustain itself in the 1850s. Mention has already been made of the contracting base of Chartism's support in the mid 1840s. Now the appeal of 'the Charter and something more' (the detailed programme of social reform adopted in 1851) withered on the vine. The underlying reasons for divisions within the working class, divisions that the temporary revival of Chartism in the year of revolution (1848) had been unable to overcome, have to be sought outside the 'subjective' arena of the movement itself.

These 'objective' factors are related to developments within the British economy which by the mid-nineteenth century had overcome many of the problems associated with the first phase of industrialisation. (These developments will be examined more closely in the next chapter.) The ensuing Victorian prosperity not only cast a rosy glow over the self-made capitalist, but also enabled a section of the working-class to bask in the reflected rays. In other words the material conditions were established whereby skilled male workers could make a reasonable living and even prosper. Hence, for them, the attraction of Chartism, particularly in its socialist phase, continued to decline in an inverse ratio to the attraction of the new-style, more defensive trade unions. These workers no longer had an interest in overthrowing a system which was capable now of rewarding them. The changes they sought were *within* the system, not outside it.

The divisions that thus emerged within the working-class had a profound impact on the development of the labour movement. In the short term they meant that the decline of Chartism was to be permanent as the conditions which had given rise to the development of revolutionary class consciousness passed. It was this developing consciousness which had characterised the labour movement in the first half of the nineteenth century, and which had found its highest expression in Chartism. It was to be almost 50 years before the working class was to form another political party of its own.

The Role of Women

Although the charter called for male rather than universal suffrage this did not mean that all Chartists were opposed to women's suffrage, nor that women were uninvolved or inactive within the Chartist movement. Quite the opposite is true. Building on the already considerable female involvement in the reform agitation, on Owenite and trade union struggles of the previous two decades, women emerged as a considerable force within Chartism as activists, theoreticians and sometimes as leaders.

Many female Charter Associations were established after 1840, and such women as Mathilda Roalfe, Mary Ann Walker, Ann Knight, Helen McFarlane, Catherine Barmby and others were well known nationally as speakers, propagandists and organisers. Helen McFarlane produced the first English translation of Marx's *Communist Manifesto*. (This was the first translation from the original German to appear anywhere in the world.)

Catherine Barmby and Ann Knight were both socialist feminists. In 1847 Ann Knight, a Chartist leader in Sheffield, published a pamphlet demanding votes for women. Catherine Barmby, in an undated essay entitled 'The Demand for the Emancipation of Women Politically and Socially', called for the charter to be amended to include female suffrage and argued that women must be emancipated domestically as well as politically. She called for economic independence and freedom from 'household drudgery'. In a later article, 'Women's Industrial Independence' (published in 1848 in the *Apostle and Chronicle of the Communist Church*) she prefigured some of the arguments of the twentieth-century women's liberation movement when she demanded 'associative arrangements' to lessen women's enslavement within the home. She also argued, earlier than any one else, for the necessity of a novel form of consciousness raising for women in an all-female environment. For this reason, although she herself was an atheist, she proposed that women should be permitted to become priests and thereby, using the power of their office, facilitate the coming together of women in order to share their common problems and experiences.

The full extent of women's involvement in Chartism is still under-researched. The above account is but a sample of what we already know, but even this fragment is sufficient to illustrate the point that within the radical and socialist tradition of the late eighteenth century and the first half of the nineteenth century, working-class women were at last beginning to find a voice in the public political arena. This voice forms the foundation of the socialist feminist tradition. As mentioned already in an earlier chapter, there was a direct link between the emergence of such consciousness among working-class women and the general level of political class consciousness in the labour movement. The defiant and daring nature of the movement in its theory and in its practice, its willingness to challenge the dominant norms and values of the bourgeoisie and aristocracy, created the space for women to extend this challenge to the usually private and sacrosanct areas of family life and personal relationships. The socialist and radical challenge was all the richer (and more frightening to the establishment) for such an intervention.

The decline of Chartism marked the temporary halt to this kind of politics and with it the active participation of women in the labour movement for at least three decades. The recollection of the radical and socialist origins of the labour movement must also acknowledge its feminist tradition. Both are as much part of its legacy as the later labourist alternative.

Further Reading

Briggs, A. (ed.), *Chartist Studies* (Papermac, 1967).

Chadwick, E., *Report on the Sanitary Conditions of the Labouring Population of Great Britain* (Edinburgh University Press, 1965, first published 1842).

Dickens, C., *Hard Times* (Dent, 1907, first published 1854).

Disraeli, B., *Sybil: or the Two Nations* (OUP, 1956, first published 1845).

Driver, C., *Richard Oastler: A Tory Radical* (Octagon Books, 1970).

Engels, F., *Condition of the Working Class in England in 1844* (Allen & Unwin, 1968, first published 1892).

Gaskell, E., *Mary Barton: A Tale of Manchester Life* (Penguin, 1970, first published 1848).

Jenkins, M., *The General Strike of 1842* (Lawrence & Wishart, 1980).

Jones, E.C. and Saville, J., *Ernest Jones, Chartist* (Lawrence & Wishart, 1952).

Schoyen, A.R., *The Chartist Challenge: A Portrait of George Julian Harney* (Heinemann, 1958).

Thompson, Dorothy, *The Chartists* (Wildwood, 1984).

Ward, J.T., *The Factory Movement 1830–55* (Macmillan, 1960).

Ward, J.T. (ed.), *Popular Movements c1830–1850* (Macmillan, 1970).

Part 2

1850–1920: The Workshop of the World and Beyond

5   Economic and Political Background 1850–1918

The economic development of Britain from the mid nineteenth century until the end of World War One falls into two distinct phases, although taken together the unifying feature of these phases is the continued prevalence of unusually high rates of profit. The source of such profit was firmly based on Britain's well-established lead in industrial production. By the 1870s, however, this early lead was being overtaken by other countries with the consequence that Britain became increasingly reliant on her colonial empire.

The Economy

1850–73: 'The Great Victorian Boom'

By mid century, having overcome the dislocation associated with being the first country to industrialise, Britain began to reap the benefit of her early lead. By the late 1840s she entered into a second phase of industrialisation – one which was much more broadly based than the first, dominated as it had been by the cotton industry. The construction of the railway network, almost complete by 1847, had stimulated the growth of a huge capital goods industry based first on coal and iron, and later on steel and engineering. The development of various branches of the engineering industry (in this period machine tools, machinery, locomotive construction, shipbuilding and marine engineering) would not have been possible without the expansion of the capital goods sector. Iron was both the agent and the symbol of nineteenth-century industrialisation. Coal was its source of motive power, used to supply first steam and then gas as the prime generators of the machine age. Together with cotton, these formed Britain's staple industries. Until the 1870s they flourished in a unique period of uninterrupted growth, punctuated only by the two short depressions in 1857 and 1866.

Alongside textiles, the manufactured goods produced in this second phase found not only an expanding home market (due to a rise in real wages and a continued increase in population) but also lucrative markets overseas, especially in America and later in Europe. By 1850 Britain had acquired a monopoly of world trade – she had literally become 'the workshop of the world'. By 1870 Britain accounted for two-thirds of the world's production of cotton goods and half of the world's output of coal and iron. Her dominance of world trade was complemented by a policy of free trade, officially espoused after 1846 from which date tariff duties on imports and exports were gradually removed. During the 1860s many European countries also removed their tariff duties, thereby allowing Britain access to some of the most profitable markets on the most advantageous terms, since at this stage she had no rival industrial competitors. The fact that America and parts of continental Europe were in the process of industrialising was at this stage a great advantage to Britain since it increased their dependence on the kind of British products essential to their own economic development, machinery in particular. Outside Europe and America the market for British man-ufactured goods, especially cotton textiles, was extensive. Whether they liked it or not, these countries were forced to trade with Britain. The colonies were an obvious case in point, but no country could escape Britain's trading and economic hegemony. Those, like China, who resisted by closing their ports or levying high import duties, were forced into submission by war (1840) and by gunboat (1856).

Apart from cotton, the staple industries did not require much in the way of technical innovation and labour-saving devices. Coal was mined in the traditional way, but more intensively and extensively than hitherto. The techniques for iron extraction and manufacture had already developed in the first half of the century, and this period saw their wider application, with a great increase in the number of blast furnaces. The major technical innovation of the period was the Bessemer converter (1856) for the production of steel.

Taken as a whole, and in comparison with the previous 50 years, the main industrial changes in these years (and for the rest of the century) are not marked by great technical progress in the forces of production. Rather the main change is to be found in the scale and extent of industry (mining, manufacturing and building), and in the way such operations were organised and managed.

In general, with the exception of engineering, the following trends emerge. First, there was a tendency toward concentration in ownership and an increase in the size of the firm. In engineering this happened 20 or so years after cotton, coal and iron. (Nonetheless, a surprisingly large number of small employers still remained in the capital goods industries, buttressed presumably by the boom conditions.) Secondly, there was a very marked pattern of geographical concentration and local specialisation. Some of this was obvious – mining industries are located where the raw material is found, and shipyards are sited on the coast – but in Britain the concentration was on Tyneside and Clydeside. The cotton industry demands damp climatic conditions, and for this and other reasons it had established itself in Lancashire, but within that relatively small area there was further specialisation. Spinning was established in a circle of towns around Manchester, with Bolton specialising in fine yarns, and Oldham and Rochdale concentrating on medium and coarse. Weaving was carried out in the north-east of the county, again with different towns specialising – patterned cloths in Nelson and Colne, shirtings and sheetings in Preston. Such specialisation was an inevitable feature of the division of labour characterising mature industrial capitalism. It meant that whole towns were dependent for employment on a single branch of one industry – not a problem when the industry concerned was thriving, but the consequences of a slump were dire.

The third industrial trend was the emergence of more intensive methods of profit making. The first half of the century had witnessed the almost genocidal tendency of the manufacturers to extend the working day beyond the limits of human endurance in order to maximise their profits. Factory legislation mainly directed at limiting working hours put a brake on such 'extensive' methods. Given the lack of any major new technology, the only way to maintain profits was to get more productivity over the legislative imperative of a shorter working day and week. This was accomplished by a variety of methods – most prominent of which were the speeding up of machinery, tighter labour discipline and the introduction of piecework payment systems.

1873–96 'The Great Depression'

The boom conditions of the middle years of the nineteenth century could not last indefinitely, if only because the economies of Britain's trading partners were bound to develop to a point at which they no longer required British manufactured goods and were even able to rival her in the production of those goods. Just when precisely this happened, and whether we can call the period following the boom years the 'great depression', is still the subject of intense historical debate. Terminology aside, there can be no doubt that first many of Britain's most lucrative markets were closed to her, secondly that Britain was now facing serious competition from Europe and America, and thirdly that prices, in the wake of a surfeit of mass production, were falling.

By 1870 the phase of economic liberalism and progressive drive for national identity in continental Europe (denied by the great power carve-up of the Vienna settlement), was over. From a mass of small states Germany and Italy both completed their unification, and the theory and practice of a more chauvinistic kind of nationalism surfaced for the first time. (The word 'nationalist' was used for the first time at the end of the nineteenth century.) This, combined with the depression which threatened the newly growing industries of continental Europe induced almost all of the governments to establish protective tariffs.

The competition that Britain now faced in manufactured goods was much more serious than contemporaries thought. Certainly there was a great awareness of the problem at the time as government inquiries and the publication of such books as *Made in Germany*, E.E. Williams (1896) and *American Invaders* F.A. Mackenzie (1902) showed. It wasn't simply that other countries had, by industrialising, caught up with Britain. The real problem lay in the fact that Britain had been overtaken by them. No matter how much she increased her production (which she did), she could never make up the lost ground without massive capital investment because they had industrialised on the basis of newer and superior technology. The great irony was that many of the inventions underlying this new technology were actually pioneered in Britain but not used here. The most obvious example was in the iron and steel industry in which Gilchrist and Thomas's development of the 'basic' process for the mass production of steel (1878) was used to revolutionise steel production in France, America and Germany.

It could be argued that the causes of Britain's industrial decline lay in her too-narrow concentration on her basic industries. But, again, the major technological inventions for the industries of the future were British. Faraday's pioneering discoveries could have led to the British, rather than the Germans or Americans, developing the electricity industry. The same story can be told of the chemical industry, where the Germans were quick to exploit the British invention (W.H. Perkin) of synthetic dyes. Hence Britain failed to keep pace on the old ground and did not even try, despite the opportunity, to set foot on the new until well after others had established themselves.

From the 1870s the general tendency of all prices, not just those of manufactured goods, was downwards. Improved communication systems throughout the world and the use of refrigeration stimulated the growth of agricultural production on a vast scale in the Americas and Australasia. Meat and grain were imported into Britain cheaply, free of tariffs, with the result that food prices were significantly reduced. This, combined with a series of poor harvests in Britain, had a ruinous effect on British agriculure resulting in a dramatic drop in the area of land under cultivation and the reduction of the agricultural labour force by about a half. The fall in prices of agricultural goods had an adverse effect on the terms of trade for Britain because it meant that her non-European markets had less purchasing power to buy British manufactured exports. In addition Britain was faced with foreign competition from her new trading rivals in these markets at prices which often undercut her less technologically advanced industries.

1896–1918

By the closing years of the nineteenth century prices had begun to rise again, but the underlying causes of the chronic problems faced by the British economy in the preceding period remained. The tendency was to paper over the cracks with a variety of short- and medium-term expedients. The real solution then, as now, would have meant a vast amount of capital investment in domestic industry in order to re-equip the declining and technologically backward basic industries, and to set up the newer science-based industries using the known technology pioneered in this country. Neither of these things happened in the period before World War One. Instead, this period saw an accentuation of the trends begun during the depression.

The Empire

Faced with the loss of her markets in Europe and America, Britain became increasingly reliant on her colonial empire. During the boom years and before, British colonies had been exploited for their raw materials; now they were just as important as markets for British exports. Their great advantage was that as 'wholly owned' territories they had no say in their own economic destinies. Whereas in the 1850s and 1860s many prominent politicians following the free trade *laissez-faire* line of the Colonial Reform Society had argued for a freer relationship between Britain and the empire, by the last quarter of the nineteenth century the tune had changed. Benjamin Disraeli's attitude mirrors this change precisely. In 1852 he referred in a speech at the Crystal Palace to 'these dammed colonies' being 'millstones round our neck'. This pre-1870 approach was hardly motivated by a liberal or humanitarian concern for the colonised. It simply reflected the fact that in the absence of serious rivalry from any other great power the objective of the colonial 'reformers' was to incur the minimum possible adminstrative and military expense without jeopardising Britain's economic domination. Certainly no colonies were relinquished in this period and any attempt at self-determination was brutally repressed, as in the case of India in 1857.

From the 1870s onwards British policy was dominated by the twin imperatives of ever tighter control of existing colonies and the relentless drive to conquer and annex new ones. She was not alone in this objective – the drive for protected markets propelled other European countries on the same course, leading to the agressive imperialism that characterised the 1880s onwards. This resulted in many 'small' wars between the colonisers and the colonised, and heightened international tension between the colonising 'great' (and not so great powers, e.g. Italy and Belgium) culminating in World War One. Britain, however, in this field if in no other, maintained her early lead! By 1914 the total of British colonial territory amounted to some 12.7 million square miles (in Asia, Africa, the far and near east, and Europe (Ireland)).

The Export of Capital

However, manufactured goods were not the only British exports to her colonies. More important was the export of capital. British capital, like any other, is not necessarily patriotic – it will be invested anywhere, or in any activity, that yields a high rate of return. In the early period of industrialisation and railway building the domestic economy provided just such an outlet for the already large capital accumulations of Britain. Later, and until the 1870s the majority of British capital exports were invested in the newly industrialising economies of continental Europe and America. Then due to the growing abundance of supplies of capital in those areas, British capital was forced to find other profitable outlets; hence capital was exported in vast amounts to other parts of the world, including British colonies. This typically involved investment in mining, oil, plantations and railways.

In 1870 British capital assets abroad were about £700 million; by 1913 they had risen to an astronomical £4,000 million. The highly profitable return on these investments was the most important aspect of Britain's 'invisible' export earnings. Other 'invisibles' including the profits from the carrying trade (the British maritime fleet was the largest in the world and was used by other countries), and her dominant position in world insurance and banking. All of this ensured that the City of London retained its early leading dominance as the world's financial centre, despite Britain's stagnation and loss of leadership in productive manufacturing.

However, this financial hegemony also served to mask and to perpetuate her industrial stagnation in two ways: first because her invisible trade distorted what was actually a balance of payments crisis (i.e. the gap between imports and exports); and secondly because it drew investment capital away from where it was most needed – in British domestic industry.

Further Labour Intensification

So, although the world market was expanding, the British share was guaranteed only in her own colonies. Elsewhere Britain had to compete with more efficient producers. She expanded sales of her traditional manufactured products in her domestic and overseas markets only slowly. The exception was in the field of coal and machinery exports – both being products essential to any country's future industrial development. Hence it is no accident that in coal and heavy machine engineering the industrial trends observed during the period of the depression were most accentuated.

Given the failure to invest in new technology, the only way to maintain profit and increase productivity to meet growing demand was by a further intensification of labour. Nowhere was this more apparent than in the coal industry where the most crude and brutal strategies were adopted, involving attempts to lengthen the hours of work and cut wages (sometimes at the same time). In engineering (and elsewhere) the more sophisticated techniques of 'scientific management' were applied. The turret and capstan lathes had the effect of breaking down the job into minute specialisms, all of which could be timed. This enabled all sorts of payment systems to be introduced, the most common being that of the premium bonus as an incentive to speed up the process. The main obstacle to all types of labour intensification was, of course, the trade union, and it is no accident that some of the most bitter industrial battles were fought in these industries during this period.

Other Industries

Any survey of the British economy which concentrated solely on the staple industries would have missed two (at least) crucial points. The first is that that these industries, despite their importance in the industrial and trading pattern of Britain, employed at their height only a minority of the workforce (roughly 40 per cent). The second point is that because the workforce in the staple industries, with the exception of the cotton industry, was male, the impression would be given that women hardly worked at all. Other industries, like pottery, tailoring, boot and shoe making, and printing, were based either in small factories or in workshops and relied on craft skills with relatively little large-scale mechanisation. This did not mean that machines were not used; power-driven sewing machines in the tailoring trade, and monotype and linotype machines in the printing industry were widespread by the end of the century. Other industries employing labour on a large scale remained unmechanised, like the building trade, agriculture, and some of the service industries like retailing and road transport, the latter remaining horse driven until well into the twentieth century. Even as late as 1914 firms employing fewer than 100 workers were responsible for roughly 97 per cent of all production.

Women in the Labour Force

Evidence of women's participation rates in the labour force are notoriously unreliable. The main source is census returns, useful for this purpose only from 1851 onwards. Then, as now, official statistics took no account of the fact that women's work patterns differed from those of men owing to the fact that their working lives had to accommodate the contradictions imposed by their domestic roles. Women often worked part time or on a seasonal basis. But a woman does not cease to be a worker simply because she is forced to work in what is considered to be (for men) a non-traditional work pattern.

The greatest problem of evidence is in the area of married women's work. For ideological and financial reasons the work of married women was grossly under-recorded, so much so that it throws the official evidence into doubt. The Victorians wanted to pretend that married women did not work – it upset the conventional morality of the sanctity of family life, as the shocking revelations about women in the cotton industry in the first half of the century had shown. However, the very fact of job segregation is a clear indication that women were still needed in the workforce. The only way to overcome this contradiction between the needs of capital and its ideological moralism was by literally and figuratively hiding women's, and particularly married women's, work.

The notion of the 'family wage' encouraged even male trade unionists to collude in this duplicity (see Chapter 6). Married women continued, of necessity, sometimes for limited periods, to supplement (or even supply) the family income by doing paid work in their own homes, like sewing, or taking in other people's washing, or looking after other people's children. Such homeworking was the most hidden (and possibly growing) area of employment; then, as now, it was never recorded in the official statistics. In times of unemployment, sickness or death of the 'male breadwinner' such earnings may have been the only way of avoiding the workhouse. Women themselves may well have played a part in hiding the truth of their own employment either because they, or indeed their husbands, saw it as a mark of shame or because they did not want a visit from the tax collector. A slightly less hidden, though still unrecorded, aspect of women's employment was their work in the sweated trades – either as industrial out-workers or in small, dingy unregulated workshops escaping the notice of the inspectorate and hence of any factory legislation.

So, although the census data shows that the percentage of 'economically active' women declined toward the end of the century, it is highly unlikely that this was actually the case, especially given the growth in male unemployment even among the better paid workers from the 1870s onwards. The official figures show that between 1871 and 1931 the proportion of women legally entitled to work ranged between 27 and 35 per cent. The table below shows the 'industries' in which these (recorded) women worked.

	1851	*1871*	*1891*	*1911*
Domestic servants	1,224,419	1,664,195	1,959,195	1,822,169
Textile workers	506,492	519,110	576,536	604,253
Dressmakers, milliners, tailoresses				469,519
Clerical workers				182,782
Agricultural workers	70,470	55,687	46,196	19,341

Politics and Ideology

1850–67
Until 1867 when the better-off section of the male working-class was enfranchised by the Second Reform Act the electorate remained very small, and the party system (Whig and Tory) retained the character of rival and exclusive interest groups unsure of the precise differences between them. The emergence of 100 or so unattached Peelites (followers of Peel who had broken the ranks of the Tory Party over the Corn Law issue in 1846) added to the fluidity of the party system. Both parties knew that they had to appease the *nouveau riche* industrialists by not rocking the free trade boat, and at the same time retain their traditional aristocratic bases. Gladstone summed it up neatly in 1858 when the Tories under Lord Derby formed a government: 'It would

be hard to show the broad differences of public principle between the
government and the bench opposite.'

Between 1846 and 1867 there were nine governments, very few of
them with stable majorities, and so it was safest to concentrate on that
which, within ruling circles, was uncontroversial – foreign policy – that
is, the maintenance of British interests abroad.

Great efforts were made in the period before the mass extension of
the franchise to instil in the working-class a sense of the Victorian values
of thrift, sobriety, hard work and discipline. The church played an
important part in this – witness the feverish church (of England) building
programme of the mid 1840s as an antidote to Chartism.

Apart from organised religion, the spirit of the attempt to incorporate the working class (or at least the better-off section of it) into the
dominant value system is best represented by the work of Samuel
Smiles. Smiles's best-known book, *Self-Help: with Illustrations of Character
and Conduct*, was published in 1859. It continued to be read throughout
the century and by 1900 its sales had reached over a quarter of a million.
It represented and advocated the self-confident spirit and individualism of the self-made men of the industrial age. The book was based on
a series of lectures delivered by Smiles to a Leeds mutual improvement
society (one of many similar organisations established by better paid,
usually skilled, workers for social betterment). The opening sentence,
'Heaven helps them who help themselves', was illustrated with examples
of the 'rags to riches' high achievers of Victorian Britain, men like George
Stephenson, James Watt, Josiah Wedgewood, Richard Cobden and
countless others. (Examples from history also served to prove Smiles's
point – Shakespeare, Copernicus, Titian, Joshua Reynolds, etc.) They
all came from humble backgrounds, but by dint of hard work and per-
severance in the face of adversity they all made their pile. The message
was clear to all working men: don't rock the boat; don't ask the state
to help you get on; do it yourself by persistent effort and endeavour.
No message could be better suited to an era of economic expansion
that was allegedly providing great opportunities for all but founded on
the unfettered free play of market forces that made almost a virtue of
the fittest surviving and the weakest being pushed to the wall. The weakest
could neither demand nor expect any help since their predicament was
due to their own character deficiencies. (For us in Tory Britain of today
there is no difficulty in recognising this message; it has been resurrected,
while collectivism – dubbed by Tory ideologues as the 'nanny state' –
has been systematically abolished in favour of the individualism of

rediscovered Victorian values – the only difference being that then it was founded on economic progress!)

1867–1906

Both Tory and Liberal parties from 1867 were conscious of the need to capture the working-class vote. It appeared initially that the Liberals had the natural advantage, having masterminded the phenomenon of 'lib-labism'. This was a means by which the Liberals graciously permitted horny-handed sons of toil to present themselves as parliamentary candidates in predominantly working-class constituencies. Needless to say, such an altruistic attempt slightly to modify the class composition of the House of Commons was destined to benefit the Liberal cause, since these candidates stood as Liberals and took the Liberal whip if elected. Hence the first 'cloth-cap' MPs were not Labour men. In fact the very success of lib-labism was one of the reasons for the great delay in re-forming an independent working-class political party.

What of the Tories? If the Liberals seemed to be doing so well in incorporating those workers who had the vote, how do we explain the fact that a Tory government was ever elected again? The question is even more pertinent given that the period between 1885 and 1906 witnessed a period of almost uninterrupted Conservative rule (the interruptions were provided by two brief Liberal administrations, one in 1886 and the other from 1892 to 1895), and all at the very time when the electorate had just been enlarged massively (1884).

The strictly political explanation points to an analysis of the great difficulties facing the Liberal Party during this period. These included a split in the ranks in 1886 over the question of Home Rule for Ireland which led to a motley breakaway group of Liberal Unionists led by Joseph Chamberlain eventually joining the Conservative Party. (Hence the name change of that organisation to the one it still holds – the Conservative and Unionist Party.) When the Labour Representation Committee was established in 1900, the old lib-labism was formally ended, and in the longer term, the Liberal revival of 1906 aside, the Liberal Party was virtually extinguished. On the other hand, although the Tories had their differences, especially on the question of the future of free trade, an open rupture was not apparent until 1903. In that year Chamberlain (that great wrecker of parties) formed the Tariff Reform League and blew open the simmering rift within the capitalist class on how best to respond to the crisis-torn British economy. Once again the old battle-ground of free trade versus protection (now modified by preferential treatment for the empire) threatened temporarily to split the Conservative Party as it had done in 1846. This division was in part responsible for the Liberal election victory of 1906.

The Tories were far too patrician to foster their own tame cloth-cap MPs. They were nonetheless very well organised in working-class areas. Traditionally their main base of support had been the counties, but very early on Disraeli realised the importance of securing a base in the boroughs. In the 1870s he had established Working Men's Conservative Associations. Randolph Churchill continued in a similar vein with the foundation of the Primrose League, although this was more successful in rural areas than among the urban working-class. One of the successes of the more democratic appeal of the Tories was the securing of a substantial part of the textile workers' vote in Lancashire (the cotton towns especially) and in Yorkshire.

However, an analysis of the working-class vote in purely political terms presupposes great differences of principle between the two main political parties. In fact none such existed in overall orientation, especially since the post-Gladstonian Liberal Party increasingly identified itself with the domininant imperialist ethos of the age. Both parties were prepared to make concessions to secure the working-class vote by offering social and trade union reform. It would be invidious and hair splitting to say which one was more generous in this sphere. They were both motivated by the same tactical imperative – to do just enough to secure the vote of the workers and at the same time avoid alienating the men of property.

Racism

Although the extension of the franchise in 1867 and 1884 produced a great sea-change in British politics, and in particular a more recognisable party system, the strength of the system was not (and still is not) a matter of party politics alone. In the era of the masses more subtle forms of social influence and social control emerged. The last quarter of the nineteenth century witnessed a great expansion, formally and informally, of the ideological apparatus of the state which was both prompted and facilitated by the rise in literacy. (By 1890 elementary education was free and compulsory for all.) This was the era of the birth, or widescale development, of the popular press (dominated by the conservative magnate, Harmsworth), the propaganda poster, the music hall, the Scout movement (and other similar youth movements), the working men's club, cheaper and more popular literature (the novels of Henty and Kipling) and great national pageants like Queen Victoria's diamond jubilee and Empire Day. The significance of this expanded mass culture was that it coincided with the new mass ideology of jingoistic imperialism. Whereas the 'self-help' ideology reflected the self-confidence of the booming mid-Victorian economy, the empire and its benefits in the form of social imperialism provided the new unifying antidote to the emerging socialist consciousness of the 1880s which threatened to expose the possible class conflict of a declining economy. The popular culture of the masses both reflected and provided great opportunities to win the masses for the national, as opposed to the class, cause.

Of course, ideology alone could not accomplish this, which is why social imperialism was so important. Social imperialism, a term first used by the Austrian Marxist Karl Renner in 1917, was summed up by Disraeli's famous dictum 'sanitas et imperium', which meant that the profits from the empire could be used in part to finance social reform. It was recognised that a mass electorate could not be wooed by self-help alone, and that imperial expansion could play a key role in winning votes for either of the two parties if it was linked materially to social betterment. The writings of all the major imperialist statesmen, Chamberlain, Cecil Rhodes, Viscount Milner, to name but a few, made this connection. The point was made earliest and clearest by the Tories, which may help to account for their ascendancy in the later part of the nineteenth century.

The ideology of racism had underpinned slavery and hence was not a new phenomenon. In the period of imperialist expansion, however, it was dressed up in a new pseudo-scientific garb and given a popular mass appeal. Hitler was later to draw upon the writing of the British white supremacists of this period – men like Benjamin Kidd and Karl Pearson, who subverted Darwin's theory of evolution by crudely using his ideas on the 'survival of the fittest' and applying them to the struggle between races. Pearson, whose only objection to socialism was the theory of class struggle, substituted instead the struggle between races as the mechanism of progress. The black races had already lost out in this struggle, having been conquered by the whites, hence proving the racial superiority of the conqueror.

Francis Galton, professor of 'eugenics' at London University, discovered this new 'science', the practical application of which could, by means of selective breeding, regulate heredity and produce a super (white) race capable of surving the struggle for existence. The following extract from *A History of England* by Fletcher and Kipling, a standard textbook in use for many years in elementary schools, shows that such racist ideas were not confined to a few quirky intellectuals.

The prosperity of the West Indies, once our richest possession, has very largely declined since slavery was abolished in 1833. There is little market for their chief products, and yet a large population, mainly descended from slaves imported in previous centuries, or of mixed black and white races, is lazy, vicious and incapable of any serious improvement, or of work except under compulsion. In such a climate a few bananas will sustain the life of a negro quite sufficiently: why should he work to get more than this? He is quite happy and quite useless and spends any extra money he has upon finery. (Clarendon Press, 1911)

1906–1920

The arrival of the Labour Party on the political scene (see Chapter 8), the culmination of the long campaign to enfranchise women, and World War One all had profound repercussions, in the long or short term, on the political system. The birth of the Labour Party led ultimately to the demise of the Liberals, despite their stunning election victory of 1906, thereby altering the form if not the content of British two-party politics. The 1906 Liberal government did all it could to head off the labour challenge. The funding of its series of collectivist social reforms led to the great constitutional crisis of 1910–11 which resulted, in turn, in the restriction of the veto power of the House of Lords. By 1918 the vote had been extended to all adult males over 21, and to women over 30 who were householders, married to householders, or graduates. (Women had to wait until 1928 to be enfranchised on the same terms as men.)

The war produced a coalition government in 1915 (which included Labour until 1917) under the premiership of Lloyd George, who managed to retain this position with Conservative support until 1922. Hence the first election in 1918 under the new franchise produced another coalition government, but the Tory participants in it were clear that they called the tune. As Bonar Law, their leader, said of Lloyd George: 'It is not his Liberal friends, it is the Unionist party which has made him Prime Minister ...'

Ireland

No survey of English politics over the last eight centuries could be complete without mentioning Ireland – England's first and probably last colony. And yet, as with all subjugated nations, it is usually overlooked by constitutional historians save for the occasional reference to the suppression of a local rising. Ireland, however, unlike the more far-flung reaches of the empire, forced its way on to the agenda of English politics in the last quarter of the nineteenth century in particular, when the nationalist cause crashed through the portals of Westminster and insinuated itself into the very fabric of the parliamentary system.

Since the famine of 1845 the Irish economy had been steadily reduced to the position of a supplier of livestock for the tables of the English. But by the 1870s even this was threatened, by the import of refrigerated meat from South America and Australasia. Constant resistance to forced rural impoverishment was met by savage coercion. Such resistance formed the backbone of the unity of all shades of nationalist opinion, regardless of religion, which was expressed in the formation of the Home Rule movement in the 1870s under the leadership first of Isaac Butt and later of Charles Stewart Parnell. Home Rule candidates stood for election to the English House of Commons and their success in returning a fluctuating group of around 60 MPs had a dramatic effect on the English party system in general. At two moments in particular, in 1885 and 1910, the votes of these MPs held the balance between the Liberal and Tory Parties, and hence determined the fate of governments.

In the nineteenth century this Irish influence resulted not in the victory of the Home Rule cause, but rather in the defeat of the Gladstonian Liberal Party. Gladstone was 'converted' to the idea of Home Rule as the only realistic alternative to the demonstrably unworkable traditional policy of coercion. Gladstone's 'conversion' was motivated as much by pragmatism as by idealism since the power of the House of Lords with its safe Tory majority would never have allowed the Bill to pass. Nonetheless his 'realpolitik' was a miscalculation, since the Home Rule Bill introduced in 1886 was defeated in the Commons and his party was split.

In 1911 Asquith's Liberal government was once again forced to pay the price for Irish support by introducing another Home Rule Bill. The possibility that this attempt would be successful, in parliament at least, given the now reduced power of the Lords, fuelled the fire of loyalist opposition based in the northern Irish provinces. Ulster Unionism was based on the interests of the settler, mainly protestant, population of the north which by now, linked with English capital, had acquired dominance of the cotton, linen and shipbuilding industries. Unwilling to lose this lucrative base of capital investment, English Tories (and the anti-Home Rule defectors from the Liberal Party), now led by Bonar Law, were prepared to condone and assist the open rebellion of Ulster Loyalists in order to prevent Irish independence. Under the slogan 'Ulster will fight and Ulster will be right' the interests of capital on both sides of the Irish Sea conspired to pervert one of the most sacred and time-honoured principles of the establishment – the rule of law. Were it not for the fact that the establishment itself was engaged in this conspiracy it would have been viewed as treason. But the forces that organised around the 'Covenant' (a document signed by Ulster protestants as a binding oath pledging resistance to Home Rule) were too powerful to be dealt with as traitors. Apart from the panoply of establishment figures, statesmen and politicians (Viscount Milner, Walter Long, Rudyard Kipling, Edward Elgar and the entire Tory Party) who actively supported the Ulster Unionists, it was clear that the forces of law and order in Ireland did so too. In an act of unpunished mutiny, Brigadier Gough, commander of the British cavalry brigade stationed in Ireland at the Curragh, along with 60 other officers, resigned rather than be forced to fight the Covenanters who had themselves in 1913 organised their own military wing, the Ulster Volunteer Force.

Against this background Asquith capitulated. The Home Rule Bill was amended to exclude the province of Ulster, and although in this amended form it was passed, its implementation was delayed until World War One was over. The war provided a convenient diversion from the Irish question in parliament at least, but in Ireland the struggle continued. The moderation of the Parliamentary Nationalist party (successor to the Home Rule Party) led by John Redmond was challenged in Ireland by an alliance of republican nationalists who not only rejected Redmond's support for the British in World War One but saw it as Ireland's opportunity to win her own war against the English. The Irish Republican Brotherhood (an alliance of the Fenians and the Gaelic republicans) organised their own fighting wing – the Volunteers – to fight against the terrorism launched by the British forces and the Orange Order. This was supplemented by the socialist republicans led by James Connolly, whose Citizen Army contained recruits who had to be (where eligible) trade union members.

Not content with waiting on the pleasure of the English to deliver home rule, the combined republican forces planned to liberate Ireland by their own efforts, and to this end organised the remarkable Irish Rising in Easter week 1916. Although this took the English authorities by surprise, after a brief moment of glory it was brutally suppressed and its leaders, including Connolly, executed. The impact of the rising had repercussions far beyond the event itself. This was clearly shown in the elections of 1918 when Redmond's party was routed in the polls and the republican forces, except in Ulster, were triumphantly returned and constituted themselves the governing body of 'the Republic established in Easter Week'. The coalition government in Westminster, which was by now strongly influenced by Unionist die-hards like Carson and F.E. Smith, did everything possible to counter this act of rebellion short of recognising the obvious fact of the existence in practice of the Irish Republic.

A reign of terror was launched by paramilitary irregulars (the Black and Tans), whilst at the same time the Government of Ireland Act was passed in 1920 which attempted to impose the Home Rule solution of 1914. Such a 'solution' was unacceptable to those who really ruled Ireland, and undeclared war continued between the Irish forces (now organised in the Irish Republican Army) and the Black and Tans.

The Truce and Treaty, signed in 1921, gave Ireland dominion status. The six (not the original nine) counties of Ulster could and did choose to be excluded. This compromise, although accepted, found little favour with the Unionists. However, a section of the nationalist republicans remained bitterly opposed and a civil war ensued in the south between the pro- and anti-treaty factions. Britain had 'solved' the Irish question at the expense of the Irish people, and although the south (the Free State) did become a republic in 1925, the price paid was high. The civil war had taken its toll, but even greater was the permanent reminder of British and Orange dominance of the economically lucrative north of the island, enshrined by partition. The legacy of the as yet unfinished struggle for Irish freedom is a devastating fact of political life today.

Further Reading

Ashworth, W., *An Economic History of England* (Methuen, 1960).

Chancellor, V., *History for Their Masters* (Adams & Dart, 1970).

Eliot, G., *Felix Holt* (Penguin, 1987, first published 1866, a novel set against the background of the 1867 Reform Act).

Goldby, J.M.(ed.), *Culture and Society in Britain 1850–1890* (OUP, 1991).

Hobsbawm, E.J., *The Age of Capital 1848–1975* (Cardinal, 1991).

Jackson, T.A., *Ireland Her Own* (Lawrence & Wishart, 1971).

Kemp, T., *Industrialisation in 19th Century Europe* (Longman, 1985).

Mackenzie, F.A., *American Invaders* (Grant Richards, 1902).

Marsden, G. (ed.), *Victorian Values* (Longman, 1990).

Sayers, R.S., *A History of Economic Change in England 1880–1939* (OUP, 1967).

Semmel, B., *Imperialism and Social Reform* (George Allen & Unwin, 1960).

Williams, E.E., *Made in Germany* (Heinemann, 1896).

Young, G.M., *Portrait of an Age: Victorian England* (OUP, 1989, first published 1936).

6 Trade Unions, Politics and the Labour Aristocracy 1850–80

There is little doubt that there was a change in both the orientation and the organisation of the labour movement in the 1850s. The form of these changes was represented by the growth of the amalgamated unions (see below), but it would be misleading to see these as a super-imposed alien creation. These kinds of union had their roots in the previous period. So, what was new? Is it valid to see the post-Chartist period as a watershed, and the 1850s as labour's turning point?

Apart from the fact that amalgamated unions gained in strength and importance, two other factors give this period its distinguishing features: first, that the organisational base of the movement was much narrower than hitherto, hence it is as instructive to analyse what kinds of worker were left on the outside of the labour movement as it is to look at who was organised by it; and secondly, the undoubted triumph within the labour movement of a particular kind of ideology, best summarised by the engineers' slogan 'defence not defiance'. The contrast between this and the emerging socialism of the Owenite and Chartist movements before 1850 was very stark.

Put simply, how do we explain the fact the the labour movement appeared for at least 20 years to be content to exclude from its ranks the majority of workers (women, the lesser skilled and the lower paid), and to find for itself a niche within the capitalist system, the very system which had been the object of such hatred hitherto? Part of the explanation is to be found in analysis of the decline of Chartism (see Chapter 4), which was greatly affected by the spectacular growth of the economy in the boom years (see Chapter 5). While this might help to explain the initial shift in orientation and ideology, it cannot explain its long-term success nor the mechanism for achieving it.

The Labour Aristocracy

The great prosperity of the mid Victorian period touched even the 'lower orders'- but not all of them. Had capitalism been able to accomplish such a miracle, poverty, unemployment and homelessness would have been eradicated. For the vast majority of the working population conditions remained almost as bleak as ever, except perhaps that there was more regularity of employment. However, a section of the working-class experienced an appreciable change in terms of a considerable rise in real wages, together with a vast improvement in living and (often, but not always) working conditions. Contemporaries like the trade unionist George Potter used the term 'aristocracy' to describe this group of workers who could be easily distinguished in habits of dress, manners and lifestyle from labourers. (Tom Mann, in his memoirs, describes his comrade John Burns thus, 'He always wore a serge suit, a white shirt, a black tie, and a bowler hat. He looked the engineer all over.') The general use, then and now, of the term 'labour aristocracy' as a description of the better-off section of the working-class is uncontroversial, although there are differences concerning its application. This aside, the real controversy lies in the theory which makes use of such a category of workers to explain the move away from the revolutionary traditions of the labour movement.

Who were the labour aristocrats? A combination of factors determined the prosperity of this group of workers. Of overriding importance was the profitability of the particular industry in which they were employed. The most prosperous undertakings were the staples (coal, iron and steel, and cotton) together with the building industry which experienced boom conditions. But that did not mean that all workers in these industries were labour aristocrats.

In some cases (e.g. engineering) higher pay was determined by skill (usually achieved after serving an apprenticeship). In industries like coal mining and cotton manufacture apprenticeships were rare, but nonetheless there existed discernible groups of higher paid workers. In mining the hewers were the best paid, and in cotton it was the adult male spinners. There is no particularly good reason for this other than custom, practice and prejudice within the industries themselves. (Prejudice because it will be remembered that the first cotton spinners in the industrialised mills were women, and very poorly paid.) If we are to find any logic in such payment systems it is probably better located in the employers' desire for social control achieved through creating a divided and hierarchical workforce. Given the immense prosperity of these industries in this period, it was now possible to create such hierarchies much more consistently than hitherto through pay differentials. Finally, higher paid workers could be found in industries which were unmechanised and still depended in part on artisan skill. Masons and joiners in the building trade fitted into this category, as did printers. The skilled craftsmen in the luxury or bespoke trades (e.g. tailoring, shoemaking, jewellery) could also be counted in this group. Underlying all this is the stark fact of a blatant sexual division of labour which automatically excluded women workers from the higher earnings league.

Given the absence of a white-collar managerial stratum, and also the small-scale nature of many industrial undertakings, it is hardly surprising that groups of privileged workers were receptive to the self-improvement ideas of the Samuel Smiles type (see Chapter 5). Social advancement, even to the point of becoming a small master, seemed well within the grasp of any hard-working and thrifty man, provided his passions were not roused by drink or 'dangerous' politics. Thus it was that the economic and social boundaries between the labour aristocrats and their 'betters' were seen by the former as more blurred, with the inevitable consequence that the gulf between the aristocrats and the rest of the working-class widened.

It is not possible to say what those who were left behind thought of the new situation, but it was quite clear that the boom years, having created for the first time the promise (maybe just the dream) of upward social mobility, had a profound impact on the thinking and the lifestyle of the group of favoured workers. In one sense there is nothing particularly remarkable about this – ingrained habits of subservience and deference have always meant that the 'lower orders' tend to ape their betters. The remarkable, though controversial, aspect is the extent to which such attitudes and ideas penetrated the labour movement. This is not to deny their force earlier – it was not the case that one day in 1850 the working-class awoke to find that it had become a reactionary mass, whereas the day before it had been revolutionary. However, after 1850, the 'defence not defiance' philosophy was the *dominant* trend, for the simple reason that it made real sense to those who advocated it.

Given the coincidence of the labour aristocracy and the organised labour movement, it would be hard to deny the ideological influence of the former on the latter. Of course, there were periods of militancy during these 20 or so years, just as there were quiet years in the preceding turbulent period. But it is also true that the dominant characteristic of each period was markedly different, despite obvious continuities. It stands to reason that those groups who dominate the movement also dominate its ideas and orientation, and it was undoubtedly the case that the labour aristocracy dominated almost exclusively.

Trade Unionism – The New Model

Although trade unionism revived after the demise of Chartism, it was clear from the start that in important respects it was very different from the trade unionism of the earlier period. Most notably, the earlier experiments in general unionism were discontinued as was its general outlook as expressed in the objective of the GNCTU – 'bringing about a different order of things, in which the really useful and intelligent part of society only shall have the direction of its affairs'. That said, most of the so-called new unions were re-formations of already existing (usually) craft organisations. For example, the most famous, the Amalgamated Society of Engineers (1851), was a grouping of smaller societies around the largest of the engineering unions, the Journeymen Steam-Engine, Machine Makers' and Millwrights' Friendly Society, formed in 1826. Many of these older (and now amalgamated or revitalised) unions were already craft dominated and fairly cautious in that they concentrated more on friendly society benefits than class confrontation. So are the Webbs correct in their description of the unions formed between 1850 and 1870 as 'new model'?

The 'newness' of trade unionism in this period resides in the contrast between these unions and the older societies from which they developed. These were usually smaller, more local and often impermanent. The new formations were nationally based, highly centralised and much stronger. Their high membership subscription made them richer, too, and hence more able to continue the already established trend of employing full-time officials and offering improved benefits. To this extent, the Amalgamated Society of Engineers (ASE) formed a model national organisation on which many others were based (for example the Amalgamated Society of Carpenters and Joiners (ASCJ)).

The other new feature was linked to the more favourable economic cicumstances which permitted those more favourably placed workers to engage more productively through their unions in forms of collective bargaining which were very rare in the earlier years of industrial capitalism. Negotiation and arbitration gradually came to be accepted practices, and were a much more common means of securing improvements in wages and conditions than strike action. The first conciliation and arbitration board, consisting of equal numbers of employers and workers, was established in 1860 for the Nottingham hosiery trade. This found imitators in many other industries and regions. Not that strikes did not take place (for example the engineers' strike of 1852 and the protracted London builders' strike of 1859–60), but caution was to be exercised in the use of the 'double edged (strike) weapon' (Applegarth, secretary of the ASCJ). William Allen, secretary of the ASE, informed the 1867 Royal Commission on Trade Unions that in his union 'The Executive Council and the members, generally speaking, are averse to strikes. They think that matters ought to be settled in a different way than coming to strikes or lock-outs.'

Whilst the economy was buoyant and expanding, and the provision of key labour (often skilled) was in short supply (owing to union control), a 'different way' in the form of collective bargaining could be used, and yielded rich rewards. The prosperity of the individual enterprise thus came to be seen as being as important to the worker as to the employer. When trade was good and profits high the well-placed worker expected to share the good fortune. Hence a boilermakers' song of 1872, after expressing sympathy with the risks that capital had to run, ended:

> So tis just and meet
> Labour should co-operate,
> And to help with all their might
> The masters to compete.

Of course, this meant the jettisoning of the notions of class consciousness in favour of a more sectional and exclusive trade (or at best trade union) consciousness. The former appeared as old fashioned rhetoric whereas the latter could, literally and figuratively, deliver the goods.

Finally, the other new feature of trade unionism was the fact that apart from the co-operative movement it was virtually the only form of working-class organisation. Gone, therefore, was the *independent* political dimension of the labour movement which had so characterised it in its formative years. Apart from some smaller, less centralised, and often more militant unions in the north of England, this was the *only* form of trade unionism, whereas in the past it had existed as but one tendency among others. The smaller craft unions like those of the tailors and shoemakers, whilst not 'new model' in their organisational form, shared a similar ideology. George Potter, editor of the trade union paper the *Beehive*, was the spokesman for these and the northern unions. So, although we know that new-model unionism was symbolised by its exclusiveness, being the organisations of the labour aristocracy, the fact is that trade unionism in general did not exist for the vast mass of British workers.

Hence it was exclusive in itself and by virtue of its dominance. It was nonetheless very successful in its own terms. In 1850 there were roughly 100,000 trade union members. By 1874 this figure had risen to over a million. Thereafter there was a sharp decline in membership, reflecting the strong associations between this type of trade unionism and Britain's economic fortunes.

Despite the decline in the years of the depression, most of the unions established in this period remained intact. Indeed many of the craft-based unions in existence today can trace their history back to the 1850s. Other organisations like the trades councils and the Trade Union Congress itself were also established at this time.

The TUC had very inauspicious beginnings and its first meeting in 1868, whilst having an historical significance, passed by virtually unnoticed at the time. Convened by the Manchester and Salford Trades Council, it was proposed that:

> the congress shall assume the character of the annual meetings of the British Association for the Advancement of Science and the Social Science Association, in the transactions of which Societies the artizan class are almost entirely excluded ... (From the circular issued in February 1868 by the Manchester and Salford Trades Council, reprinted in V.L. Allen, *The Sociology of Industrial Relations*, 1971)

In other words, there was the assumption that the annual congress should be little more than a debating society dealing with the 'merits and demerits' of 'papers, previously carefully prepared' on a twelve-point list of subjects broadly connected with labour and trade union interests. Other than agreeing to meet annually, no permanent structure or organisation was established after the first congress. A greater cohesion and immediacy was given to these leisurely and somewhat scholarly proceedings by the fear that the government's sudden interest in trade unionism in the 1870s might produce hostile legislation.

Women and Trade Unionism

What happened to the vast mass of workers who were excluded from the unions of the labour aristocracy? Why did not those workers, the low paid and lesser skilled who gained little or nothing from Britain's prosperity, organise themselves? They, the most exploited, were divided only by a generation from the revolutionary traditions of Chartism, Owenism and early trade unionism.

Other than the evidence we have of their misery, through contemporary novels and social surveys, we know next to nothing about this majority group. There were some tentative attempts to organise unskilled labour, including agricultural workers, in the 1870s in the wake of the strikewave inspired by the engineers' fight for a nine-hour day in the north-east. Despite the efforts of the Labour Protection League the only survival of this was the stevedores' union (which later played a key role in the London dock strike of 1889).

Women workers were a special case. The dominant sexist ideology, punctured slightly in the previous period, now permeated fully the more class-collaborationist mood of the labour movement. Women workers suffered a great defeat. The only trade in which they still remained organised in any numbers was that of weaving. The aim of trade unionism, according to Henry Broadhurst, secretary of the TUC, speaking in 1875, was '... to bring about a condition ... where wives and daughters would be in their proper sphere at home, instead of being dragged into competition for livelihood against the great and strong men of the world'.

From this kind of thinking sprang the widespread acceptance of the notion of the 'family wage' to be won by the male breadwinner. Hence not only was unequal pay accepted as a norm, but women's work was tolerated only if not threatening to the man. In any case, it was seen as a mark of shame if a man permitted his wife to work, hence the widespread practice, hardly contested by the unions until the twentieth century, of barring married women from employment altogether. Such attitudes and practices help to explain women's increasing job segregation and the fact that so much female labour was literally hidden (see Chapter 5). It is not surprising therefore that the unions of this period demonstrated a studied indifference if not downright hostility to women workers.

Any attempts to organise women in this period came from outside the labour movement, often through the work of philanthropic women. The most notable example is the formation in 1874 of the Women's Protective and Provident League (later the Women's Trade Union League). Under the leadership of Emma Paterson the league fostered the growth of separate associations of women working in such trades as dressmaking, millinery and upholstering. Between 1874 and 1886 over 30 such associations were formed on the same plan, using a model constitution devised by the league. Most of these societies were very small, weak and short-lived. They hardly merit the description 'trade union' since their stated aim was 'to promote an entente cordiale between the labourer, the employer and the consumer'. Strike action was deprecated as 'rash and mistaken' and instead emphasis was placed on friendly society benefits. But such attitudes were derived from the craft unions, so perhaps our judgment should be more even-handed. The difference was that in the women's case their unions were not nearly so successful and the impetus to organise came from the outside. The only matter of real controversy was the league's opposition to protective legislation for women on the grounds that it restricted women's choice of employment and their earning capacity. Apart from the still topical debate on this question, the lasting achievement of the league was to get the first women delegates to the TUC.

Co-operation and Friendly Societies

In a way the trade unionism that evolved can be seen, and indeed was seen by the governing class, as part of a legitimate attempt by law-abiding workers to better themselves in the approved self-help tradition. This partly explains the improvements in the legal status of trade unions achieved in the 1870s (see section on 'politics' below).

The development of the co-operative movement provides an even clearer indication of this trend in the labour movement towards self-improvement through self-organisation. Co-operation in the first half of the nineteenth century, whilst it took many forms, was essentially political in character in that it was inspired by a vision of a different and better society. Although consumer co-ops existed, this was not the only, or indeed the dominant trend until the second half of the century.

The establishment of the Rochdale Pioneers' Equitable Society in 1844 heralded a great expansion of co-operative shops throughout Britain which followed the Rochdale model of inducing custom by paying dividends on purchases. Later, in 1863 in England and 1868 in Scotland, wholesale societies were established on sound business principles. At one level these development were a practical and very successful way of encouraging workers' self-improvement by nurturing the saving and investment habit whilst at the same time satisfying material needs in the form of better quality and usually cheaper items of common consumption. However, at another level the movement in its very pragmatism marked a turning away from the 'new moral world' type ideals of earlier co-operation. This was reflected in the changed aims of the Rochdale Manufacturing Society, which by 1860 stated 'the present co-operative movement does not seek to level the inequalities which exist in society as regards wealth', but rather, according to Abrahan Howarth (president of Pioneers' Society), to unite individual talent 'for the mutual benefit of each' through 'a common bond of self-interest'. The spirit of this kind of co-operation was very much in keeping with the spirit of trade unionism in the same period; both were in tune with the spirit of the age.

Closely connected, in fact symbolic of this spirit, was the spectacular growth of friendly societies. The origin of friendly societies goes back much further but their growth in the second half of the nineteenth century reflects the increasing need of an urban population wholly dependent on their own purchasing power unsupported by any form of self-sufficiency to sustain them when they fell on hard times through sickness, old age or unemployment. The lack of any state support whatsoever rendered the friendly society the ideal type of self-help organisation through which the thrifty, sober worker could make provision for himself without being a burden to others and avoiding the threat of the hated Poor Law. As a result the ruling classes were quite prepared to look kindly on friendly societies, seeing them for what they were, agents of social accommodation rather than agents of social change. Thus it was that such strangely named organisations (with strange rituals to match) as the Independent Order of Oddfellows, the Loyal Order of Ancient Britons, and the Antideluvian Buffaloes, became the fastest growing working-class organisations, far outstripping in membership both trade unions and co-operative societies. By 1872 they could claim around four million members. Of course it was only the better paid workers who had the spare cash to invest in such organisations.

Politics

Although no independendent working-class political organisation was yet formed, or even contemplated, trade unions did exert some political influence in these years. The fluid state of the party system in the mid Victorian period witnessed the development of middle-class inspired popular radicalism which cut across class boundaries. The more forward looking of British capitalists together with their parliamentary allies captured progressive sentiment with a new form of internationalism that welcomed the national movements within the Italian and German states. Hostility was shown to the autocratic and semi-feudal governments of the Austrian and Russian empires. General Haynau, the Austrian butcher of the 1848 Hungarian revolution, was given a rough reception by British workers when he visited Britain in 1850. Palmerston, the Foreign Secretary, having already labelled the Austrians 'the greatest brutes that ever called themselves by the undeserved title of civilised men', now added fuel to the fire by saying of the Haynau incident that the workers should have 'tossed him in a blanket, rolled him in the kennel and sent him home in a cab'.

The fact that most British trade union leaders affiliated their organisations to the First International (1864–72) was little more than a continuation of this already acceptable type of internationalism, born during a period when Britain reckoned she had much to teach a world emerging from feudalism about democracy. When the issue of working-class state power arose as a result of the Paris Commune, 1871, the leaders of Britain's trade unions recoiled in horror and were the first to turn tail, thereby precipitating the downfall of the International.

Sections of the middle-class, including prominent 'captains of industry' like the cotton magnate John Bright, favoured the extension of the franchise. They formed the Reform Union for the purpose of campaigning for household suffrage, and in so doing emasculated the more radical and working-class Reform League which advocated manhood suffrage. Trade unions were quick to exploit the new opportunities presented by the extension of the franchise in 1867 to better paid urban male workers by taking on some of the functions of a parliamentary pressure group. This was exemplified by the formation in 1871 of the TUC's Parliamentary Committee – forerunner of the General Council and successor to the informal grouping of general secretaries of amalgamated unions based in London (dubbed the 'Junta' by the Webbs). The name of this body described its function – to exert pressure on members of parliament to pass legislation favourable to the functioning of trade unions and collective bargaining. There was ample opportunity in the 1860s and 1870s. A flurry of interest and attention was showered on the trade unions. Two royal commissions were established in the space of seven years. The first in 1867, was to inquire into the trade unions, following the so-called Sheffield 'outrages', and the second, on labour laws, was appointed in 1874.

Of the six major pieces of factory/trade union/industrial relations legislation passed as a result the main consequence was that the status of trade unions, although not their power, was accentuated. The old Master and Servant Law was modified by the Employers and Workmen Act 1875 which meant that not only employers, too, could be sued for breach of contract, but that such an offence was now a civil and not a criminal one. The 1874 Factory Act set a ten-hour limit on the working day – the unions were campaigning for eight. The 1871 Trade Union Act recognised unions as legal entities as corporations, and as such they were entitled to protection under the law. (This provided an end to the anomaly revealed by the *Hornby* v. *Close* case in which it was deemed *not* to be unlawful to abscond with the funds of a union – in this case the Boilermakers'.) The question of whether or not unions could take effective strike action by picketing the workplace was the subject of much controversy. Interestingly it was a Liberal government which criminalised picketing (Conspiracy and Protection of Property Act 1871), and a Tory government which decriminalised it (Criminal Law Amendment Act 1875).

So, had the ruling class been converted to the trade union cause? George Howell, Secretary of the TUC Parliamentary Committee, appeared to think so. In 1875 he resigned his post on the grounds that the 'work of emancipation' was now 'full and complete'. Two factors combined to make the ruling class look more favourably on trade unions than they had done at almost any other time (the 1824 repeal excepted). One was that, despite their historic paranoia of workers' combinations, they could see that the unions formed after 1850 were quite different from their predecessors and that in some senses they were positively advantageous. The Majority Report of the 1869 Royal Commission expressed it thus:

> … the habitual code of sentiment which prevailed between employers and workmen in times when the former were regarded both by law and usage as the governing class is now greatly relaxed, and cannot be revived. A substitute has now been found for it, arising from the feelings of equity, and enlightened self interest, and mutual forbearance, which should exist between contracting parties who can best promote their several chances of advantage by aiding and accommodating each other.

This substitute was trade unionism.

Secondly, it was clear that the working-class vote was important to both parties, and that the Tories were as keen as the Liberals to use it to advantage. The phenomenon of lib-labism has already been mentioned (see Chapter 5). It yielded its first results in the 1874 election with the return of a miner, Thomas Burt, as the Liberal MP for Morpeth, and Alexander McDonald (Secretary of the National Miners' Association) as Liberal MP for Stafford. The Tory government under Disraeli that took office after the election saw the danger of working-class liberalism and hence remedied the defects of Gladstone's trade union legislation. This came as something of a surprise to the TUC who had declined to give evidence to the 1874 Royal Commission on the grounds that its establishment was a delaying tactic. In fact the recommendations of the commission were unhelpful, but the ensuing legislation, which ignored its findings, was not.

So, although lib-labism was a force, the Tory strategy to combat it must have worked, for otherwise Liberal governments would have been a permanent fixture. In any case the TUC Parliamentary Committee advised tactical voting at election time by submitting a series of 'test questions' to the candidates seeking their attitudes on current questions of concern to trade unionists. Thus it was that modern trade unionism had discovered that its economic and political interests could be accommodated within the framework of the existing system, and that the system was expansive and pragmatic enough to incorporate those interests. In this sense the British labour movement was unique in Europe. In almost every other European country, with the possible exception of Belgium, the development of trade unions was a product of the political activity of the working-class, usually in the form of the creation of a socialist party. In Britain the reverse was the case. By the 1880s a strong, although narrowly based, trade union movement had been created, the very success of which in its interdependent harmony with the existing economic and political system banished all thoughts, let alone practical steps, of political independence. The surprise is that such a situation remained so long after the material conditions to which it had given rise passed. However, by the 1880s there were the stirrings of a challenge. The boom was over and the ensuing depression questioned the complacency of the self-help ideal.

Further Reading

Allen, V.L., *The Sociology of Industrial Relations* (Longman, 1971).

Gray, R., *The Labour Aristocracy in Nineteenth Century Britain* (Macmillan, 1981).

Hobsbawm, E.J., 'The Labour Aristocracy in Nineteenth Century Britain' (in *Labouring Men*, Weidenfeld & Nicolson, 1968).

Hobsbawm, E.J., 'Trends in the British labour movement since 1850' (in *Labouring Men*, 1968).

Hutt, A., *British Trade Unionism – A Short History* (Lawrence & Wishart, 1975, first published 1941).

More, C., *Skill and the English Working Class 1870–1914* (Croom Helm, 1980).

Rothstein, T., *From Chartism to Labourism* (Martin Lawrence, 1929).

Simon, B., *Studies in the History of Education* (Lawrence & Wishart, 1964).

7 The Rise of a Mass Labour Movement – Trade Unionism 1880s – 1914

The years up to and including World War One witnessed the rise of a mass labour movement. Trade unionism spread to previously unorganised workers and its initial militancy rocked the complacency of the old leadership. The new mood was inspired by a revival in socialist activity beginning in the 1880s. This presented a challenge to the dominant reformist ideology of the movement but was not strong enough to displace reformism completely (although it seemed close to so doing) despite the turn in the economic tide. Ultimately this political challenge was emasculated, leaving the strange British paradox of militant trade unionism with (apart from small and often sectarian socialist sects) a very weak political voice in the form of the Labour Representation Committee (1900). This body, which was the forerunner of the Labour Party, was the child of the trade unions but reflected the reformist ideology of their cautious leaderships. Whereas in much of continental Europe mass Marxist/socialist parties were in the vanguard of similar pre-war militant struggles, in Britain not only was the reverse the case, but such a political party barely existed. Hence apart from the socialist groups and later the Communist Party, the mass movement was left without the kind of political leadership that reflected its growing militancy. This partly expains why syndicalism (see below), especially in the immediate pre-war years, was such a force.

The trade unions were not the only mass movement. The women's movement, almost unnoticed by the labour movement, had attracted a mass following by the turn of the century. The importance of its early allegiances to the labour movement and its roots among working-class women failed to be fully recognised industrially or politically by the male-dominated labour leadership (with a few notable exceptions). Syndicalism, too, despite its socialist inclinations, offered little to women industrially or politically in an era when their main struggle was for the franchise. Thus it was that the opportunities offered by the 'votes for women' campaign were lost by the labour movement, and the Women's

Social and Political Union eventually severed its links with organised labour.

So, were these the decades of lost opportunity in which reactionary and chauvinistic male leaders of the labour movement squandered the immense revolutionary prospects offered by an increasingly powerful and class-conscious movement of women and men? This may well be a descriptive picture but it offers no real explanation beyond the 'evil men' approach to history. The fact is that although politics do not obediently follow economics, the ending of Britain's boom, whilst upsetting the Victorian equipoise of the previous period, did not mean that the material conditions for the continued advancement for at least a section of the working-class had finally ended. This period was one of adjustment rather than breakdown, in which the old labour – capital consensus was ultimately renewed.

Imperialism and the Labour Movement

The renewal of the consensus was dependent on a renewal of its supportive ideology. The expansion of the British empire provided the material basis for this. It helped to maintain low prices, especially of food, at a time of economic adversity, thus preventing a drastic drop in real wages for those who had jobs. By providing protected markets it assisted in the maintenance of high profits in certain traditional export industries (the staples) which had lost their competitive edge elsewhere. Those industries thereby retained a privileged sector of workers who continued to identify their interests with the fortunes of their own firm against 'foreign' encroachment. The increased importance of capital exports to the colonies and elsewhere assisted in the creation of further class divisions as a growing army of white-collar clerical workers mushroomed to staff the finance sector of the economy. Finally, there was some truth in the social imperialist argument that the profits from the empire could be used to finance social reform in Britain. The real substance of the limited social reforms introduced should not be exaggerated, but for those who were unconvinced by the socialist alternative they gave continued hope of further improvement within the existing system.

Of equal importance, however, was the fact that imperialist ideology, with its outspoken racist overtones, made skilful use of popular culture (see Chapter 5) and undoubtedly, in an atmosphere of heightened national and racial chauvinism, made it much harder for a comparatively weak socialist movement to gain much ground. The degree to which imperialist and racist ideology penetrated the collective psyche of the labour movement is hard to quantify and is the subject of continued debate. It would be difficult to imagine that it had no impact given its prevalence in every walk of life and the fact that the working-class was the special target of the social imperialists who were quick to spot the dangers of the appeal of socialism at a time when the majority of male workers were enfranchised (1884) and the economy was in the doldrums. The following oft-quoted statement made in 1895 by Cecil Rhodes illustrates perfectly the concerns of the social imperialists:

> I was in the East End of London yesterday and attended a meeting of the unemployed. I listened to the wild speeches which were just a cry for 'bread, bread, bread' and on my way home I pondered over the scene and I became more than ever convinced of the importance of imperialism ... My cherished idea is a solution for the social problem i.e. in order to save the 40,000,000 inhabitants of the United Kingdom from a bloody civil war, we colonial statesmen must acquire new lands to settle the surplus population, to provide new markets for the goods produced by them in factories and mines. The Empire as I have always said, is a bread and butter question. If you want to avoid civil war, you must become imperialists.

Apart from the anti-imperialist stance taken by some (although by no means all) of the socialist organisations, the attitude of the mainstream labour movement leadership to the empire was at best silent and at worst aggressively pro-imperialist. The partition of Africa appeared to escape the notice of the TUC. Its only comment on the enslavement of India was a resolution asking for factory legislation to be introduced in the subcontinent. In 1899 the TUC 'took note' of the Boer War. The 1901 TUC decided to support the war, and in 1902 it criticised the government for its 'clumsy handling' of the issue.

A surprising array of pro-imperialists appeared as opinion formers on the intellectual left. The non-Marxist Fabian Society, formed in 1884 (the 'think-tank' of reformism and later of the Labour right wing), was aggressively pro-imperialist. Its classic text on the subject, *Fabianism and the Empire*, drafted by Bernard Shaw and published in 1900, could have been written by Cecil Rhodes or Joseph Chamberlain. For the Fabians, the empire provided the means of accomplishing the social reforms they consistently championed and it led them not in the direction of labour independence but rather towards political unity with all those who wanted to promote the 'national interest', as opposed to sectional or class interests. Many of them, like H.G. Wells and Shaw himself, were outspokenly racist and accepted without question the prevalent white supremacist ideology. Hence they were the prime movers behind a project to form a new party of 'national efficiency'. Ultimately they contented themselves with regular meetings of the Coefficients, a 'brains trust' formed by the Fabians (notably the Webbs) and consisting of leading Liberal and Tory imperialists, at which the 'aims and methods of Imperial policy' were discussed.

Although it might be suspected that the rarified middle-class intellectualism of the Fabian Society was hardly representantive of the labour movement as a whole, the trend it reflected had far-reaching resonances. It was imperialism, particularly social imperialism, rather than the Fabians which gave credence to idea of the 'national interest' and the 'white man's burden'. This was most sharply expressed in times of war and affected even those with more respectable left-wing credentials than the Fabians. In this connection the Boer War and later World War One were testing grounds and turning points for the politically conscious section of the labour movement. The leader of the Social Democratic Federation, H.M. Hyndman, opposed the Boer War, as did the Independent Labour Party (founded in 1893). However their grounds for opposition had nothing to do with any recognition of the interests of the indigenous black population. Their pro-Boer sentiment was based on their dislike of 'Rand capitalists' who were frequently referred to as 'financial Jews'. Later, Hyndman and Robert Blatchford (editor of the popular socialist paper the *Clarion*) became ardent supporters of Britain's 'big navy' programme – the policy of increasing naval expenditure to protect the empire from rival European imperialism. Hyndman's views did not reflect the majority opinion within his own party but the fact that he, as its leader, articulated them meant that valuable time and energy was spent waging an internal struggle rather than conducting an anti-imperialist crusade.

The attitude to imperialist Britain among the majority within the leadership of the British labour movement was not much worse than the labour movements of other European countries. The main difference was that the wave of tub thumping, flag waving chauvinism caught independent labour politics in Britain at its very infancy and gave the older, incorporated political tradition a new lease of life. All over Europe there were great divisions on the issue, usually dividing hitherto united socialist parties into pro- and anti-marxist groupings. By the time of World War One the scene was set for the breakdown of international class solidarity, expressed in organisational form through the Second International, into national labour movements all of which supported, to varying degrees the war efforts of their own country's governments.

New Unionism

It is against this background that political (see Chapter 8) and trade union developments during the years 1880–1914 must be understood. Trade unions grew at a faster rate than at any time in their history between 1888 and 1918. The estimated membership figure stood at roughly 750,000 at the beginning of the period, rising to 6.5 million in 1918. This spectacular growth took place in three main periods: from 1880 to 1891; from 1910 to 1914 during 'the great unrest', a period of extensive strike action inspired largely by syndicalism; and during the war years 1914–18 which not only continued the militancy of the previous four years but witnessed the development of the shop stewards' movement.

1888–91

Inspired by the successes of the women matchworkers' strike at the Bryant and May factory in 1888 (known somewhat belittlingly as the match girls' strike),[1] the gasworkers' and the dockers' strikes of 1889, trade unionism among unskilled, semi-skilled, white-collar and professional workers spread rapidly. The term 'new unionism' is properly applied to this short period. Not only were many new unions formed, but a new approach to trade unionism permeated both the older and the new organisations. Tom Mann and Ben Tillett criticised the old outlook in a penny pamphlet, *The New Trades Unionism – a Reply to Mr. George Shipton*, published in 1891:

1 This strike was significant not just because it was organised and led by women. In itself this is not a unique occurrence. Its importance lay in the fact that it took place in one of the notorious 'sweated trades' and that the involvement of socialist 'outsiders' like Annie Besant ensured that it achieved great publicity. It is perhaps a sign of the tendency to regard women as victims rather than fighters that the popular historical representation of the strike consists of faded photographs of faded waif-like women suffering from the occupational disease of 'phossy jaw' (the debilitating effect of the phosphorus component of the match tip which ate into the women's facial bones). The Bryant and May factory, in use until the 1970s, still stands today in Bow, East London. Its exterior remains, for those who know or care, a stark and gaunt reminder of the women's suffering and their brief moment of victory. Despite this, save for a small and easily missed plaque, no memorial remains, and the stain of the past is now buried, symbolically, in the building's current use as 'concept dwellings' for the new stylish incomers to today's East End.

... many of the older unions are very reluctant to engage in a labour struggle, no matter how great the necessity, because they are hemmed in by sick and funeral claims, so that to a large extent they have lost their true characteristic of being fighting organisations ...

Why was it that this outlook was finally challenged at the end of the 1880s? It had been clear since the mid 1870s that the 'old unionism' had not been successful, even in its own limited terms. Only the very largest and richest unions had been able to withstand the pressures of the depression and the drain on their funds due to unemployment. Many craft unions now fell by the wayside, and of the two mining unions one was dead and the other moribund. The example of the initially successful attempt to organise agricultural labourers in 1872 may have served to indicate that trying to organise among the unskilled was fruitless, especially at a time when trade unionism for the skilled was beginning to experience difficulties. The key factor in explaining the change in outlook in the 1880s is a political one.

The outlook of old unionism was challenged by class-conscious socialists (see Chapter 8) some of whom, like Tom Mann and John Burns, were already, as ASE members, experienced trade unionists. Indeed there was a growing left opposition within some of the craft unions which was to have important repercussions later. The strike activity which led to the breakthrough among the unskilled was often led or inspired by socialists. Annie Besant (a member of the Fabian Society) played a key role in the matchworkers' strike. Tom Mann and John Burns, both of whom played a key role among the dockers, were members of the Social Democratic Federation, as was Will Thorne, the gasworkers' leader. Prominent socialists outside the trade union movement, like Eleanor Marx, Keir Hardie and H.H. Champion were frequent speakers at mass meetings of trade unionists and also assisted in recruitment drives. The organising principle was that of mass recruitment. Whereas old unionism had relied on the skill and scarcity value of labour, new unionism was dependent for its success on sheer force of numbers. Thus women were welcomed as members from the start, accounting for the first recorded real increase in women's trade union membership from roughly 50,000 in 1888 to about 432,000 in 1913. (However, the gains for women should not be over-emphasised, see the section on women below.) The central slogan of this forward movement was that of the demand for an eight hour day – a demand of the international labour movement, popularised by the newly formed Second International (1889–1914). The huge May Day 1890 demonstration in favour of the eight hour day took even its organisers by surprise. So effective was this agitation that it penetrated the bastions of the old unionism; the ASE declared itself in favour of the eight hour day in 1889, as did the TUC at its 1890 congress.

Many of the unions among the unskilled did not survive beyond 1891, although the collapse of some of them was temporary. The irony was that the new unions which survived the 1890s often did so by becoming a bit more like the older unions. They concentrated their efforts on particular groups of workers rather than spreading themselves generally, and consolidated their gains where they were already strong. During the 1890s the only new unions to be formed and to weather the storm were unions among white-collar and professional workers. Three unions formed in 1891 are indicative of this trend – the Post Office Workers' Union, the National Amalgamated Union of Shop Assistants, and the Postman's Federation. The National Union of Teachers was formed in 1889.

In fact the more tangible achievements of the spirit of new unionism were to be found within the older unions. In 1891 Tom Mann came within a 1,000 votes of winning the general secretaryship of the ASE, and in 1892 that union began to recruit more widely among less skilled engineers. In 1889 a new, initially more militant, miners' union, the Miners' Federation of Great Britain, emerged from the collapse of the older societies. It recruited more widely than among just the hewers (the base of the old miners' unions) and declared in favour of the eight hour day from its inception. The Amalgamated Society of Railway Servants abandoned much of its exclusiveness in the 1890s and began to recruit from all grades.

Employers' Counter-offensive

Part of the reason for the collapse of so many of the newly formed unions was the determined resistance of the employers, aided by state legislative action. This was the period in which determined efforts were made to counter trade union growth by more effective and co-ordinated employers' strategies, as witnessed by the formation of employers' associations within, and ultimately across, industries, and their widespread adoption of the tactics of the lockout and the use of 'scab' labour.

The first of their targets were the new unions. By these means even the biggest of the new unions, the London gasworkers and the dockers, were smashed. The job of breaking the older unions was not so easy, but it was even more vital. Trade union resistance in the staple industries was delaying employer determination to introduce new work methods and wage cutting associated with the drive for labour intensification –

their preferred strategy, in the absence of capital investment, to ensure the maintainance of their profits in an increasingly competitive world market (see Chapter 5).

Thus it was that attempts were made by the employers to reduce wages in the cotton and mining industries in 1893, and to defeat the engineers' struggle for the eight hour day following the national lockout of 1897. The settlement which ended the cotton spinners' strike and the engineers' lockout resulted in a form of collective bargaining which incorporated the unions' leaderships in an industrial truce which impicitly acknowledged the main objective of the employers – the 'right to manage' at a time of great internal change in their industries. The 1893 Brooklands Agreement (cotton) was the prototype. It established a National Procedure Agreement whereby all disputes at a national or local level had to be referred to a central joint council of the industry (consisting of union and management sides) before strike action was 'permitted'. Other industries apart from engineering followed suit – the boot and shoe industry in 1895, the building industry in 1904 and shipbuilding in 1908. This new departure in industrial relations also helps to explain the period of industrial peace between 1888 and 1907.

Thus, although the employers had met with determined resistance the great forward push of trade unionism appeared to have halted. This strengthened the hand of the 'old guard' of union leaders whose outlook had been temporarily challenged but who remained in post despite the militancy of the rank and file. They, having entered into these novel forms of national collective bargaining, were as keen as the employers to see the system work. Further, they took advantage of the lull in militancy to consolidate their own position. The change in the standing orders of the TUC in 1895 was a symbolic representation of this. The block vote was intoduced, and trades councils were barred from sending delegates to congress as were those not working at their trade. This last was a move to bar socialist 'agitators' from attending future congresses.

The hostility of the employers to trade unionism was re-enforced by two infamous legal decisions that challenged the legislative gains made by the respectable leadership in the 1870s. The case of *Lyons* v. *Wilkins* in 1896, upheld by the High Court and the Court of Appeal in 1897, set a precedent for outlawing even peaceful picketing. In 1901 the Taff Vale judgment, whilst not outlawing strike action directly, enabled the employer (the Taff Vale Railway Company) to sue the union (in this case the Amalgamated Society of Railway Servants) for losses sustained during a strike. The fact that this decision was upheld by the House of Lords, thereby reversing a ruling of the Court of Appeal, indicated that in essence this action, inspired as it was by the Employers' Parliamentary Council, was intended to prevent strike action altogether.

Syndicalism

On the face of it, therefore, it seemed that by the twentieth century trade unionism had achieved very little. The gains of the old leadership had been undone both by the courts and by the vicissitudes of the economy, and the new unions, with the exception of the continued organisation of white-collar and professional workers, had little to show for themselves. The only new union to be formed during the period of industrial peace was an unlikely but significant one in that it foreshadowed the ideas which inspired 'the great unrest'. This was the as yet tiny Workers' Union formed in 1898 by Tom Mann as a general union along the lines of the old GNCTU.

Trade union membership, which stood at just over two million in 1900, actually declined slightly between 1903 and 1906. Thereafter, however, its rise was steady until 1914, with spectacular increases recorded from 1910. This growth was a product of the extraordinary militancy of the pre-war years which exploded in a huge wave of strike action, dubbed 'the great unrest'. It owed little to leadership of the industrial and political wings of labour movement. Indeed its very hostility to such leadership, which was condemned as class collaborationist, inspired its alternative – syndicalism. Syndicalism, whilst being the inspiration, was not necessarily the cause of the massive strikewave, rooted as it was in the worsening material conditions of employed workers. Syndicalists were a minority current in the labour movement, but nonetheless they offered a simple alternative to the continued employers' offensive – that of direct action in order to regain some form of workers' control over workplace pay and conditions, utilising the strategy of the mass strike and rapid trade union recruitment.

At a deeper level syndicalism represented the much grander project of winning, through industrial action, workers' control of the means of production as a whole, thereby consigning capitalism to the dustbin of history. Although within it there were different and cross-fertilising ideological currents, syndicalism was an international phenomenon which took hold in many European countries and in America during roughly the same period. Whereas in Britain syndicalists operated as a force *within* the existing trade unions, in France, America, Spain and Italy they broke away from a much weaker and divided movement to form their own trade union confederations. Small anarchist and socialist political groups like the Industrial League, the Central Labour College and the Plebs League (both a product of a breakaway from Ruskin College), popularised syndicalist ideas in Britain. However, had the movement not attracted the support of trade unionists such as Tom Mann, James Connolly and Jim Larkin, it is likely that it would have remained the property of small sects without mass influence.

Mann, Connolly and Larkin all learned the syndicalist message in their travels abroad, and all three rejected the notion of 'dual unionism' – the establishment of separate syndicalist unions alongside the existing ones. Rather, they sought to change the existing trade unions from within, whilst rejecting the ineffective political forum of parliament and labourist politics.

The South Wales Miners' Federation gave practical form to syndicalist theory. In the wake of the defeat of the often violent (e.g. Tonypandy, 1910) strike movement in the South Wales Coalfield 1910–11, syndicalist miners led by Noah Ablett (an ex-Ruskin student) set about reconstructing the union along the lines contained in a pamphlet widely discussed by rank and file miners and published in 1912 under the title *The Miners' Next Step*. This was the best and most popular expression of the syndicalist tradition. Its opposition to the encrusted and collaborationist miners' union leadership was matched only by its class hatred of the coal owners. It advocated a wholesale repudiation of the existing system of conciliation and collective bargaining in favour of rank and file control of the union, and workers' control of industry. To this end it proclaimed the syndicalist tenet that:

> an industrial vote will affect the lives and happiness of workmen far more than a political vote ... Hence it should be more sought after and its privileges more jealously guarded. (*The Miners' Next Step*, 1912, p. 9)

The vacuum created by the absence of political leadership together with the ineffectiveness of old unionism meant that syndicalism, with its clarion call to direct action by the rank and file, found a ready response within the conditions of pre-war industrial militancy.

Women, New Unionism and Syndicalism

Despite the fact that the number of women trade unionists had increased by 1914, 90 per cent of all trade unionists were men, and over 90 per cent of women workers remained unorganised. Of the 10 per cent of organised women almost half were members of unions in the textile industry (the only industry in which they had maintained continuous organisation), and a high proportion of the remainder were members of teaching, clerical and shopworkers' unions.

Although the periods of growth in women's trade union membership usually coincided with overall union expansion, the unions themselves cannot claim the sole credit for organising women workers. As in the previous period, that task fell to women themselves. This time, however, the new unions of the late 1880s actually admitted women members, although they did little to attract them. The open access policy of the new unions and the general militancy giving rise to their creation had an effect on the existing organisations promoting women's trade union membership. The Women's Trade Union League (formerly the Women's Protective and Provident League 1874, re-named the Women's Trade Union and Provident League in 1891) became more militant and abandoned some of the policies of its predecessors. The league supported strikes and encouraged women to join existing trade unions. Far from opposing protective legislation as the WPPL had done, the league campaigned for its extension.

Other organisations were formed in this period which championed the cause of working women and campaigned for their unionisation. A member of one of these, Clementina Black of the Women's Industrial Council, moved the first successful equal pay resolution at the 1888 TUC. This was not such a victory for women's rights as it may have seemed. Quite apart from the fact that nothing was done to campaign for equal pay, it was hoped that in the unlikely event of its implementation women would price themselves out of the labour market thereby ceasing 'competition for livelihood against the great and strong men of the world' (Broadhurst).

In membership terms the two most important women's organisations were the Co-operative Women's Guild, formed in 1883 (by 1931 it had 67,000 members organised in 1,400 branches), and the National Federation of Women Workers, founded in 1906. The guilds were very active in the north – their membership was drawn from working-class women. They campaigned to improve conditions for women at work and at home, and they were vital educators and mobilisers in the fight for the vote (see Chapter 8). The National Federation of Women Workers under the leadership of Mary Macarthur probably did more than any other organisation (including the unions) to unionise women especially during the mass strikewave of 1910–14. The federation saw strikes as the chief means of unionising unorganised workers. The NFWW was entirely unselfseeking in that its efforts were purely for the benefit of the unions rather than its own prestige. Although its membership had risen to 20,000 by 1914, its leaders never intended that the NFWW should remain permanently as a women's union. In fact, in 1920 it quietly merged with the General Workers' Union (now the GMB).

The federation also played another role which was seen by some as contrary to the interests of trade unions. Along with many of the other women's organisations it campaigned to expose the evils of the sweated trades. Their propaganda was very effective and played a major part in inducing the Liberal government to pass the 1909 Trade Boards Act which was an attempt to fix minimum wages in certain of the most exploitative trades, usually the ones in which women predominated. This was seen by some trade union purists as an attempt to bypass union organisation and to rely instead on state regulation. Even those male trade unionists like Will Thorne, whose politics should have taught them better, persisted in writing off such reforms as the work of middle-class do-gooders. Such attitudes to the trade board system blinded male activists to the union recruitment side of the NFWW's work, which had in any case been particularly successful in some of the small 'sweated' factories in London like biscuit making, jam and pickle making, bottle washing and a host of others. But for the work of the NFWW such women would have been ignored even by the more revolutionary syndicalists. Syndicalism, for all its successes in promoting the massive spread of trade unionism in the immediate pre-war years, concerned itself by its very nature on large concentrations of labour in factories and mines, and these tended to be male dominated. The ideal of industrial unionism leading to workers' control of industry had very little to offer women workers in small workplaces and in industries which were hardly central to the motor of the capitalist system. A strike in a pickle factory, in syndicalist terms, could not be equated with a strike in an industry at the heart of the productive process like mining or engineering.

Thus it was that syndicalism was a mixed blessing. Whilst it inspired the trade union militants of the pre-war years in a way that the small socialist sects failed to do, its appeal was nonetheless limited to the big industrial battalions from which women were largely excluded. But in any case its total focus on workplace struggles meant an explicit rejection of wider political issues, like the franchise for women. It confused a healthy cynicism of the existing political system with a disregard for all those who sought to work within it, regardless of their political standpoint. The political vacuum created by the left in the labour movement was

readily filled by the right wing, thus fuelling the self-fulfilling syndicalist prophesy of the corruption of established politics.

Further reading

Ablett, N. et al., *The Miners' Next Step* (South Wales Miners' Federation, 1912).

Bell, T., *Pioneering Days* (Lawrence & Wishart, 1941).

Holton, B., *British Syndicalism 1900-1914* (Pluto Press, 1976).

Hyman, R., *The Workers' Union* (Oxford, 1971).

Lenin, V.I., *Imperialism, the Highest Stage of Capitalism* (Progress, 1968, first published 1917).

Lenin, V.I., *British Labour and British Imperialism* (Lawrence & Wishart, 1969).

Lovell, J., *British Trade Unions 1875–1933* (Macmillan, 1977).

Mann, T., *Memoirs* (MacGibbon & Kee, 1967, first published 1923).

Mann, T., *Social and Economic Writings* (Spokesman, 1988).

8   Socialist Politics 1880s–1914

The three decades before World War One witnessed a socialist revival. Socialism was one of the chief factors inspiring the trade union expansion and militancy of these years, while the fact of mass industrial struggle undoubtedly increased the appeal of socialism. The stage appeared to be set for a political counterpart to the industrial unrest. Yet the early political promise of socialism remained largely unfulfilled. Aside from the underlying influences of social imperialism (see Chapter 7), British socialism emerged as a peculiarly eclectic and contradictory product of Christian moralism, militant class consciousness, radical individualism, deferential conformity, reformism and Marxism. These trends were represented by the plethora of organisations that emerged between the 1880s and 1920, but they could also be found *within* individual organisations.

Apart from the Fabian Society and, later, the Communist Party, no single organisation could be said to be a pure reflection of any single variety of socialist thought. Hence by 1900 when a dominant organisation emerged in the form of the Labour Representation Committee (the LRC, known from 1906 as the Labour Party) its only distinctiveness was that it championed parliamentarianism. It did not, as yet, represent a distinct socialist current; it was not even a party in the accepted sense of the term, rather a federal organisation – a broad church. However, through it, and its successor the Labour Party, parliamentary socialism stamped its imprint on the entire labour movement.

This was accomplished despite, (or possibly because of), doctrinal inertia which, tempered by the parliamentary obsession, was able to accomplish an achievement unique to Britain – the unification in one organisation of the industrial and political wings of the labour movement. However, although such a merger, achieved as it was during a period of heightened class consciousness, was a potentially revolutionary accomplishment, this was far from its purpose. Rather it sought accommodation within the parliamentary system so that through it the best possible deal for the workers could be won. Doctrinal inertia, through the medium of parliamentary socialism, thus, by sleight of hand, was converted almost without knowing it to reformism.

Marxism

The fact that reformist parliamentary socialism ultimately became the distinguishing political hallmark of the British labour movement, and remains so to this day, would have surprised socialist activists of the 1880s and 1890s for two reasons: first, because in the beginning the ideological appeal of socialism was strongly counterposed to reformism; and second because the attachment of the leaderships of the main trade unions to liberalism was opposed altogether to the notion of independent labour representation. When, by 1901, most of the trade union leaders were eventually won round to the idea of an independent workers' party, the resulting compromise produced in the form of the LRC was further evidence to the Marxists of the bankruptcy of reformism, and induced in them and their rank and file militant supporters a distrust and even hatred of the whole parliamentary system. Mass extra-parliamentary activity, especially during the syndicalist wave, was posed by the trade union militants against participation in 'bourgeois' parliaments, although the political left was not averse to standing candidates in local and national elections.

Most of the Marxist organisations were small in membership terms but they exercised an influence far beyond their numbers. The first such organisation, the Social Democratic Federation (SDF), was not Marxist when it was formed as the Democratic Federation in 1881. It was initially a federation of London radical clubs under the leadership of the ex-Tory stockbroker H.M. Hyndman which, by 1883 had gravitated to Marxism. Hyndman's brand of Marxism was, to say the least, peculiar, and the SDF was initially very sectarian both in relation to other labour movement organisations and in its own internal squabbles. Nonetheless, the organisation and its immediate successors had a long history and contained within its ranks at one time or another most of the leading trade union and socialist militants of the next 30 or so years. This is all the more surprising given that the SDF leadership was at first opposed to trade unions, having written them off as bastions of a corrupt labour aristocracy. This view was unmodified even during the new unionism of the late 1880s the leaders of which, like Mann, Tillett and Burns, were or had been SDF members.

The SDF initial attitude to strikes was similarly out of keeping with 'the great unrest' of 1910–14. Strikes were viewed as a waste of time in that they induced in workers the unrevolutionary belief that they could really achieve something within capitalism, the wage system of which was fixed against them anyway. The justification for this was based on the un-Marxist theory of the 'iron law of wages' propounded by Ferdinand Lasalle and explicitly rejected by Marx himself in the early 1870s. And yet much of the impetus for the strikewave came from militants who had learned their socialism from the SDF. Similarly, Hyndman's attachment to nationalism and imperialism owed nothing to Marxism and promoted disunity and ideological confusion at a time when the force of the countervailing jingoistic propaganda demanded clarity from those who had always posed as the educators of the workers.

Thus, for all that was positive in the other aspects of the agitational and educative role of such groups as the SDF and its splinter group, the Socialist League, the opportunities presented to them of a working-class awakened to mass struggle was dissipated on the altar of their sectarianism. *Justice*, the journal of the SDF, and to a lesser extent *Commonweal*, the Socialist League's paper (edited by William Morris), conducted valuable propaganda for the socialist cause in general, but did little to lead or even reflect the day-to-day struggle except in relation to the important campaign against unemployment in the mid 1880s. Overall their propaganda was concentrated upon the political rather than the economic struggle, and in this they did not reject the campaigns to use parliament and local government to win social reforms such as free school meals, affordable housing and the eight-hour day. In fact the breakaway groups, first the Socialist League and then the Socialist Labour Party (1903), were highly critical of the parent organisation for being too willing to use the existing structures to win reforms. The concentration on the political, as opposed to the economic, struggle was in itself a product of a much older political tradition dating back to Chartist days, witnessed in particular by the failure of the Chartist leadership to see the importance of the 1842 general strike. Nonetheless, given the well-established position of the trade unions and their changing nature, it is hard to appreciate avowedly Marxist organisations falling into the same trap some 50 years later. For all this, and despite the vagaries of its leadership, the SDF was for many years the only socialist organisation to pay consistent attention to theory and the ideological struggle. Its ability to attract working-class militants helped to provide and enrich the labour movement with a wider socialist ideological dimension.

The pressure of syndicalist militancy did, however, by 1911 induce the British Socialist Party (BSP as the old SDF was then called, having already changed its name once before, in 1909, to the Social Democratic Party) to modify its attitude to trade unions and strikes. The BSP was later to become the main organisation behind the formation of the Communist Party in 1920. But meanwhile much of the fertile ground of mass militancy had been lost to non-Marxist organisations – politically in the form of the Independent Labour Party and industrially in the form of syndicalism. Thus it was that although Marxism had been an inspirational force ideologically in popularising socialism, it remained in organisational terms outside the mainstream of the labour movement in these years.

The fact that organisations are usually judged by the stance and characters of their leadership often obscures the reality of the contribution made at grassroots level on the part of the rank and file. In the case of the SDF its ability to attract, albeit for short periods, almost every subsequently well-known socialist, owes more to the consistent propaganda and presence of the branches than to Hyndman. Quite simply, the SDF before 1893 was the only place for class-conscious socialist activists. After 1893, when the Independent Labour Party (ILP) was formed, the SDF retained its footing as the only organisation in Britain which professed Marxism.

Ethical Socialism

The fact that Marxist organisations failed to attract a mass following does not indicate that British workers were solely preoccupied with trade unionism and hostile to Marxism in particular or to politics in general. The steady growth of the Independent Labour Party in the north of England belies such an assumption. It is probably true, although impossible to prove given the peculiarities of British Marxism, that the ground was more fertile for the spread of a non-Marxist socialist party. After all, the liberal tradition within the working-class was by now deeply embedded. Those to the left of this tradition were, like Keir Hardie in the 1880s, 'advanced' radicals. In popularising socialism, the Marxist groups impacted on such radical class-conscious workers to the extent that they developed a moral critique of capitalism and an acceptance of the moral values of socialism without necessarily implying an acceptance of Marxist theory. The clearest and most popular expression of this was found in the writings of Robert Blatchford, whose paper the *Clarion* started in 1891, achieved a circulation of upwards of 30,000 and a readership of thousands more. His book *Merrie England* (1893) was probably the most influential book since Tom Paine's *Rights of Man*.

Paradoxically such ethical socialism gained the best reception in areas where strike action had been relatively unsuccessful. This is not to say that trade unionism was weak in such areas, but rather that its traditional strength could no longer be relied upon to protect working-class living standards at a time when they were under severe attack by the employers.

One such area was the West Riding of Yorkshire, where male and female textile workers had a long and continuous history of active trade unionism. The American McKinley tariff of 1886 had a disastrous effect on textile exports, and the mill owners had resorted to the old methods of wage reduction coupled with labour intensification in order to preserve their profits. A wave of strikes resulted, the most famous of which, the Manningham Mills strike of 1890–91 (in which women workers played an active role), was a last-ditch attempt by the textile unions, now aroused from their torpor, to halt the employers' attack. The fact that the strike ultimately failed, although it was well organised and well supported by the community as a whole, did more than anything to induce the workers to turn to politics. It may thus have been one of the main reasons for the spectacular growth of the Independent Labour Party which was founded in 1893 in Bradford, the very heart of the industrial struggle. Liberalism was no longer the answer; it was too closely identified with the employers. Class-conscious workers were increasingly receptive to the kind of independent labour politics which gave expression to their concerns at work and in the community. Of the 305 ILP branches formed within the first year of the party's existence, 105 were in Yorkshire.

Some of the most active organisers promoting the ILP's growth had been, or still were, members of Marxist groups. Tom Maguire and Fred Jowett had joined the Socialist League in the 1880s, and Tom Mann of the SDF was elected to the secretaryship of the ILP in 1894. Jowett was also a committed Christian, remaining active in the Congregational chapel in Bradford until at least 1892. The connection between nonconformist religions and socialism has sometimes been exaggerated, but it remains the case that some of the moral tenets of the Christian gospel inspired the socialist pioneers. In fact, much of the language and practice of socialism was borrowed from religion, with socialist churches, socialist Sunday schools and socialist preachers attracting a wide following and helping to boost ILP membership.

The ILP brand of socialism was unsectarian in a practical and an ideological sense. Women and men came to it from Marxist, Christian or radical traditions provided they agreed that:

> the interests of Labour are paramount to, and must take precedence of, all other interests, and that the advancement of these interests of

Labour must be sought by political and constitutional action. (London
ILP 'Declaration of Adherance')

This declaration of adherence drawn up by the London ILP gives the
real clue as to the historical significance of the ILP. It worked consistently to win the entire labour movement for the simple and
straightforward project of the creation of a political party of the working-
class which would stand its own candidates in elections, independent
of existing parliamentary parties. Its lack of doctrinal consistency was
an asset in this campaign, but at the same time it prefigured its outcome
in that its achievement involved a compromise formula in which
socialism itself was a casualty.

The Beginnings of Parliamentary Labourism

The uniqueness of the ILP's early success in bridging the gap between
trade unionists and socialists set its course in the direction of the much
more grandiose task of cementing this unity formally on a national scale
in the form of a political party capable of fighting elections and giving
the labour interest a voice in parliament. This relatively limited objective
was hard to achieve given the trade union leadership's attachment to
liberalism, and could only be accomplished by an appeal to pragmatism
rather than idealism. The Taff Vale decision of 1901 was more important
in a practical sense in convincing the trade unions of the need for a parliamentary voice than countless socialist exhortations on the bankruptcy
of liberalism. By this date only the Miners' Federation remained outside
the labour coalition. (It eventually affiliated in 1909.) A parliamentary
voice was all that was offered by the LRC. Its purpose as stated at its
founding conference in 1900 was simply 'to establish a distinct labour
group in parliament who shall have their own whips and agree upon
their own policy'. Affiliated organisations would finance their own
candidates but would receive LRC backing.

Keir Hardie of the ILP characterised the 'philosophy' of the new organisation not as socialism but as *labourism*, which he defined as:

theory and practice which accepted the possibility of social change
within the existing framework of society; which rejected the revolutionary violence and action implicit in Chartist ideas of physical
force; and which increasingly recognised the working of political
democracy of the parliamentary variety as the practical means of
achieving its own aims and objectives. (Quoted in D. Coates, *The
Labour Party and the Struggle for Socialism*, 1975)

Labourism thus became the successor to nineteenth-century lib-labism but it did not supersede it entirely, as the new lib-lab pact of 1903 was to show. This was a secret electoral agreement between Ramsay MacDonald of the LRC and Herbert Gladstone of the Liberal Party whereby the Liberals agreed to stand down in over 30 constituencies in return for labour support for other Liberal candidates elsewhere and a promise of support for a future Liberal government. Such cautious tactics may seem surprising in view of the ILP's fervent belief in political independence and the fact that three independent labour MPs had been returned without Liberal support in the general election of 1892 (Keir Hardie for West Ham; Havelock Ellis, the seamen's leader, for Middlesborough; and John Burns for Battersea). However, a series of election defeats for Labour followed, notably in the 1895 general election and 1901 by-election. This resulted not in an analysis of the jingoistic atmosphere of those years which made victory for any progressive candidate a near impossibility, but rather a conviction that three-cornered fights were the essence of the problem. Thus emerged the unselfconfident vision of Labour's future prospects in which not its socialism but also its independence was to be jettisoned for the sake of its parliamentary ambitions. This did not pose a problem for Ramsay MacDonald, the new secretary of the LRC, whose vision of the Labour Party from the outset was hardly even labourist. His stated aim in 1903 was for:

> a united democratic party appealing to the people on behalf of a single, comprehensive belief in social reconstruction. The party may not be called Liberal, and will be as far ahead of Liberalism as Liberalism itself was of its predecessor Whiggism. (Quoted in Miliband, *Parliamentary Socialism*, 1961)

Even though the ILP might not have shared MacDonald's view, it is clear that Hardie at least knew of the liberal electoral alliance and went along with it. In fact implicitly the green light was given to such an alliance in 1900 when the stated objectives of the LRC also said that it must 'embrace a readiness to co-operate with any party which for the time being may be engaged in promoting legislation in the direct interest of labour'. This 'readiness to co-operate' was responsible for the disaffiliation of the SDF in 1901, leaving the socialist current in the Labour Party even weaker.

The euphoria of the electoral success in the 1906 election in which 29 labour candidates were returned had the effect of confirming the MacDonald strategy. The landslide Liberal victory, ushering a period of long-awaited social reform, also served to justify the uncritical support of Labour for the Liberal legislative programme, blinding it to the significance of the remarkable victory of the Independent Labour candidate, Victor Grayson, in a three-cornered by-election without official labour support in Colne Valley in 1907.

Although in the two elections of 1910 there was an increase in the number of labour MPs (42 in January, 44 in December), this was largely due to the transfer of miners' votes rather than a significant electoral upsurge. Again most of these seats were won as a result of an accommodation with the Liberals. By now, however, there was a much more outspoken criticism of Labour strategy from the left. The so-called 'green manifesto' was published in 1910 (officially entitled 'Let us Reform the Labour Party'), condemning Labour for clinging to the coat-tails of liberalism. But the dye was already cast, and Labour's parliamentary leaders were already sufficiently well entrenched to weather the storm, especially since their critics offered little in the way of a viable alternative. Had they managed to make common cause with the industrial militants outside parliament and linked the industrial to the political struggle, socialism rather than syndicalism might have been given a new lease of life.

However, the logic of the parliamentary process locked Labour's left wing into its familiar role of being the socialist conscience of a party firmly committed to a one-dimensional strategy. The left was an irritant within this strategy, but was perforce also limited by it. MacDonald and Philip Snowden each published a pamphlet in 1912 in which they attacked syndicalism. Working-class industrial militancy was an embarrassment to them – far from seeking to give it a political voice, it had to be condemned for fear of damaging an electoral strategy which was so closely tied to liberalism. This was the first of many such episodes in which Labour showed itself to be as hostile to mass extra-parliamentary struggle as any Tory or Liberal. In the years prior to World War One this naturally fuelled the syndicalist strategy of direct action and workers' control of industry to bring about socialism, by-passing altogether the parliamentary scene.

Reformism

Unlike reformist social democracy in continental Europe, the British strain emerged without the theoretical underpinnings that characterised the sharp ideological battles of both the Second International and the largest of the European workers' parties, the German SDP in particular. The Fabian Society, formed in 1884, the most 'theoretical' of the non-

Marxist organisations, distanced itself initially from labour politics. Although there was a representative of the Fabian Society, E.R. Pease, on the LRC, the Fabians played a very little role in the fight for independent labour representation, preferring instead their policy of permeating the Liberal Party. Once the Labour Party was up and running, the Fabians saw its possibilities and switched their intellectual efforts in its direction. Their theory and practice provided a suitably harmonious counterpoint for Labour's new parliamentary leaders.

The Fabian track record was fairly impressive. As a predominantly middle-class organisation much of its effort was devoted to scholarly research into all manner of social and political questions, with leading members like Sidney and Beatrice Webb becoming acknowledged 'experts' in their fields. On a practical level it was the proud Fabian boast that they had defeated Marxism in London through their assiduous work in nurturing the lib-lab alliance which had captured control of the newly formed (1888) London County Council. Their 'gas and water' municipal socialism established a tradition of attention to detail at local government level. This, its supporters argued, brought more tangible benefit to the working-class than all the Marxist polemic put together. So, although labourism had already emerged on the national scene in a pragmatic way, Fabianism gave it its reformist intellectual underpinnings, freeing its leaders to get on with less cerebral tasks.

Fabianism itself, however, was not immune to intellectual challenges from within. During the 'great unrest', opposition to its non-revolutionary gradualist philosophy emerged. The main rebel was G.D.H. Cole whose breakaway group of Guild Socialists took with them the Fabian research department and converted it to the Labour Research Department. (The latter still survives to fulfil its original purpose to provide a service for active trade unionists.)

Women, Politics and Socialism

None of the labour or socialist organisations made the enfranchisement of women, or women's rights in general, a campaigning priority. Indeed, the SDF was for a time downright hostile, while the ILP and the Labour Party were late converts. The issue of votes for women had been debated on countless occasions in labour movement forums but it was always sidelined by the device of passing an alternative resolution (usually proposed by Harry Quelch of the SDF) calling for full adult suffrage. Although there were individual men, like Keir Hardie, George Lansbury and Ben Turner (woollen workers' union), who saw through this ploy and supported women's suffrage, it was not until 1907 that the ILP was won over, and it was 1912 before the Labour Party finally followed suit. Apart from the outright misogynists like Belfort Bax of the SDF, the arguments that united the political spectrum of the labour movement in opposition to the demands of the women's movement ranged from sheer political expediency advanced by the Ramsay MacDonald tendency to the 'class politics' line of the SDF leadership. The former reckoned that a bill to enfranchise women was simply unachievable and would alienate Labour's Liberal supporters, while the latter argued that the vote for women was undesirable since it would add too many middle-class votes to the electoral register and hence would work in the interest of the bourgeois parties. The fact that neither the Tories nor the Liberals saw it that way yet remained hostile to the demand had little effect on the dubious logic of both camps.

The fight for the vote was the single demand around which the disparate strands of the women's movement could rally in the late nineteenth century. There had been many separate challenges to women's non-status as citizens throughout the century. The Victorian ideal of passive womanhood had always been a hollow sham for working-class women, but increasingly women from more well-to-do backgrounds were forced to question a society that conferred humanity upon them only if they were dependent wives, daughters or sisters. Unmarried or widowed women, whatever their class background, were often forced to live in dire poverty. Opportunities for 'gentle-women' to obtain paid work outside the home, other than as governesses, were extremely limited. Within marriage, although they had the status of wives, they were owned by their husbands – it was not until 1888 that the Married Women's property Act allowed women to retain their own property after marriage. Thus it was that the frequently dismissed 'bourgeois' women's movement, whilst not challenging the dominant sexist ideology as a whole, nor even seeking to make common cause with 'lower-class' women, did produce pioneers who broke through the wall of male prejudice and hostility against all the odds.

Women novelists like Jane Austen (writing secretly and living in poverty in her brother's house) articulated the plight of such women. All her heroines sought marriage because, as she put it in *Pride and Prejudice*, this 'was the one honourable provision for well educated women of small fortune, and, however uncertain of giving happiness, must be their pleasantest preservative from want'. Other writers, like the Brontë sisters and Mary Ann Evans (George Eliot), had to adopt male pseudonyms in order to get their works published. Elizabeth Garrett Anderson,

Sophia Jex Blake and others had to undergo appalling male hostility, including physical violence, in order to qualify as doctors. Mary Seacole, a black Jamaican, did as much as the more famous Florence Nightingale to establish nursing as a respectable profession for women, contending with both sexism and racism in the attempt. Josephine Butler did more than any male politician to win, in 1886, the repeal of the notorious Contagious Diseases Act. (This act entitled the authorities in naval and military areas to classify any woman as a 'common prostitute' and thereby subject her to a medical examination which, if refused, would result in imprisonment.) Dorothea Beale and Frances Mary Buss contended with ignorant prejudice in order to establish the propriety of education for girls outside the home, as did Emily Davies and Jemima Clough in winning the right for women to obtain a university education.

Such initiatives and many more besides rarely attracted the interest, let alone the support, of the political wing of the labour movement. Assuming, charitably, that the reason for this was more to do with class hostility than male prejudice, no such similar excuse can be found for the failure to support the women's suffrage campaign which by the end of the century had a mass following among working-class women. Indeed many of its leaders, like Selina Cooper, Ada Nield Chew, Annie Kenney, Hannah Mitchell, Helen Silcock and many others, were well known as socialists and sometimes as trade unionists, besides having the working-class credentials lacking in some of their lofty male socialist opponents. These women, the radical suffragists, had a dramatic impact on the older and more cautious women's suffrage societies whose aim was to win the vote for women 'as it is, or may be accorded to men'. Instead they formulated the demand for 'womanhood suffrage' – the vote without a property qualification for all women over 21.

This demand electrified and mobilised women in the Lancashire cotton towns and beyond. They worked through and with a variety of organisations including local branches of the ILP, the Women's Co-operative Guilds, the North of England Society for Women's Suffrage and the trades councils, as well as establishing their own – the Lancashire and Cheshire Women Textile and Other Workers' Representation Committee. By the time the Pankhursts formed the Women's Social and Political Union (WSPU) in 1903 they were already latecomers on the scene. In the years before the WSPU moved from Manchester to London in 1906, it too had strong ILP connections. The fact that the labour movement was so slow to respond to the growing mass movement for women's suffrage provided Emmeline and Christabel Pankhurst with the excuse for severing the link, but in doing so they also turned their back on working-class women. The WSPU achieved its fame precisely because of this. It concentrated its efforts on influential and 'well-placed' women in a less democratic, pressure-group style of campaigning, differing only from the salon style of the older middle-class suffrage societies in its less orthodox tactics. Individual acts of arson and terrorism captured the headlines, as did the strong-arm response of the Liberal government. Despite the heroism of such exploits, they alienated and upstaged the mass campaigns of working-class women with which Charlotte Despard of the SDF and Sylvia Pankhurst (incurring the wrath of her mother and sister) identified themselves.

The division within the women's suffrage movement was more about its class orientation than any question of short-term tactics. This was in evidence when Sylvia was expelled from the WSPU in 1914 because of her activities among working-class women in the East End of London. She reported her sister Christabel's comments on this occasion:

> a working women's movement was of no value; working women were the weaker portion of the sex: how could it be otherwise? Their lives were too hard, their education too meagre to equip them for the struggle! Surely it is a mistake to use the weakest for the struggle! We want picked women, the very strongest and most intelligent! ... we want all our women to take instructions and walk in step like an army. (Sylvia Pankhurst, *The Suffragette Movement* 1931,1977)

The military metaphors proved to be appropriate – just a few months later these 'intelligent' women were instructed by their high command to ditch the battle for the vote in order to support the real army fighting the Germans in the 1914–18 war! Happily the women of 'meagre education' did not respond to this call and the fact that the first instalment of the women's vote was enacted in 1918 is a tribute to their continued mass campaigning before and after the war. The commonly accepted story that the vote was granted as a reward for women's work in support of the war effort is a hardly credible, though convenient, explanation for the government climb down.

As with the government, the conversion of the Labour Party and the ILP owed little to arson and bombs but rather to mass and sustained pressure in working-class areas. However, the lateness of the conversion meant that a golden opportunity of linking this mass women's movement with the predominantly male labour movement was dissipated to the ultimate disadvantage of both. In Germany and in Russia the socialists had shown an early understanding of the 'woman question' and had, not without opposition, declared their support for equal rights, the women's franchise and for women's self-organisation within the socialist movement. The writings of Lenin, Bebel and Clara Zetkin consistently advocated such policies and were debated within the Second International. International Women's Day (8 March) was celebrated in 1910 by women in 17 different countries (Britain was not one of them), on the initiative of the women's section of the Second International, to highlight primarily the demand for the vote. The British socialist and labour organisations, had they chosen to support women's rights, had ample international examples to follow.

Further Reading

Callaghan, J., *Socialism in Britain Since 1884* (Blackwell, 1990).

Coates, D., *The Labour Party and the Struggle for Socialism* (CUP, 1975).

Cole, Margaret, 'Guild Socialism and the Labour Research Department' (in *Essays in Labour History 1886–1923*, ed. A. Briggs and J. Saville, (Macmillan, 1971).

Collins, H., 'The Marxism of the SDF' (in A. Briggs and J. Saville,1971).

Hobsbawm, E.J., 'The Fabians Reconsidered' (in *Labouring Men*, Weidenfeld and Nicholson, 1968).

Levine, Philippa, *Victorian Feminism 1850-1900* (Hutchinson, 1987).

Liddington, Jill, *The Life and Times of a Respectable Rebel: Selina Cooper 1864–1946* (Virago, 1984).

Liddington, J. and Norris, J., *One Hand Tied Behind Us: The Rise of the Women's Suffrage Movement* (Virago, 1978).

Miliband, R., *Parliamentary Socialism* (Allen & Unwin, 1961).

Mitchell, Hannah, *The Hard Way Up: Autobigraphy of Hannah Mitchell, Suffragette and Rebel* (Virago, 1977).

Pankhurst, Sylvia, *The Sufragette Movement* (Virago, 1977, first published 1931).

Pelling, H., *The Origins of the Labour Party 1880–1900* (OUP, 1965).

Pierson, S., *Marxism and the Origins of British Socialism* (Cornell University Press, 1973).

Ramelson, Marian, *The Petticoat Rebellion* (Lawrence & Wishart, 1972).

Strachey, Ray, *The Cause: a Short History of the Women's Movement in Britain* (Virago, 1978, first published 1928).

Thompson, E.P., *Homage to Tom Maguire* (in A. Briggs and J. Saville, 1971).

Thompson, E.P., *William Morris: Romantic to Revolutionary* (Merlin Press, 1977).

Tsuzuki, C., *H.M. Hyndman and British Socialism* (OUP, 1961).

9 Labour, the Shop Stewards' Movement and World War One

War disrupts society. World War One was no exception, but far from disrupting the existing trends within the labour movement it had the effect of concretising them. The militancy of labour's rank and file continued unabated, whilst the exigencies of war gave labour's leaders the chance to become fully enmeshed within the state apparatus. The gulf between the two widened to such an extent that it was difficult for them to co-exist within the same organisations. The 'unofficial' opposition, reflecting the chasm between leaders and led, generated its own structures in the form of the shop stewards' movement and workers' committees. Although no longer unofficial, the shop stewards of today can trace their origins to this wartime period during which rank and file workers kept effective trade unionism alive in the face of their leaders' surrender.

The War and the Labour Leadership

The British labour leadership was not alone in finally capitulating to the nationalist seduction of a war between rival imperialisms. Similar patterns were repeated throughout the European labour movement, with the exception of Russia and Serbia. The resolutions of the Second International, in condemning colonialism (1907 Stuttgart Congress) and calling for workers to oppose war (1910 Copenhagen Congress) were promptly forgotten in the rush to arms, and the International itself collapsed. British labour leaders maintained an anti-war stance up until the point, on 4 August 1914, that the government finally declared war on Germany. Thereafter, their opposition transformed itself not just into support but into wholesale co-operation in the war effort. By the end of August the Labour Party and the TUC declared an 'industrial truce' for the duration of the war and lent their support to an all-party recruitment campaign. The British Socialist Party, led by Hyndman, supported this position until the party leaders were defeated in 1915–16 and Hyndman himself was removed in 1916. On a primarily ethical basis, the ILP maintained an anti-war policy from the start, even though some of its leading parliamentary members did not. (As an ILP member, Ramsay MacDonald surprised his detractors by opposing the war. In consequence he resigned as leader of the Labour Party. His place was taken by Arthur Henderson.)

Labour compliance was more than welcomed by a government faced with the problems of wartime production and mass mobilisation of fighting men. As it became clear that the war would not be over by Christmas, the government became more dependent on a compliant labour leadership to act as their conduit to the masses. In order to achieve its wartime aims, it was clearly desirable for the state to operate through a process of consent rather than coercion, even if this meant, from the viewpoint of the leaders of organised labour, a hitherto unimagined degree of status in the machinery of government.

Not that coercion was far below the surface, as the draconian measures adopted in 1915 showed. Apart from the Defence of the Realm Act, under which the government assumed the right to commandeer any factory and workers it deemed necessary for war work, the Treasury Agreements and the Munitions of War Act were both concluded with explicit Labour and/or trade union support. (By May 1915 there were three Labour MPs in the coalition government, one of them, Arthur Henderson, in the cabinet.) The two Treasury Agreements signed by government and trade union representatives confirmed labour's promise to abandon strike action for the duration of the war. It also drew the unions (including the ASE, whose members were principally affected) into agreeing to suspend 'restrictive practices' in skilled trades by agreeing to the use of unskilled or semi-skilled labour (particularly that of women) in the war industries. (This was known as 'dilution'.) To press home their advantage, the government rushed through the Munitions of War Act, which made these agreements legally binding, extended their coverage to other industries, and introduced the infamous 'leaving certificates'. This was a device whereby a worker could obtain other employment only on production of such a certificate, and was clearly aimed at preventing sacked militants from working again. Promises that the government, in return for these massive concessions, would take steps to clamp down on the enhanced opportunities for prof-iteering were seen as a fair quid pro quo by the labour leadership, although in practice this turned out to be quite meaningless.

Thus opened, in Lloyd George's phrase 'a great new chapter in the history of Labour in its relations with the State'. In a way he was correct. As a result of the war Labour was transformed from a pressure group struggling to gain a foothold in consensus politics into a party semi-incorporated in the state machine. The incorporation was partial in the sense that although the ambition of the leadership was flattered by the role they were now asked to play, that role was a very limited one. They were never real insiders in that they had no effect whatsoever on the formulation of policy; they were tolerated as useful brokers in the execution of policies decided by those who really held power. Provided they accepted that and toed the line, which meant not driving too hard a bargain (even though they had more bargaining strength than they realised), the infinitely flexible British state was prepared to confer prestige upon them.

The Labour Movement and the War

The Clyde

As it turned out the labour leadership proved to be singularly ineffective in delivering a compliant labour movement to serve the nation's war effort. Apart from the ILP there was a considerable body of political opposition to the war which generated a host of anti-war organisations like the Union of Democratic Control and the No Conscription Fellowship. Socialists played a part in these alongside radicals from the liberal tradition whose internationalism and pacifism was affronted by the wasteful carnage inflicted in the name of national self-interest. As the war progressed the lack of war aims coupled with the blundering stupidity of the military commanders made it clear that the price of peace was to be paid through mass slaughter. The 'war to end wars' was reduced to the stalemate of the western front (the Gallipoli campaign to open an eastern front having ended in ignominious disaster). Ever-increasing supplies of cannon fodder in the form (by 1916) of conscripted soldiers were dumped in trenches and made to face certain death when they were ordered to go 'over the top' in pointless battles to advance the front a few miles.

The most serious threat to the patriotic consensus came, however, from industry. Wartime industrial struggles were not linked directly to the anti-war movement, and there was no equivalent in Britain to the anti-war strikes that took place in continenal Europe. The main effect of the strikewave in Britain was that it posed a real challenge to the incorporation of labour, which labour's leaders had attempted, so tamely, to deliver. Whether consciously anti-war or not, it was clear from 1915 that industrial workers were not going to be bound by the surrender of their leadership, nor were they to be cowed by the legal strictures against strike action. J.T. Murphy, a prominent leader of shop stewards in Sheffield and later nationally, put it thus:

> None of the strikes which took place during the course of the war were anti-war strikes. They were frequently led by men such as myself who wanted to stop the war, but that was not the actual motive. Had the question of stopping the war been put to any strikers' meeting it would have been overwhelmingly defeated. The stoppages had a different origin and a different motive. They arose out of a growing conviction that the workers at home were *the custodians of the conditions of labour for those in the armed forces, as well as for themselves*. (J.T. Murphy, *New Horizons*, 1941 p. 44 Murphy's emphasis.)

The sharpest and earliest expression of this mood of defiance came from the very engineering workers whose quiescence was so vital for wartime production. A strike of engineers on the Clyde in February 1915 (ASE members) in support of a wage demand of 2d arising from the expiry of a pre-war agreement had important repercussions. The strike was, of course, unsupported by the ASE leadership. In addition, it was of dubious legality, occurring as it did in munitions factories. (The blanket ban on strike action was not in force until July when the Munitions of War Act became law.) Aided by the hastily formed Central Withdrawal of Labour Committee the strike spread rapidly throughout the Clyde. Signs of mass defiance were not limited to Scotland. In the same year there was a mass strike of 200,000 South Wales miners which, like that of the Clydeside engineers, arose from a claim arising from the expiry of a pre-war agreement. The vital need for coal in wartime lent this strike a special importance, and far from using any of the strong-arm powers at his disposal to crush it, Lloyd George went in person to South Wales to negotiate a settlement by which the miners' demands were, in the main, satisfied.

In themselves there seemed nothing to distinguish these strikes in the early years of the war from the normal run of trade dispute over wages and conditions. Apart from the fact that they occurred in the difficult conditions of war hysteria and repressive legislation, they seemed unremarkable. The Clydeside workers were ultimately defeated and the South Wales miners won only the same deal as miners elsewhere in the country had achieved without strike action. However, on Clydeside, the Central Withrawal of Labour Committee was replaced by a permanent organisation, the Clyde Workers' Committee (CWC), whose aims were:

to obtain an ever increasing control over workshop conditions, to regulate the terms upon which workers shall be employed, and to organise the workers on a class basis and to maintain the class struggle until the overthrow of the wages system, the freedom of the workers and the establishment of industrial democracy have been attained.

This body provided the model for similar organisations in other urban industrial centres. Its language was syndicalist but its practice was not, in the sense that it sought to link the industrial struggle in which it was firmly rooted to wider, community-based campaigns. Hence it transcended the narrower horizons of syndicalism to include women and unorganised workers in a more general *political* onslaught on capitalism. In this way the often limited and defensive demands of the strike movement were given a broader character, in that they acted as mobilisers for the working-class as a whole.

The new structures developed in the factories in the absence of official union backing aided this process. Narrow sectionalism preserved by individual unions crumbled as new directly elected workplace representatives took the place of the by now immobilised full-time officials. These representatives, the shop stewards, were not in themselves a new creation – they had existed in some unions, particularly the ASE, for some time, mainly to recruit new members and to collect union dues. Now, however, their function changed beyond recognition. They not only dealt with the myriad of problems caused by the abandonment of pre-war industrial practices (especially dilution) but they represented workers across craft and union divide, thereby aiding the process of working-class unity. The strength of the shop stewards' movement among the engineers was significant given their key importance in wartime production and the fact that their union, despite its traditional craft exclusiveness, was well established and well organised. The explanation for this is a political one. Socialists in all unions, albeit a tiny minority, were quick to seize upon the vacuum left by the abrogation of their union leaders and acquired an influence out of all proportion to their numbers. The shop stewards on the Clyde, even if they were not already socialists, came under the socialist influence of the Clyde Workers Committee (CWC), the body that united them. The influence of the BSP, the SLP and the ILP was very strong in the west of Scotland, although the latter organisation did not have the industrial influence enjoyed by the other two. John Maclean's (BSP) Marxist education classes attracted hundreds of workers. Socialist militants like William Gallacher (BSP, and the chairman of the CWC), Arthur MacManus, J.W. Muir (both of the

SLP) and others gave practical and theoretical leadership to the growing mass movement in the factories and the wider community where rent strikes were common.

Dilution

However, it soon became evident that the parodox of socialist militants rooted so strongly in the most skilled and craft-conscious section of the workforce was both a strength and a weakness. The issue of dilution posed the great contradiction between craft and class. By 1916 it tested the ability of socialists to give principled but practical leadership, as distinct from revolutionary phrase mongering, on an issue of immediate concern. The government, for their part, clearly saw the importance of the dilution question in Scotland, not just for its own sake but because they saw it as the chief means of breaking the influence of the CWC. The militant craft union approach to dilution would be to oppose it root and branch on the simple grounds that it would break the long established craft control of the engineering industry which had been won in the teeth of employer opposition. Maintaining such controls in wartime implied great militancy because it meant opposing the state itself and the union leadership. But what of the socialists? They had always railed against craft exclusiveness and had sought to broaden the appeal of their union. Now it would seem that the state and their own previously blinkered leadership were on their side. In addition there was the little acknowledged question of sexism. Could socialists identify with the backward male chauvinist opposition to the entry of women into the engineering industry? These issues had to be faced elsewhere, but the very strength of the socialist base within Scottish engineering and the predominance of that industry (together with ship building) on the Clyde, meant that the dilution issue was particularly sharply focused there.

The CWC showed that it was not afraid to tackle the issue head on, but in doing so it revealed an internal division and an overestimation of its political (although not its industrial) strength. Courageously both the SLP and BSP factions in the CWC leadership did not oppose dilution *per se*. The majority position was to call upon munitions workers to refuse to negotiate its terms and to campaign instead for the nationalisation of the engineering industry under workers' control. Maclean opposed this line because implicit within it was an acceptance of the unpalatable fact that engineers should be more effectively self-organised to do the government's war work. As it turned out, the government strategy of attempting (through their commissioners specially appointed for the purpose) to go over the heads of the CWC directly to the factories to negotiate individual agreements was at least partially successful. The matter was thus taken out of the hands of the CWC as the dilution agreement at Parkhead Forge showed. This left the CWC to fight a rearguard action on less revolutionary terms not of its own choosing. Revolutionary socialism was temporarily defeated, but militant trade unionism was not. Within weeks of the Parkhead agreement the workers at that factory went on strike over the right of their convenor, David Kirkwood (an ILP member who negotiated the dilution agreement!), to walk freely around the different departments of the factory in the course of his trade union work.

It was richly ironical, therefore, that the very factory which proved to be the weakest link in the CWC's chain turned out to be the one which prompted the second wave of strikes on the Clyde. Sensing its advantage, the government used the full force of its repressive powers to deal with the strikers' leaders. Maclean, Gallacher, Maxton and Muir were gaoled, others were deported, and the socialist paper, *The Worker*, was suppressed. However, this temporary body blow to the CWC does not prove that it or its socialist message were defeated because they were too politically advanced and hence out of tune with the sectional interests of defensive, albeit militant, trade unionism, as later events were to show.

Outside Scotland

'Red Clyde' was in the vanguard of the the wartime workers' movement, but mass protests led by revolutionary socialists developed with as much force in other parts of the country. The election of shop stewards and the formation of shop stewards committees was commonplace in most large factories that had been turned over to wartime production. In Sheffield a workers' committee under the leadership of J.T. Murphy was formed on the model of the CWC. Other industrial centres like Manchester, London and later Birmingham also had workers' committees, but they survived for briefer periods than their Sheffield and Clyde counterparts. In Sheffield it was not dilution but the introduction of conscription in 1916 and the fear that it would be used as a means of removing industrial militants that prompted the formation of their workers' committee. The Sheffield Workers' Committee (SWC) attempted to involve women and unskilled workers from the start. Many local strikes in London (at the Woolwich Arsenal), on Tyneside, in Southampton, in the Midlands and elsewhere erupted throughout 1915 and 1916 in munitions factories, with craft workers, particularly engineers, at the forefront. It was not until May 1917 that this localised movement acquired a national character, although not yet an effective national leadership.

Two government decisions of especial concern to skilled workers provoked the May 1917 strikes. One was the plan to extend dilution to non-war work and the other was to abolish the Trade Card scheme whereby skilled craftsmen were exempted from military service. Beginning in Manchester, the strike spread rapidly during May to nearly 50 towns throughout Britain. An attempt had been made before the strike to convene a national conference of workers' committees, but this got off the ground only during the strike and hence cannot be said to have led it. The government, typically, reacted by arresting the strike leaders, but displayed its worries about this mass militancy by appointing a Commission on Labour Unrest. One of the commission's recommendations was to capitalise on the craft sectionalism that had prompted the May strikes by offering a 12 per cent wage increase to skilled workers. The fact that this divisive tactic was met with a further upsurge, this time by unskilled and semi-skilled workers also demanding wage rises, is an indication of a deepening awareness which was doubtless influenced by the revolutionary events in Ireland (the 1916 Easter Rising) and the first Russian Revolution in 1917. So although the May strikes had their origin in craft sectionalism and defensiveness, their outcome was to lay the basis for a nationally co-ordinated and ultimately broader and more political movement in 1918 and 1919. Without the previous political groundwork and subsequent leadership of the workers' committees such an outcome would not have been possible and the struggle might have exhausted itself in its own whirlwind spontaneity.

Women Workers and the Unofficial Movement

The Clyde Workers' Committee was reconstructed by the end of 1917. According to Gallacher, the first Russian revolution 'was one of the most potent factors in the revival'. Significantly, its first action was to call a mass strike in support of the reinstatement of four sacked women workers at Beardmore's factory. The Sheffield Workers' Committee, having given active support to the non-craft workers' fight for the 12 per cent wage increase, was now clearly established as an all-grades committee. This was an important development since it ensured henceforth that the militant movement was broadened from its original base among skilled workers. Furthermore the SWC, although a male dominated organisation, outspokenly condemned both craft sectional-ism and sexism. In its founding document written by J.T. Murphy the

SWC expressed criticism of the prevailing view whereby seven million women workers were 'tolerated with amused contempt as passengers for the war'. It went on to explain that the cheapness of their labour was due to 'man's economic dominance over women which has existed for centuries', and that now 'content to treat women as subjects instead of equals, men are ... faced with problems not to their liking'.

These attitudes were mirrored in other parts of the country where, despite the lack of workers' committees, the (by now almost universally recognised) shop stewards' committees sought closer co-operation with unions representing the unskilled – in particular the Workers' Union, the most militant of them. This meant that for the first time women workers, the subject of so much exploitation and the object of so much suspicion, were drawn into the mainstream of the struggle. Female trade union membership increased by about 160 per cent during the war, but apart from the National Federation of Women Workers, the Workers' Union (WU) was the only union to make a serious commitment to organising women. By 1918 the WU employed 20 women full-time officials and had a female membership of over 80,000. This was more than any other general union and represented a quarter of the WU's own membership.

There is little evidence, however, that the demands of women trade unionists, especially for equal pay, were ever placed high on any bargaining agenda during the war. Early on, in 1915, a conference called by the Women's War Workers' Committee drew up a comprehensive list of demands including the rights to training, trade union membership and pay parity. However, when in 1918 the first equal pay strike occurred, it was initiated, led and ultimately won by women. This was the strike of women tramway workers starting in London and spreading to other towns in the south east over the offer of an unequal war bonus.

1918–19

All that was now required was a national leadership and a national focus. The former was achieved when in January 1918 a national delegate conference of shop stewards was held in Leeds. This elected a National Administrative Council of the Shop Stewards' and Workers' Committee Movement (NAC). The government provided the national focus in the form of a renewed attempt, temporarily defeated in May, to conscript skilled men engaged in war production. The Military Service Bill, introduced for the purpose, could have proved divisive if the NAC had opposed it on the same grounds as the skilled workers previously. After all, why was it less desirable to send skilled men to be slaughtered in a senseless war? Were their lives of more value than unskilled workers? This time, however, in the wake of the Bolshevik victory in Russia and the Russian withdrawal from the war, the NAC's opposition to the Military Service Bill took a more general anti-war stance. All further conscription was opposed and the NAC called on the government to follow the Russian lead and sue for peace.

The full force of this now open attempt to unite the political and the industrial was not really effective until 1919. With the exception of the Clydeside May Day strikes, despite failed attempts in other parts of the country, there were no other anti-war or anti-conscription strikes in 1918. There were two reasons for this. One was the fact that conscription remained, despite the NAC's attempts to broaden it, a sectional issue the opposition to which was of greater appeal to skilled workers. Secondly, the government embarked upon a far more thorough process of victimising militants than it had attempted in 1916. Nonetheless, the widespread political debates which were generated by the NAC's initiative, laid the basis for the mass industrial/political action of the following year even though the NAC, by 1919, was virtually moribund. It held two further conferences, one in 1920 and the next in 1921, but formally dissolved itself in the following year.

The war ended in November 1918 but it did not bring peace on the home front. The following year witnessed the broadest and most serious strikewave yet seen. Some 35 million working days were lost in strike action – six times as many as in in the previous year. This included strikes of those normally relied upon to carry out the repressive functions of the state – the police and the armed forces. Miners, transport workers and printers joined those who had been taking action throughout the war. Their mood was influenced by news of the workers' risings in Germany and Hungary, and their strong support for the fledgling Soviet Russia.

At the forefront, once again, was the Clyde Workers' Committee, which organised a mass strike in January 1919, accompanied by mass picketing, for the 40-hour week. Unlike the wartime strikes, this one was not defensive – it was a political offensive against the power of capital. It was all the stronger for its well-established links with discharged soldiers and sailors. (Even before the war ended these latter were organised in the Federation of Discharged Soldiers and Seamen.) Women, too, were fully involved in the action and on the picket lines. The huge demonstration in George Square, Glasgow, resulted in a battle with the forces of law and order, supported by young troops sent there by a panic stricken government anxious to nip the 'Bolshevik spirit' in the bud. Strike leaders were arrested and Glasgow fell under virtual military occupation. In Belfast, too, a huge strike-wave paralysed the city.

However, two fatal weaknesses were revealed in what otherwise appeared to be a revolutionary situation. The first was the lack of co-ordinated national leadership, and this enabled the government to pick off individual struggles one by one. The second weakness, linked to the first, was that the kind of leadership that did exist, for example on the Clyde, was not equal to the *political* challenge demanded by the situation. That is not to say that the CWC was not a highly political organisation, but its limitations were inherent in the fact that it remained a loose federation of workplace organisations. While having a clear line on the daily struggles, there was little in the way of a clear revolution-ary perspective beyond general support for socialist principles. This point was later expressed thus by Gallacher: 'We were carrying on a strike when we ought to have been making a revolution' (*Revolt on the Clyde* 1936).

The Communist Party

A turning point had been reached by revolutionary industrial militants in 1919. The peculiar British paradox, that of a mass movement without a political voice, and a tiny socialist (as opposed to labourist) movement without the masses, was by now glaringly obvious. Syndicalism had shown itself capable of confronting individual employers but incapable of sustaining lasting advances in the face of the full repressive power of the state. The wartime industrial struggles had witnessed the emergence of a much closer unity between some of the hitherto aloof socialist organ-isations like the SLP and the BSP with the shop stewards, but the special conditions of war, during which the state was forced to make conces-sions for its own survival, blurred the distinction between industrial and political action. The theories of Marx and Lenin as well as the practical lessons of the Russian and German revolutions pointed to the necessity of a united revolutionary socialist party to lead the movement to a more permanent advance in the battle against the capitalist system as a whole.

Events in Russia were followed with close interest, and when it became clear that British troops were being used with those of other capitalist countries against the revolution a powerful solidarity movement emerged in the form of the Hands Off Russia Committee. Initiated by the BSP, SLP and left-wing shop stewards, it even won the support of the labour leadership. Its president, A.A. Purcell, a member of the TUC's Parliamentary Committee, was also a member of the BSP. Practical solidarity, following intensive agitation, was shown by east London dockworkers when they refused in 1918 to load a munitions ship destined for Russia, the 'Jolly George'. The threat that Britain might actually declare war against the Soviet Republic resulted, in August 1920, in the formation of Councils of Action (over 350 were established in all parts of the country, largely based on trades councils), which pledged, with the support of the TUC and the Labour Party, to mobilise mass strikes should the threat prove real.

In this atmosphere the talk of communist unity became at once more urgent and more realistic. Attempts had been made to unite the disparate socialist parties and factions during the war on the initiative of the BSP, but it was not until after the war that any real headway was made. Earlier attempts (1917) at unity between the BSP and the ILP had failed due to the latter's rejection of Marxism as the guiding theory for a new socialist party. It was apparent therefore that the minimum condition for participation in the post-war unity talks was an acceptance of Marxist theory. Agreement on theory (and *in* theory) proved to be much easier than agreement on strategy and tactics. The talks in 1919 and 1920 revealed deep disagreements on two major questions – whether or not to affiliate to the Labour Party and whether or not to participate in local and parliamentary elections. The intervention, by letter, of Lenin in these debates certainly helped the less sectarian position to triumph, even though it failed to convince some of its supporters like Sylvia Pankhurst of the Workers' Socialist Federation.

By August 1920 the Communist Party of Great Britain existed. It was, and for many years remained, tiny. Its influence, however, was immeasurably greater than the sum total of its membership. From the very beginning it had within its ranks the leading industrial militants who had led the massive pre-war strikes and who had formed the core of the Shop Stewards' movement during the war. To these were added in (1920 or later) other individuals and small groups who had either been 'converted' to Marxism or induced to jettison pure syndicalism because of the war and the Russian Revolution. The South Wales Socialist Society, a descendent of the pre-war Miners' Reform Movement and some of the Guild socialists (like R. Page Arnot, Ellen Wilkinson and Walter Holmes), fell into this latter category. A left-wing group within the ILP, including such individuals as Shapurji Saklatvala, R. Palme Dutt, Emile Burns and Helen Crawfurd, may be counted among the former.

It would be wrong to lay false claims about the significance of the formation of the Communist Party in 1920 given the stranglehold of the by now well-entrenched reformist and labourist traditions in Britain. Such traditions, nurtured and abetted by social imperialism, had deprived Marxism of a mass following. Equally, however, it would be wrong to deny the importance of the Communist Party's existence. For at least 60 years it was the only significant Marxist organisation in Britain providing a focus for the activities of the left politically and industrially. As such it was a force with which the ruling class and the right-wing labour leadership had constantly to reckon.

Further Reading

Foster, J., '*Strike action and working class politics on Clydeside,* 1914–1919, *International Review of Social History,* XXXV, 1990.

Gallacher, W., *Revolt on the Clyde* (Lawrence &Wishart, 1936).

Hinton, J., *The First Shop Stewards' Movement* (Allen & Unwin, 1973).

Murphy, J.T., *New Horizons* (Bodley Head, 1941).

Murphy, J.T., *The Workers' Committee: an Outline of its Principles and Structure* (Sheffield Workers' Committee, 1917).

Klugmann, J, *History of the Communist Party of Great Britain,* vol. 1 (Lawrence & Wishart, 1969).

Rosenberg, Chanie, *1919: Britain on the Brink of Revolution* (Bookmarks, 1987).

Stewart, B., *Breaking the Fetters* (Lawrence & Wishart, 1967).

Part 3

1920–1951: Readjustment

10   Economic and Political Background 1920–51

World War One and the temporary post-war boom had the inevitable effect of camouflaging the underlying chronic economic problems associated with Britain's loss of status as a prime manufacturing power. The inter-war years brought these difficulties, with their attendant social effects, to the surface once more, in a political climate that was far less stable nationally and internationally than it had been during the latter part of the nineteenth century.

This was a period of readjustment, economically and politically. The growing internationalisation of capital meant that Britain as a debtor nation could not fully control her own economic decisions. A new tension emerged between the interests of finance and industrial capital. Politically a new adjustment was necessary in the era of the mass franchise (universal after 1928) to accommodate a new two-party system brought about by the decline of the Liberal Party and its replacement by Labour as the main opponent of the Tories. The international tensions caused by the rise of fascism in the 1930s meant that national politics too was played in the context of a world stage which ultimately led to world conflagration in the form of World War Two. The aftermath of that war presented an altered world balance in which socialism, no longer confined to the Soviet Union, was seen by the capitalist world as the main enemy at home and abroad. The resultant Cold War was the backdrop against which the labour movement had to operate by the mid twentieth century and beyond.

The Economy

The Staple Industries
The decline in Britain's staple industries, already noted in Chapter 5, was, after the war, an irreversible fact. The boost they had received under the impetus of the demand for munitions and uniforms during the war evaporated once the war was over. Coal, heavy engineering, ship building, iron and steel, and textiles, the original foundations of Britain's industrial supremacy, already challenged by foreign competitors after

1870, paid the price for failure to respond adequately to this earlier challenge which was now compounded by the loss of export markets to old rivals and to new ones in the form of Japan and the USA. Britain's return to the gold standard in 1925, with a currency that was overvalued, had a further detrimental effect on the competitive position of her exports in the world market.

The inter-war period witnessed the inevitable results of this deep economic decline. Although most industrialised countries suffered as a result of the world depression after 1921, Britain was in the worst possible position to recover. Even in comparison with Germany, the vanquished power who lost all her colonies, some of her own industrial territory and much else besides, Britain's economy with all the built-in advantages of her greatly expanded empire lagged sadly behind.

The continuing decline of the staple industries was in part responsible for the persistent high unemployment of the 1920s and 1930s. Although new industries began to develop these were located mainly in the Midlands and the southern part of England and did not compensate for, much less solve, the problems of the declining industries. A new phenomenon, that of the 'distressed areas', emerged as a characteristic feature of the inter-war years. Such areas, South Wales, the west of Scotland, Lancashire, Tyneside and West Yorkshire – the old industrial heartlands, remained impervious to faint-hearted attempts by governments to resolve their social problems. These were due, above all, to the absence of any concerted attempt by capital or the state to deal with the underlying economic causes of their plight. Unemployment in the distressed areas never fell below a million in the 1920s, but the 'great crash' at the end of the decade produced a prolonged slump in industry as a whole with even higher rates of unemployment in the 1930s. By 1932 a fifth of the employable population was out of work and although the end of the year witnessed an economic recovery lasting for about five years the staple industries were only marginally affected by it. Unemployment in the distressed areas remained at shockingly high levels of between 40 and 60 per cent and had even risen to 80 per cent in some of the most blighted regions.

The End of Laissez-Faire

The war had seen, for the first time in the history of industrial capitalism in Britain, the abandonment of *laissez-faire* economics as the state interfered, regulated and commandeered those aspects of industrial production most vital to the war effort. Such controls were speedily relinquished after the war in the rush to resume traditional economic orthodoxy but the experience of centralised state planning, even in the very modest form of wartime production, provided a vision of its future possibilites. It may have been that such planning, coming so late, could have done little to rescue the fortunes of Britain's declining industries but it could have given a boost to the newer ones struggling to emerge. As it was, industries like electrical engineering, aircraft production, motor cars, man-made fibres, chemicals and glassmaking acquired a tenuous hold in the 1920s and became really successful only in the economic upturn after 1932. By this time, however, they had lost any potential they might have had for gaining a foothold in the export market. Thus, unlike the old staples, they contented themselves with satisfying home demand. They thrived in this valuable but more limited market, largely because they were protected from foreign competition due to the final and belated abandonment after roughly 100 years of the traditional British policy of free trade. The first protective tariff was introduced, without too much controversy, in 1932.

Although goverment intervention stopped short of the kind of central planning advocated by socialists and that seemed to be so successful in the Soviet Union, governments in the inter war years involved themselves in the economy to a far greater extent than hitherto. Apart from the introduction of protective tariffs, the state played an important role in encouraging new forms of industrial organisation which, by 1939 had transformed the structure of British business. In Britain, although some industrial giants had emerged before the war, the small firm based on single or family ownership retained a dogged existence. The growth of industrial concentration, the expansion of joint-stock enterprises, the development of cartels and monopolies, was commonplace elsewhere by 1918 but it took off in Britain only after that date.

The attitude of the government, which had always looked upon cartels, monopolies and the like as unwanted forms of restrictive practice, undoubtedly changed to the extent that by the 1930s it was even prepared to pass legislation to enforce or encourage the process, particularly in the staple industries. The Coal Mines Act of 1930, which compelled the establishment of a cartel in that industry, and the 1935 Finance Act, which granted tax relief to successful monopolies, are examples of both aspects of the new policy. Related to these developments was the changing character of the ownership of British industry. The larger the firm the more capital was required for its operation, rendering single individuals, no matter how rich, less likely to be able to supply it. Boards of directors representing major shareholders, among whom could be counted banks or finance houses, replaced the old-style owners/managers. The now familiar fact of separation between ownership and day-to-day control established itself in the inter-war years. However, restrictive and monopolistic practices did almost nothing to revive the fortunes of the declining industries, even though they boosted the profits of the smaller number of employers who remained. Employers preferred to tinker with these new forms of organisation than to address the central question of investment in new plant and machinery in order to modernise their undertakings.

The New Industries

As has already been noted, the new industries, unlike the staples, were based on the domestic market. How was it that they succeeded in tapping home demand when unemployment was high and the economy (except for a few years in the 1930s) stagnated? The answer in part lies in the fact that for those who had work real wages improved due to the fall in the cost of living, a fall accounted for chiefly by cheaper food imported from Britain's colonies. This meant that surplus income was available to be spent on consumer goods, and this, coupled with a growth in population (due in the main to longer life expectancy), led to expanded domestic demand. Added to this was the considerable disposable income of the middle and upper classes, who, due to the decline of the servant population, had both the incentive and the spare cash to purchase the increasing array of consumer durables. It is also the case that for the employed population working hours were shorter and paid holidays more common (particularly for those in the new industries), giving rise to more leisure time that could be spent shopping (witness the massive growth of the chain and departmental stores) or relaxing by going to the cinema and listening to the radio. These and other forms of entertainment either took off or underwent a tremendous expansion in this period.

Most of the new industries were based in purpose-built factories using electricity as their source of motive power. Not dependent on coal supplies, and not needing to be near a port (because they were not export oriented), they could locate themselves where they liked. Because they chose such unlikely places as Oxford, Luton, Bedford or the outskirts of London and Birmingham, these industries stimulated a boom in house building as workers flocked to them. However, the extent to which, despite government hopes, there was a wave of internal migration away from areas of high unemployment was greatly exaggerated. Such industries displayed other common characteristics. Early on in their development they were almost always dominated by monopolies, duopolies or a small number of very large firms operating in a cartel. Their products thus became associated with such household names as Austin and Morris (cars), ICI (chemicals), Courtaulds (man-made fibres), Morphy Richards and Hoover (domestic appliances), GEC and AEI (electrical engineering), Marks and Spencer and Woolworths (chain stores) and Unilever (food and much else besides). The factories established by such firms were very large and were based on the most advanced methods of mass production, utilising the technique of the assembly line and so-called 'scientific management'. This latter took the form of time-and-motion study, the most common of which was the Bedaux system. The assembly line stimulated the demand for cheaper semi-skilled and unskilled labour, much of which was filled by women who had been unceremoniously turned out of their posts when the men returned after World War One.

Unemployment

The inter-war period was thus one of contrasts. The poverty and despair of the depressed areas contrasted sharply with the hope and affluence promised by jobs and products of the mass consumption industries. It was as if two nations existed not just between workers and employers but also between workers who had a job, or the prospect of one, and those who were resigned to a life of almost permanent unemployment and doomed to the stigmatised pittance of a means-tested benefit. Not for them were the gleaming, tantalising products of the new industries displayed so temptingly in all the chain stores that mushroomed on every high street. Novels like Walter Greenwood's *Love on the Dole* captured such hopelessness and misery.

Unemployment in itself was nothing new, and indeed in comparison to figures we have got used to, the highest estimated total in September 1932 of 3,750,000 jobless is not all that startling. However, the sheer duration of the problem for almost the entire span of years between the wars and its resistance to upturns in the economic cycle endowed the unemployment of this period with an intrinsic character. It persisted even at a time when the building boom and the new industries were creating thousands of new jobs. Some labour from the depressed areas migrated to fill the vacancies, competing with the indigenous workforce. This created a situation in which the high unemployment in the regions of declining industry was transported in diluted form to the growth areas. Thus even in the high growth industries in a boom year like 1937, 17,000 car workers and 15,000 chemical workers were unemployed. Hence there was never a year between 1921 and 1939 when unemployment fell below the million mark. This is probably an underestimate since then, as now, the official figures hardly reflect the problem. They record only insured workers who registered as unemployed. This meant that any worker, like those in local government or agriculture who were not part of the national insurance scheme (established in 1911 and dependent on the payment of contributions by both worker *and* employer) were automatically excluded from government unemployment statistics, as were a large number of married women who would have been excluded from benefit anyway.

It was plain for all to see that this could not be passed off by the usual subjective dogma which held the jobless responsible for their own plight – the problem was a structural one. Governments, although becoming more interventionist, did nothing to deal with the underlying causes of unemployment beyond attaching the term 'special areas' (1934) to its structural foundations. They also did next to nothing to remedy the social consequences, and a Labour government actually added insult to injury by cutting unemployment benefit by 10 per cent in 1931 during the most severe economic crisis.

The Economy in War and Peace 1939–51

As during the 1914–18 war, World War Two saw the government taking control or directing much of industry in the interests of wartime production. The extent of the intervention was greater than before, but this time the new Keynsian economic orthodoxy encouraged the state to maintain many of the controls once the war was over. Whereas in 1919 the influence of classical economics had encouraged the state to pull out, the inter-war years, as we have seen, had produced a contradiction between economic theory and economic practice. The state had become increasingly interventionist. By 1939 due to industrial concentration it was relatively much easier for the state to plan and deliver its wartime requirements. Once the war was over, having created a huge centralised economy, there was little objection even among Tories for some degree of central control to remain in order that the state could now plan for its peacetime needs.

Women Workers

Although unemployment was high for almost the entire inter-war period the proportion of women who worked actually increased slightly, from about 32 per cent in 1921 to 34 per cent in 1931. No census was conducted during the war, hence no figures are available for 1941, but as in World War One women made a mass entry into social production during the war years and hence it is likely that the figure would have been unusually high. In 1951 it had readjusted to the norm but did not decline nonetheless, standing at almost 35 per cent. Unemployment, as we have seen, hit the older staple industries most severely, and apart from textiles these were the ones in which men predominated. The new industries were keen to use female labour on their modern assembly lines, which explains the fact that the south east (the main locus of such industry) accounted for over one-third of the total number of women employed. The second largest geographical region giving employment to women was the traditional one – the north west, where women had been heavily involved in the manufacture of cotton and woollen cloth for almost a century and a half. The textile trade, as one of the staples, was also adversely affected by the decline in the export market but its crisis was not as severe as that of the other older industries. Its decline was very slow in comparison and hence unemployment rates were not so high.

Despite the open recognition of the need for female labour in the new high profile industries the attitude to women workers was the same as in Victorian times. An official (as in local and national government service) or ideological (elsewhere) marriage bar operated within the labour market to ensure that married women understood that their proper place was to attend to their *real* functions as wives and mothers. This line was reinforced by a cult of domesticity popularised by the huge growth of women's magazines in the 1920s and 1930s the most popular of which, *Woman*, had a circulation of nearly one million by 1940.

Although World War Two saw an all too brief respite for women in the traditional pattern of job segregation, the post-war scene witnessed its resurgence. By 1951 women were confined to six main occupational groups. Even though these were somewhat different from the pre-1914 pattern they displayed the same characteristics, in that women's employment was defined by the kind of sex stereotyping which attempted to view it as a natural offshoot of the domestic role. It was undervalued accordingly. The decline in the textile trade and domestic service was more than amply compensated for by the huge increase in demand for women clerks, typists and shop assistants. Of course, there is nothing intrinsically feminine about clerical or shop work. Indeed, such work in the nineteenth century was conventionally regarded as a male preserve. But the very process of feminising such labour fulfilled the vital economic function (for the employers) of cheapening it. Hence the very real fact of 'women's work' is also an ideological construct, founded upon the huge economic gains to be made from the historical

inequality of women's position within the labour force due to their sub-
servient role within the family.

Politics

For the labour movement this period is particularly significant in that
it produced what might be regarded as the zenith of all their aspirations
– Labour governments. There were three of these, the first two (1924
and 1929–31) were both minority administrations. Only the third
(1945–51) had a sufficient majority to act alone and to accomplish
anything. All three will be discussed more fully in later chapters.

The fact that Labour emerged as the main party of opposition should
not cloud the fact that the Tories were still very strong and were effectively in office in one guise or another with or without Liberal (and
Labour!) support (mainly as the National government) throughout
most of the period. World War One had divided the already weakened
Liberal Party, with Lloyd George having formed his own National Liberal
Federation, still clinging to Tory support and organisationally distinct
from the mainstream Liberals led by Asquith. No less than seven general
elections took place in the 17-year period between 1918 and 1935, four
of these held by 1924. (No elections were held between 1935 and 1945.)
Clearly, however strong the Tories were, this was a time of adjustment
for them as they struggled to reassert themselves in the face of the mass
franchise, considerable industrial unrest and a Labour Party which
seemed set to take advantage of the situation. The fact that the Conservative Party, in spite of in-fighting and leadership struggles, maintained
its ascendancy until 1945 was helped by in-built advantages in its favour
in the electoral system after 1918. Second votes for graduates and
owners of businesses helped Tories, as did the redrawing of boundaries
which gave them a solid bedrock of suburban seats to add to their rural
vote. Irish independence after 1921 removed around 80 anti-Tory
seats in what was now the Republic of Ireland, while the Ulster
Unionist MPs in the north accepted the Tory whip until 1972. To these
Tory blessings can be added the weakness of the opposition which never
succeeded in challenging the ideological grip of individualism and
property rights.

Apart from the issue of the social consequences of poverty and unemployment which forced its way occasionally on to an unsympathetic
parliamentary arena, politics until 1945 was dominated by foreign affairs
the course of which Britain no longer controlled. She reacted to rather
than initiated world events. The 'threat' of the Soviet Union and the

obsessive desire to isolate it took second place to the real menace of
the alarming growth of fascism in Italy and Germany, the territorial
ambitions of which remained largely unchecked until it was too late.
The Versailles settlement, drawn up by the victor powers at the end of
World War One, created an unstable balance of power in which the
old Austro-Hungarian, Ottoman, Russian and German empires had been
dismembered in favour of a host of small and weak 'nation' states in
central and eastern Europe.

The League of Nations established to maintain the peace in the new
world order proved to be unequal to the task and was in any case ill-
disposed to accomplish it since it too parodied the anti-Sovietism of its
member states by refusing the Soviet Union the right to participate in
its proceedings, even though Germany who had been made to sign the
'war guilt clause' was admitted in 1925. International politics after
World War One was overshadowed by the might of the most powerful
country to emerge after 1919 – the United States of America. Britain,
whether her rulers recognised it or not was now a second-rate power
economically and politically. Even the lavish protuberance of her vast
empire could no longer hide this fact. Indeed, she was even forced to
recognise changes in her autocratic relationship with her colonies under
the pressure of the emergent movement for national liberation within
them. The colonies dominated by white British settlers – Canada,
Australia, New Zealand and South Africa – were granted Dominion
status in 1931. The prolonged struggle for independence in Ireland had
been crowned by the liberation from the British of all but Ulster. The
mass movement in India and Egypt following savage repression resulted
in some reforms, although not independence.

In Europe Britain tamely tagged behind American initiatives. These
were largely focused on aiding the economic and military recovery of
Germany, in defiance of the Versailles Treaty, in order to provide
America with a strong foothold in Europe while at the same time
building a buffer against the presumed danger of Communist expansion.
Hitler put paid to any idea that Germany would be a client state, but
at the same time his own aspirations to world domination were openly
publicised in his book, *Mein Kampf*. Together with Mussolini he
proceeded to put his expansionist aims into practice under the very noses
of the major powers. In 1935 Italy invaded Abyssinia. In the same year
the Germans, by now well underway to reverse Versailles, re-took the
Saarland and in 1936 they reoccupied the Rhineland. These two prime
industrial areas greatly aided not just Germany's economic recovery but
also her military potential. This latter proceeded by leaps and bounds,

and in 1936 German rearmament was fully sanctioned by the powers. Sanction or no, it was clear from the German supply of military hardware to the fascists in Spain during the Civil War (1936–39) that her arms industry was already very productive.

It was quite evident that Germany was preparing for war, but provided Tory statesmen like Neville Chamberlain could be seduced into believing that a forthcoming war was to be fought against the Soviet Union, the goverment was more than happy to ride the international crises and to tolerate Hitler's excesses. This meant turning a blind eye to the anti-semitic and anti-democratic horrors of Nazi domestic policies. This was not too difficult since many leading British Tories shared views similar to Hitler and Mussolini even if they expressed slight unease about some of their methods. In this sense the Tory policy of appeasing Hitler was not confined to Chamberlain and the aristocratic wire-pulling Cliveden set. Although such views, culminating in the infamous Munich agreement of 1938 with Hitler, have been roundly condemned since, and the opposition to appeasement supposedly led by Churchill venerated as the real Tory orthodoxy, the fact is that hardly any Conservatives and not all that many Labour MPs had taken the fascist threat seriously at home (in its Mosley-ite guise) and abroad since its inception. Indeed of the two 'isms', most of them, if forced to choose, preferred fascism to communism.

When Britain was pushed finally and reluctantly to declare war on Germany in September 1939 her motive was not to rid the world of an evil creed but to safeguard British interests. The more realistic anti-appeasers under Churchill (in a coalition with Labour) proved better able to accomplish this more limited task when they ousted Chamberlain from office in May 1940 after the disastrous nine months of the 'phoney war'. The main difference between those who sought in 1940 to combat Germany more vigorously and their pusillanimous predecessors was that the latter had realised earlier that Hitler's plans were not simply to smash Bolshevism, nor, despite his Munich and other promises, were they confined to grabbing non-German territories like Poland and Czechoslavakia, much less simply to consolidating the German *volk* in an expanded Reich. The Nazi policy of *lebensraum* (literally, 'living space') required much more, including a colonial empire. The collapse of France, aided by her own fascist collaborators and the temporary Nazi-Soviet non-aggression pact (1939–41) left the Germans a free hand to pursue their plans for world domination and brought them ever closer to overrunning Britain. The entry of the Soviet Union into the war in 1941 took the pressure off the western front for a while as operation

Barbarossa (the German code name for the elimination of the Soviet union and its people), deflected the Nazi war machine.

Domestic politics during and after the war provided the Labour Party with its greatest opportunity ever. It played an essential role in Churchill's wartime coalition government, and was the government between 1945 and 1951. How successfully it made use of this is the subject of Chapter 14.

Further Reading

British Labour Statistics : *Historical Abstracts 1886–1968* (Department of Employment, 1971).

Constantine, S., *Unemployment in Britain Between the Wars* (Longman, 1980).

Glucksmann, Miriam, *Women Assemble: Women Workers in the New Industries in Inter-war Britain* (Routledge, 1990).

Greenwood, W., *Love on the Dole* (Penguin, 1972, first published 1933).

Halsey, A.H. (ed.), *Trends in British Society Since 1900* (Macmillan, 1974).

Hannington, W., *The Problem of the Distressed Areas* (Gollancz, 1937).

Laybourn, K., *The Rise of Labour* (Edward Arnold, 1988).

Mowat, C.L., *Britain Between the Wars 1918–1940* (Methuen, University Paperbacks, 1968).

Pugh, M., *Women and the Women's Movement in Britain 1914–1959* (Macmillan, 1992).

Stevenson, J., *Social Conditions in Britain Between the Wars* (Penguin, 1977).

11 Labour Governments and Unemployment 1920–31

The economic problems of the 1920s and 1930s obviously had consequences for the labour movement, but these were by no means predictable. Mass unemployment helped to account for the fall in trade union membership from around six and a half million in 1920 to its lowest point in the inter-war years of three and a quarter million in 1933. (Membership rose slowly but steadily thereafter.) But a decline in membership did not mean a decline in militancy. Strike action was almost as prevalent as hitherto and culminated in the biggest display of working-class strength yet seen – the General Strike of 1926.

The vibrancy of the movement cannot be measured simply by the number of days lost in strikes. Other indices include the existence and viability of a range of organisations capable of giving expression to working-class aspirations outside the workplace. Two such organisations were particulary significant in this period. One was the campaign, begun in the London Borough of Poplar, to defend living standards in working-class areas by reducing the domestic rate (Poplarism) and the other was the movement to organise the unemployed and draw attention to their plight. In addition, in some areas, paricularly in compact mining villages, trade unionism and community politics fused to produce a revolutionary outlook in such a singular fashion that such places earned the nickname of 'little Moscows'. The fact that two (albeit minority) Labour governments took office in this period could also be said to be an indication of a more general political belligerency, but the experience of Labour in office only served to underline the continued need for extra-parliamentary organisation and showed once again the huge gap between leaders and led, or more accurately, between left and right.

The influence of the Communist Party in most of the mass campaigns in the inter-war period had the effect of politicising such protests, but at the same time sharpened the divisions between those who participated in them and the official leadership of the trade unions and the Labour Party. Divisions had always existed, but the fact that Labour became a party of government made it especially important for it to present its ultra cautious and respectable face if it was not to incur the wrath of a state machine which saw the Soviet Union and hence communism as its main enemy. The labour leaders had managed to regroup themselves after they had lost the popular initiative in the wake of the mass struggles during and immediately following World War One. Given their continued commitment to reformist parliamentarianism, they were unlikely to learn the lessons the left was anxious to teach them. Rather, they attempted to strengthen their grip on the movement and in doing so helped to reduce the movements of protest.

The Labour Party

In 1918, the Labour Party, in belated recognition of its official existence, adopted a constitution and a programme. It also permitted individual members to join it as distinct from affiliated organisations. This did not mean, however, that it transformed itself into a mass campaigning party. Although it developed constituency organisations these remained, as now, primarily vehicles to mobilise votes in local and national elections. However, in 1918 socialists could be forgiven for thinking that the party they had fought to create had fulfilled their cherished dreams of becoming a mass socialist party. The new constitution adopted the famous socialist clause four which committed the party

   to secure for the workers by hand or by brain the full fruits of their industry and the most equitable distribution thereof that may be possible, upon the basis of the common ownership of the means of production and the best obtainable system of popular administration and control of each industry and service.

The other still surviving feature of the constitution (but probably soon to be changed after 64 years) was the introduction of a centralised method of electing the party's leadership at the annual conference on the basis of reserving seats for different categories of member. Five seats were allocated to local constituency organisations, four were for women, and the remaining 14 went to affiliated organisations. The fact that no distinction was made between political affiliates (like the ILP) and trade unions meant in practice that the latter now dominated the National Executive, resulting in a loss of influence of the socialist current. Thus the ILP which had done so much to create the party was now marginalised and the body it created lost the most active political guardian of its implied socialist conscience. The 1918 manifesto, 'Labour and the New Social

Order', also heralded a distinctive and uncharacteristic break with liberalism. It advocated nationalisation of some of the major industries and called for the 'scientific reorganisation' of the economy. But whilst the programme, drafted by Sidney Webb, was a radical departure, its essence expressed the Fabian desire to create a mixed economy rather than a socialist one. The fact that it and the constitution seemed so advanced is a reflection of and a tribute to the revolutionary spirit which had engulfed the labour movement worldwide in the course and the wake of World War One. Socialists, particularly those in the ILP, may well have been pleased that the party even came this far, at least in theory, but their hopes were soon to be dashed when it came to the acid test of Labour politics practically applied to concrete issues.

The First Labour Government 1924

The test came soon enough. The party increased its representation in the House of Commons in the general elections of 1922 and 1923 (142 and 191 seats respectively), by which time Ramsay MacDonald had been re-elected leader – the choice of the left! No-one, including MacDonald, expected that he would become Prime Minister in 1924. The Tories were in disarray over the issue that had historically divided them – tariff reform. Unable to unite his party and with no overall majority in parliament, their leader, Baldwin, dissolved it, leaving Labour as the next largest party free to form a government provided it obtained Liberal support. Such were the formal (and unfavourable) circumstances in which the minority Labour government of 1924 came into being. Regardless of the wisdom or otherwise of accepting office in these conditions, the fact is that Labour was so blinded by the lure of office that it unwittingly fell into a trap created for it by the other two parties. Tariff reform, whilst a problem for the Tories, was but a fig leaf to cover a more sinister manoeuvre. In a situation of high and rising unemployment, and with no policy to alleviate it, the Tories were genuinely concerned that it would only be a matter of time before a majority Labour government was elected. Such a government, if its 1918 manifesto was to be taken seriously, would pose a serious threat to the owners of wealth. Baldwin expressed this openly at a meeting of the Conservative Party after the 1923 election:

> It was on unemployment that the Labour Party relied on coming to power within two or three years. Their calculations were that the discontent in the country coupled with want of action on our part

would have swept them into power and us out by 1926. (Quoted in Allen Hutt, *The Post War History of the British Working Class*, 1937)

Asquith agreed with him. For the Liberals a Labour government 'with its claws cut' was infinitely better than one that was truly independent; as he said:

If a Labour government is ever to be tried in this country, as it will sooner or later, it could hardly be tried under safer conditions. (Quoted in Ivor Bulmer-Thomas, *The Growth of the British Party System*, 1965)

This explains why the Liberals did not, as was in their power, help save the Tory government and instead threw in their lot for nine months to prop up, while it suited them, this first Labour government.

The establishment parties showed undue alarm at the prospects of Labour's radicalism, let alone its socialism. Although dependent on Liberal votes this was not a coalition government and hence the fact that Ramsay MacDonald went outside the ranks of his own party to find cabinet ministers was a matter of some concern to the Labour rank-and-file. He selected Lord Haldane, a former Liberal minister, as Lord President and the posts of Lord Chancellor and First Lord of the Admiralty went to two Conservatives (Lords Parmoor and Chelmsford respectively). Such matters were decided at a secret meeting at the Webbs' house. The reason given by Philip Snowden (in his autobiography) for the choice of non-Labour cabinet ministers was quite simple:

... the most timid conservatives and the most frightened capitalists took heart from the presence in the cabinet of men like Lord Parmoor, Lord Chelmsford and Lord Haldane; they could hardly believe that these men would be the instruments for carrying out the socialist revolution.

Further evidence for the groundlessness of the fears of the establishment was to be found in the Labour government's attitude to the rising wave of strikes. It elevated its hostility to them almost to a point of principle. As J.R. Clynes, the Lord Privy Seal, proclaimed, in its handling of strikes, the government

played the part of a national Government, and not a class Government, and I am certain that any Government, whatever it might be, could not in the circumstances have done more than we have done to safeguard the public interests. (Quoted in Allen Hutt, 1937)

Even moderate trade union leaders like Ernest Bevin complained of the threats emanating from the parliamentary leaders of the Labour Party during the dock strike. Such threats were made real during the strike of London's transport workers when the government went to the lengths of invoking the hated Emergency Powers Act, the force of which was not activated only because the strike was settled.

It is thus surprising, given the extent of the government's hostility to mass action, that the establishment went to the lengths it did to discredit Labour. This came in the form of the infamous 'Zinoviev Letter', the publication of which was a classic example of establishment conspiracy and cost Labour, as intended, the 1924 general election. The government could have been toppled at any time, but the issue that finally settled its demise was the Campbell case. J.R. Campbell, acting editor of the communist *Workers' Weekly*, published the famous 'Don't Strike' open letter to the army forces urging them not to act as strike breakers. For this he was charged under the 1797 Incitement to Mutiny Act, but when the charge was dropped the government was held responsible and lost a vote of censure in the Commons. Three days before the ensuing general election a letter purporting to come from the Communist International, signed by its president, Zinoviev, was leaked by the Foreign Office to the press and published in the staunch Tory paper the *Daily Mail*. In it was a promise of 'Moscow gold' to finance armed insurrection in Britain. Although the letter was addressed to the Communist Party the fact that it alluded to the draft treaties on trade and co-operation between Britain and the Soviet Union which had been negotiated by MacDonald's government meant that a connection was supposed to be made between the Labour Party and communism. The fact that the letter was an obvious forgery and that anyone who was seriously concerned with the truth could not believe for one moment that MacDonald had any sympathies with communism, did nothing to prevent the 'red bogey' distorting reality and doing the sinister job for which it was intended. The Tories obtained a comfortable majority.

The Second Labour Government 1929–31 – 'the Great Betrayal'
Although much had happened in the five years between the first and second Labour governments, the circumstances and the issues giving rise to the second were remarkably similar to the first. Once again the Tories' inability and unwillingness to deal with the sore of unemployment dominated the political scene, although this time the problem was compounded by a worldwide financial crisis which had a particularly

sharp impact in Britain. The 1929 general election, the first in which all women over the age of 21 could vote, had produced great gains for Labour. The return of 287 Labour MPs made it the largest party in the Commons, although once again without an overall majority should the 260 Conservatives and 59 Liberal members combine against it. The fact that for two years they chose not to do so was partly because of the gulf between them on tariff reform but also because they found it preferable to let Labour face the dilemma of having to take unpopular measures to deal with the economic crisis and thereby court the odium of its own electorate. Lloyd George said that he did not see why the Liberals should 'carry the ladder and hold it in its place for five years whilst the socialists are on the scaffold and doing all the building' (Quoted in Ivor Bulmer-Thomas, 1965).

Although, following the experience of the previous minority admin-istration, there was some discussion this time as to the wisdom of putting Labour into a similarly unfavourable situation, the matter was quickly resolved in favour. Only the left Labour MP James Maxton proposed a serious alternative. This suggested getting the party to prepare a socialist legislative programme and getting a mandate to pursue it following a fresh election. The fact that this was hardly discussed is a reflection of the move to the right in TUC and Labour Party circles following the defeat of the General Strike. This was reflected too in the watered-down version of the 1918 programme which appeared in 1927 under a new title, 'Labour and the Nation'. The left openly opposed it and offered their alternative in the form of the Cook-Maxton manifesto (named after its authors, A.J. Cook, the miners' leader, and James Maxton MP, both leading ILP figures). The official manifesto made an appeal to the nation as opposed to class. Its tenor was reflected in MacDonald's opening speech to the new House of Commons in which he wondered

> ... how far it is possible without in any way abandoning our party positions ... to consider ourselves more as a Council of State and less as arrayed regiments facing each other in battle ... so far as we are concerned, co-operation will be welcomed ... so that by putting our ideas into a common pool we can bring out ... legislation and admin-istration that will be of substantial benefit for the nation as a whole. (Quoted in C.L. Mowat, *Britain Between the Wars 1918–1940*, 1968)

On the main issue of the day, unemployment, Labour showed itself to be as reluctant as its predecessors to do anything constructive. Quite the reverse – it actually proposed to make the plight of the unemployed worse by cutting their already miserly benefit. Although not accepting in full the drastic remedy(!) of a 30 per cent cut in unemployment pay proposed by the Royal Commission on Unemployment, the terms of reference of the May Committee set up by the government with the aid of the Liberals had an ominously similar objective. This was to recommend ways of 'effecting forthwith all practical and legitimate reductions in the national expenditure consistent with the efficiency of the services'.

Implicit in this was an acceptance of orthodox treasury economics which sought to place the burdens of the financial crisis on those who could least afford it. It was not simply a question of rejecting socialist solutions – these had long been consigned to a never-never land. Labour was also about to reject alternative, more progressive capitalist solutions of the type advocated by the economist J.M. Keynes which were by now finding favour in TUC circles.

The report of the May Committee thus precipitated a crisis within Labour circles the outcome of which proved both unexpected and disastrous. The logic of the timidity of a minority government that was dependent on Liberal support, assailed by the Tories and their friends in the newspaper world, and above all caught in the web of its own ideological confusion meant that when the crisis came it was incapable of doing anything other than that demanded of it by its political opponents. In this sense MacDonald and the eleven members of his cabinet who supported him in making the required cuts were only acting more consistently, albeit more treacherously, than the ten who did not. Faced with the unpalatable decision to make such cuts to the tune of £78 million, which in the light of the projected budget deficit were now demanded by Britain's foreign creditors if further loans were to be forthcoming, the cabinet was split, not on the substantive issue, but on its severity. The May Committee and others backed this demand, which included a 10 per cent cut in unemployment benefit at a time (1931) when the numbers out of work were rising rapidly.

The cabinet did nonetheless agree to a cut of £56 million but this proved, as MacDonald was aware, to be too little for the other two parties. MacDonald thus went to the king to tender the government's resignation, but to the surprise even of his own cabinet supporters, he did not offer to resign himself. In a weird scenario, obviously prepared in advance, MacDonald suggested that he stay on as Prime Minister of a national government. In so doing he was consistent with the views he had announced in his speech to the Commons in 1929 – the national interest, second only to his personal ambition, came before class and party.

The fact that his unusual offer was accepted with alacrity indicated prior planning. The Liberal Herbert Samuel advised George V on these lines:

> in view of the fact that the necessary economies would prove most unpalatable to the working-class, it would be to the general interest if they could be imposed by a Labour government. The best solution would be if Mr. Ramsay MacDonald ... could propose the economies required. If he failed ... then the best alternative would be a National government composed of members of the three parties. It would be preferable that Mr. MacDonald should remain Prime Minister in such a National Government. (Quoted in R. Miliband, 1961, pp. 176–7)

Outside the Corridors of Power

Events in Westminster, while capable of adding to the burdens of the working-class, were nevertheless remote from it even when Labour was in office. However, as Bevin observed during the dock strike of 1924, there was greater pressure for political conformity during a Labour government so as not to cause it embarrassment. The pressure to conform was felt strongly in the trade unions given their organic connection with the Labour Party and this led to the formation of organisations outside their control in order both to escape the dead hand of officialdom and to encompass issues wider than the established labour movement was prepared to acknowledge. Prime among such issues was the vexed question of unemployment about which the official movement displayed at best perplexity and at worst unconcern.

The National Unemployed Workers' (Committee) Movement

The NUW(C)M, established in 1921 from the host of unemployed committees of ex-servicemen, sought with varying degrees of success to organise among the unemployed and to campaign for the next 25 years under the slogan of 'Work or Full Maintenance'. It was responsible for using daring and innovative methods of protest including hunger marches, factory raids to protest against overtime working, and mass demonstrations often aimed in particular at Poor Law Guardians who were still responsible for the adminstration of poor relief under the archaic provisions of the 1834 Poor Law Amendment Act (see Chapter 4). Women played a prominent role in the movement. Lillian Thring was the editor of the NUWM paper *Out of Work* and from the outset a place was reserved on the National Administrative Council for a women's organiser. This position was held first by Lillian Thring and later, from 1929, by Maud Brown when a women's department was also established. (In 1929 the movement dropped the word 'Committee' from its title and it became known more simply thereafter as the NUWM.) Women's contingents were a regular feature of the hunger marches of the 1930s especially when, owing to the introduction of the means test in 1931, whole families bore the direct burden of the unemployment of one or more of their members.

At its peak in 1933 the NUWM had upwards of 100,000 members, but in contrast there were periods in the 1920s when the movement seemed close to extinction. Its peaks and troughs not surprisingly roughly coincided with unemployment levels. The fact that its leadership was dominated by members of the Communist Party did not lessen its mass appeal, although this fact undoubtedly influenced the attitude of the TUC which by 1928 was outspokenly hostile. This hostility showed itself in two ways. The TUC either ignored the issue of unemployment altogether in the hope that it would simply go away, or when in the early 1930s it resurfaced with even greater force, half-hearted attempts were made to set up rival organisations. Wal Hannington, the able full-time organiser of the NUWM, together with other leading communist activists like Harry McShane, Sid Elias and many others, managed to steer a relatively independent course for the movement through the troubled sectarian path of communist politics during the so-called 'third period' of the Communist International (1929–31) and beyond. The Comintern's temporary rejection of the strategy of the 'united front' of all working-class organisations in favour of the narrow 'class against class' outlook in which previous social democratic potential allies were now looked upon as social fascists, did not have the devastating effect on the NUWM that it had on 'official' labour movement organisations. The NUWM was already unofficial and hence untainted in Comintern-speak with the bourgeois outlook of such putative supporters, who anyway had decided earlier to hold the movement at arm's length. Although the politics of the movement's leaders were quite open, it was never the case that it was simply a front organisation of the Communist Party. It achieved its support because it paid meticulous attention to the general and individual problems of the unemployed. Its legal department assisted countless victims of the system to challenge the parsimonious jurisdiction of the Poor Law and later the Public Assistance Committees established in 1931.

Local Government, Poplarism and 'Little Moscows'
The extension of the franchise had an impact on local as well as national government. Labour steadily gained ground on local elections both for

Poor Law Boards of Guardians and borough councils and in the capital for the London County Council (LCC). By 1919 Labour had a majority for the first time on the LCC to complement majorities won on eleven London councils in working-class areas. Outside London the Communist Party was so influential at local level in some areas that it shared power with Labour, extinguishing liberalism for good as a force in local politics. The best known of these 'little Moscows' as they came to be known were the mining villages of Mardy in the Rhonda Valley (South Wales) and Lumphinnans in West Fife (Scotland) along with the textile villages of the Vale of Leven in Dumbartonshire, Scotland.

At a local level Labour leaders had to be more responsive to local issues. Labour locally would have got nowhere if its leaders had adopted the same Olympian aloofness that characterised national politicians. Poverty and unemployment dominated the local as well as the national stage, with local responses clearly contrasting with the paucity of the national initiative. The imaginative and daring response in Poplar to such issues resulted in the imprisonment of the majority of its councillors and at the same time achieved such notoriety that it added a new noun to the English language – 'poplarism'.

Essentially the Labour councillors in Poplar under the leadership of George Lansbury (editor of the *Daily Herald*) attempted to do all in their power to alleviate the problems of poverty and unemployment in the borough. This involved a variety of methods including increasing the pay of council employees, in particular of women by paying them the same as men, creating more jobs, improving local roads and sewers through a big extension of public works, and increasing the scale of outdoor relief to the poor. Controversial as all this was, the issue that brought the council into direct confrontation with the state was its decision in February 1921 to use its own local rates for its own purposes. It refused to levy the rates for outside bodies like the LCC, the Metropolitan Police Authority and other London-wide organisations which were financed from the coffers of all the London boroughs with little regard to their ability to pay. Poplar did not object in principle to paying something towards London-wide services but questioned why the same principle did not operate in reverse. Rich boroughs could levy lower rates because they had no poor for whom to provide. Since the financial burden of poor relief rested with local councils, the poorer ones had been forced to increase their rates. The Poplar argument was simple – if the poor boroughs had to pay for London-wide services, then the richer ones should be forced to contribute to a pooled fund for the provision of local schemes to relieve poverty in those boroughs who could least afford to bear its rising cost. Hence arose the demand for the 'equalisation of the rates' and until this was conceded Poplar, at a council meeting in March 1921, voted (with one vote against) not to levy rates on behalf of central London bodies. This decision in itself helped the poor since it meant that rates were reduced, as were rents since many paid rate and rent together.

The wrath of the establishment was quick to descend – writs were served on 30 of the Poplar councillors. Despite the opposition of the London Labour Party orchestrated by its secretary, Herbert Morrison, the councillors stuck to their policy and were arrested and imprisoned in September 1921 amid mass demonstrations in their support. Despite Morrison's backstage manoeuvres to reach a compromise with the government represented by Lloyd George and Sir Alfred Mond (chairman of ICI), the imprisoned councillors made it clear that no deal could be struck on their behalf unless they were involved in negotiations which they insisted could take place only if they were freed and the principle of rate equalisation accepted. The fear of the Poplar action spreading to other supportive councils like Stepney and Bethnal Green induced the government to agree, after six weeks' incarceration, to the release of the prisoners and acceptance of their principal demand.

Poplar had won, at least for the time being. Instead of using this victory as a shining example of the best kind of Labour politics acting in the interests of the working-class, Morrison capitulated to the inevitable propaganda of the Tories to discredit poplarism as the antics of a 1920s style 'looney left' bunch of irresponsible spendthrifts. He did all he could to disassociate the London Labour Party from poplarism, as was shown clearly in a leaflet issued for the borough council elections which proclaimed in cold type:

> The London Labour Party does not associate itself with the demands for public assistance of a character which cannot be regarded as practicable in existing circumstances. (Quoted in Noreen Branson, *Poplarism, 1919–1925*, 1979)

Such calculations, based on the presumption that the politics of caution would bring Labour continued electoral success, were proved disastrously wrong in the local elections in London in 1923. Labour lost control in five boroughs including Morrison's base, Hackney. Whilst this was partly explained by the evaporation of the revolutionary mood that had brought Labour success in 1919 the fact is that in Poplar, Labour defied the trend and increased its share of the vote. This, although Morrison and his allies would not acknowledge it, indicated the success of Lansbury's vision of municipal socialism, which was a far cry from the 'gas and water' Fabian variety. While he understood that socialism in one borough would not bring about the end of capitalism, he argued nonetheless that:

> the workers must be given tangible proof that Labour administration means something different from capitalist administration, and in a nutshell this means diverting wealth from the wealthy ratepayers to the poor. (Quoted in Noreen Branson, 1979)

But although Poplar was able to withstand the opposition of its Labour critics in London, it was more difficult when such opposition was voiced by the Labour leadership at national level especially when, as in 1924, Labour formed the government. Initially Poplar had cause to place its hopes in the fact that the only left-winger in MacDonald's cabinet, John Wheatley, a supporter of poplarism, was made Minister of Health and Local Government. But Wheatley was a lone voice, prevented from doing anything practical to assist the beleaguered council which was now embroiled in further controversy over its policy of paying a £4 minimum wage to its own employees. The Labour Party establishment joined the chorus of disapproval against this further Poplar 'crime' deemed as profligate at a time when workers throughout the country were faced with savage wage cuts in the interests of economic efficiency. The hope that a Labour government would be sympathetic or even supportive was forlorn. Sensing the isolation of Poplar, the ensuing Tory government made clear its intention to take legal action, and in 1925, to prevent this, the council climbed down. The Poplar submission was not cowardly. It marked a realistic recognition that one council on its own, however well supported locally, could not fight the system indefinitely in conditions in which the movement was in retreat and the Labour leadership remained preoccupied with labourism rather than socialism.

Further Reading

Branson, Noreen, *Poplarism 1919–1925* (Lawrence & Wishart, 1979).

Bulmer-Thomas, Ivor, *The Growth of the British Party System* (John Baker, 2 vols., 1965).

Croucher, R., *We Refuse to Starve in Silence: a History of the National Unemployed Workers' Movement 1920–1946* (Lawrence & Wishart, 1987).

Hannington, W., *Unemployed Struggles 1919–1936* (Lawrence & Wishart, 1979, first published, 1936).

Hutt, A., *The Post War History of the British Working Class* (Victor Gollancz, 1937).
MacIntyre, S., *Little Moscows* (Croom Helm, 1980).
Miliband, R., *Parliamentary Socialism* (Allen & Unwin, 1961).
Mowat, C.H., *Britain Between the Wars 1918–1940* (Methuen, University Paperbacks, 1968).
Shinwell, E., *I've Lived Through It All* (Victor Gollancz, 1973).

12   Trade Unions, the General Strike and the Aftermath

Despite the decline in trade union membership in the inter-war years (see Chapter 11) the continued militancy of its activists, which reached its climax in the General Strike of 1926. This posed the greatest challenge this century to the power of capitalism, and by implication to the labourist ideology which had always shrunk from such confrontation. 1926 marked a watershed. Trade union militancy was pushed to its ultimate limit in an unfavourable economic climate. It was faced with a powerful and well-prepared state machine which seized with gusto the opportunity to deal a death blow to union defiance once and for all. The leadership of the trade union movement was also put to the test. As unwilling strike leaders in 1926, the TUC's concern had little to do with winning, much more to do with ensuring that it prevented the unleashing of forces on both sides of the industrial divide over which it would have little control or influence. The aftermath of the strike proved to be disastrous for the trade union and labour movement, despite the fact that its leaders bent over backwards to accommodate themselves to a new situation in which both government and employers capitalised on their victory with barely concealed contempt for the power of labour which they had been forced to tolerate hitherto.

The Trade Union Leadership

One aspect of syndicalist philosophy infiltrated official trade union circles, albeit for motives which were far removed from the revolutionary aims of its protagonists. The trend to union amalgamations proceeded apace after 1920. The impetus for this had been created during the war when centralised pay bargaining for discrete industrial groups had been accomplished by national federations of trade unions and employer organisations. A federation of engineering employers had been long established, thus it was no surprise that, albeit belatedly, the Amalgamated Society of Engineers joined with smaller craft unions in the industry to form the Amalgamated Engineering Union in 1920. Among unskilled and semi-skilled workers amalgamations of unions of general labourers and of dockers and carters produced the Transport and General Workers' Union in 1922. Under its first general secretary, Ernest Bevin, this was soon to become the largest union and it exercised considerable influence on the Labour Party. The Gas Workers' Union was the satellite around which a number of smaller general unions, including the National Federation of Women Workers, clustered and produced in 1924 the National Union of General and Municipal Workers. Similar trends of amalgamation were evident among white-collar workers – in the post office (Union of Post Office workers, 1920) and in the civil Service (Civil Service Clerical Association, 1922). Another syndicalist principle used for pragmatic purposes was evident in the seemingly innocuous formation in 1921 of the General Council to replace the TUC's Parliamentary Committee. The new body had more extensive powers than the old, but from the beginning it was clear that it was not going to be used to promote a co-ordinated onslaught on capital! Indeed Bevin hoped that strikes would be fewer because of the power of this new organisation. While not treading on the toes of affiliates, the General Council hoped to promote better relations between them and to present an effective and hopefully united trade union front in its dealings with outside bodies.

Thus it was that a tighter and more centralised leadership, dominated by a small number of large unions, emerged from the mass struggles of the previous ten years, and whilst this had the potential for promoting effective solidarity between groups of workers in struggle it could also be used with great effect for precisely the opposite purpose. The fact that sectionalism rather than solidarity remained the hallmark of trade unions and hence of TUC leaders (who always reflected change rather than initiated it) was in a paradoxical way assisted by this greater centralisation. The development of national collective bargaining which had stimulated union amalgamation and federation betokened an industrial 'coming of age' of the trade union movement. It went together with official employer recognition of unions at workplace level alongside local bargaining procedures. The collective bargaining process even spread to industries in which trade unionism was not well developed. The system of joint industrial committees of employer and union representatives recommended in the 1917 report of the Whitley Committee indicated the willingness of the government to encourage what it saw as a more orderly and centralised system of industrial relations.

By 1921 73 such Whitley Councils, as they came to be known, had been established and those that survived in the public and private sectors (many of them, in the public sector, intact until the Thatcher years) concluded national pay and conditions agreements for their respective industries. Thus it was that the interests of government, employers and the trade union leaderships, all worried by the challenge to their authority during the war years, were served by snatching the initiative from the militants through the creation of these new centralised structures. The very militancy which had induced this development was turned to the advantage of the leadership which now claimed credit for the concessions and in doing so both emasculated and incorporated its initial driving force – the shop stewards. Although the revolutionary organisation of shop stewards had collapsed, the post-war compromise between capital and labour could not ignore them. In most unions and collective agreements stewards were given an officially recognised role far beyond their original dues collector and recruiting agent function. Nonetheless, workplace militancy continued in the years after the war and this forced a persistent tension between the potential of centralisation to achieve more effective class solidarity and the pressure to confine it within the bounds of traditional sectional interest. This tension reached its breaking point in 1926, the year of the General Strike.

The Miners

The decline of Britain's staple industries, as we have seen, was a prime cause of mass unemployment in the inter-war years. The position of the workers who remained employed in such industries was grim. They were faced with a concerted attempt by the employers to cut wages and increase productivity. Due to the fact that the coal mining industry accounted for one-sixth of the male labour force and was the strongest and best organised in trade union terms, miners were at the centre of the employers' offensive and bore the main brunt of the post-war attack. A defeat for the miners would enable managerialist domination, which had taken such a knocking in the war years, to be reasserted and open the way for a successful attack on other groups of workers. The coal owners also had another aim. During the war the state had assumed some measure of control over mining as an essential wartime industry. This had boosted the miners' demand for the nationalisation of the industry – a policy supported by the Sankey Committee (appointed by the government in 1920 to avert a threatened strike for a 30 per cent pay increase). Needless to say, the owners were vehemently opposed to any form of state intervention, let alone nationalisation. In the less revolutionary atmosphere of the 1920s Lloyd George dropped all pretence at concession and brought forward his plans to de-control the mines. This coincided (probably not accidentally) with the owners' announcement of savage wage cuts to well below pre-1914 levels and an ending of national wage agreements. The fact that employers in other industries were attempting similar tactics helps to account for the wave of support given by the labour movement to the miners when, as a result of their determined refusal to accept the demands of the mine owners, they were locked out. The Triple Alliance (formed in 1914 of mine, railway and transport unions) called a rail and transport strike, but due to the backstage manoeuvring of some of the union leaders, notably Frank Hodges and J.H. Thomas (secretaries of the Miners' Federation and the National Union of Railwaymen respectively), the strike was called off at the eleventh hour. The *Daily Herald* echoed the widely held view that this incident (unfortunately dubbed 'black Friday') 'was the heaviest defeat that has befallen the Labour movement within the memory of man' (quoted in G.D.H. Cole, *The Common People*, 1938, 1971). This perhaps exaggerated opinion was explicable in the light of the *Herald's* earlier analysis that the attack on the miners represented 'a frontal attack on the whole working-class by the capitalists and their Government' (quoted in Hutt, 1937). The miners were eventually starved into submission, leading as predicted to lockouts to enforce wage reductions on engineers, cotton operatives, builders, shipyard workers, seamen and others.

This appeared to mark the end of the trade union militants' forward offensive which had characterised industrial relations since 1910, leaving only the unemployed struggles to challenge the hegemony of the capitalist and labourist establishments. However, this defeat was by no means the dying gasp of a spent revolutionary creed, as the renewed attack on the miners in 1925 was to show. By the time the coal owners, due to another slump in their badly run industry, demanded in 1925 yet another round of wage cuts and a lengthening of hours, they were faced with more formidable opposition from a re-grouped coterie of militants who had for the first time gained leading positions in their own unions and on the TUC General Council.

The National Minority Movement

The National Minority Movement (NMM) shared similar aims with the syndicalist movements of rank-and-file militants which preceded it in that it encouraged workshop organisation and industrial unionism. But unlike them it fought to ensure that the aspirations of the membership of the unions in which it had influence was reflected in the election of a new type of leadership. The movement's founding statement, *What the Minority Movement Stands For* (1924), was critical of the existing trade union leadership which it condemned as 'a bureaucracy ... often under capitalist influence' and 'which frequently acts as a barrier to swift and conscious action on the part of the workers'. It listed as one of its activities 'contesting all trade union office elections with supporters of the Minority Movement of proved loyalty to the working-class as candidates, and endeavouring to secure their return'. It thus built upon the traditions of rank-and-file organisation but did not erect 'rank-and-filism' into a principle. Although the NMM was formed, in June 1924, under the auspices of the Comintern's Red International of Labour Unions (RILU) it was neither separatist nor sectarian. The RILU had already attracted support among militants, especially in the Miners' Federation but also among engineers and transport workers. The NMM sought to unify the separate industrial groupings but stressed that:

> It is *not* a separatist movement. It does *not* aim at bringing into being new and rival organisations to those already existing. On the contrary it actively opposes any attempts that are made to split the trade unions, and to establish brand new organisations. ('What the Minority Movement Stands For')

Whilst it would be wrong to make exaggerated claims of the success of the NMM, its influence was undoubtedly behind the election of a left trend in some trade unions, notably in the Miners' Federation in which the militant A.J. Cook replaced Hodges as secretary in 1923. Although Cook was not a member of the TUC General Council, by 1924 there was, for the first time, a left grouping on that body – A.B. Swales (Engineers), George Hicks (Bricklayers) and A.A. Purcell (Furnishing Trades). Amazingly, between 1923 and 1925 the General Secretary of the TUC, Fred Bramley, was a left-wing socialist. Obviously the NMM can claim no credit for his appointment, but its effort in building rank-and-file organisation was complemented by a man who was sympathetic in general terms to their aims as shown by the formation of a joint TUC/Soviet trade union committee. Of greater significance was the fact that when, in 1925, the next round of cuts in miners' pay was proposed and Baldwin warned that the return to the gold standard meant that all workers would have to face wage reductions, the General Council responded immediately and planned, in the event of another miners' lockout, to call a strike of the Triple Alliance. This determined action, unlike that of 1921, took Baldwin by surprise and led to a climb down, the reason for which, as he later told his biographer, G.M. Young, was because 'we were not ready'. On the day the strike would have started, Friday 11 July 1925, the government announced that it would grant a subsidy to the coal industry for nine months, obviating at least temporarily the necessity for wage cuts while a Royal Commission conducted an inquiry. This victory, accomplished without strike action, was hailed in banner headlines in the *Daily Herald* as 'Red Friday', although as events were to show, Red Friday, significant as it was, was more of a truce than a victory.

The General Strike 1926

Although the government was caught unaware by the resolve of the TUC and the mass support for the miners in 1925, this did not indicate a lack of preparedness or willingness for a confrontation with militant trade unionism. Indeed, Red Friday served to galvanise the cabinet into taking the active preparations for conflict which the hawkish Churchill had long advocated. The government established the Organisation for the Maintenance of Supplies (OMS) – a volunteer 'private' strike-breaking body whose pretence at independence was belied by the fact that it received state funds for its operation and that its leadership was approved by the cabinet. By the time of the General Strike over 100,000 volunteers were ready, having been secretly trained by the OMS, to take over the running of essential services. At the same time the government made its own military-style preparations. Ten Civil Commissioners were appointed with their own staff and with the full authority conferred upon them by the Emergency Powers Act, to run the ten regions into which Britain was to be divided. Thus all the arrangements for running the country were in place to be triggered in the event of a one-word signal from Whitehall – 'Action'.

In contrast the TUC made no preparations whatsoever. They had made no plans to escalate the conflict after Red Friday, and indeed the fact that they had achieved a victory without direct action confirmed the right-wing labour leaders in their view that Baldwin's government was prepared to be reasonable. According to Beatrice Webb, as recorded in her diary, this view was shared by her husband, Sidney, who believed that:

the Conservative Government will go forward in our direction ... Public opinion will insist on the *middle* way ... it will be a collectivist middle way. (Quoted in Miliband, *Parliamentary Socialism*, 1961)

This was surprising considering the militant tone of the TUC Congress of 1925, but resolutions were one thing and decisive leadership quite another. In fact, although adopting resolutions to overthrow capitalism, condemning imperialism and supporting the extension of workshop organisation, all of which were socialist in content, the 1925 TUC congress did not address itself to concrete strategy. Furthermore the hand of the right wing was strengthened in the elections to the new General Council, which included again, after his brief spell as a cabinet minister in the Labour government of 1924, J.H. Thomas. Thomas had expressed himself as 'far from happy' about Red Friday

> because nothing is more dangerous to the future of this country than when employers of labour and the government are compelled to concede to force what they have refused to concede to reason. (Quoted in Wal Hannington, *Unemployed Struggles 1919-1936*, 1936, 1979)

He was to find a ready ally in the new TUC General Secretary, Walter Citrine (acting until 1926). However inadequate though, the general tone of this congress stood in sharp contrast to the Labour Party conference of the same year which concerned itself primarily with an anti-communist crusade, resolving that CPGB members should be barred from Labour Party membership and appealing to unions not to elect them as delegates. The government must have taken comfort from this since it exactly mirrored its own plans, in preparation for the coming conflict, to isolate the communist 'ringleaders'.

In October 1925 the government authorised a raid on 16 King Street, the Communist Party headquarters. Many documents were seized and twelve leading members of the party were arrested and imprisoned. The CPGB and the Minority Movement had consistently warned since Red Friday that the labour movement must prepare for the 'greatest struggle in the history of the working-class' that would inevitably follow the termination of the mining subsidy. The party paper *Workers' Weekly* counted the weeks remaining in a box headed 'Warning'. The accuracy of their analysis was far too uncomfortable for the government.

That the warnings of communists were not taken seriously by labour's leaders is only partly explained by their anti-communism. The resolve of the government begs the question as to why it chose this moment to assert the full power of the state to crush the labour movement rather that resort to the more traditional strategy of dividing and ruling, especially when it knew that the dominant labourist position would do all in its power to avoid class confrontation. Although the mountain of evidence does not provide us with an easy answer it is fairly clear that the Tory strategy was based on its understanding of the weakness rather than the strength of British capitalism in the inter-war years which gave it much less room for manoeuvre and compromise than hitherto. Although trade unionism was much weaker in membership terms in the 1920s than it had been during and immediately before and after the war, the militant trend led mostly by communists was still powerful enough to block the restructuring of the British capitalism which, as we have seen, was to be accomplished at the expense of the workers in the staple industries. The defeat of this older and better organised section of the workforce was essential if a new climate of industrial relations was to be made to stick in the newer industries. A victory for the labour movement at the weakest point of capital formation, the coal industry, would have reverberations far wider than that industry, particularly when the weakness of British capital as a whole stood in sharp contrast to the development of socialism in Soviet Russia, a point repeatedly made by the trade union militants. Hence the Tories chose in their propaganda to represent the fight of the miners and the widespread solidarity it attracted as a challenge not just to the coal owners but to civil society itself. Their own intelligence sources informed them that given the effect of mass unemployment in sapping the strength of the trade unions this was as good a time as any to deal the final blow and tame the movement once and for all.

The report of the Royal Commission (the Samuel Commission) was delivered in 1926. It recommended a reorganisation of the industry but *not* its nationalisation. On the crucial question of wages it rejected a continuation of the government subsidy and approved the wage reductions that the owners had tried to enforce the previous year. The gloves were off. The miners swiftly announced their intention to fight under the slogan 'not a penny off the pay, not a second on the day'. The owners posted the lockout notices and after fruitless attempts at negotiation between the government, the coal owners and the TUC a special conference of trade union executives was convened on 1 May to approve plans for a 'national' strike in defence of the miners. The strike began on 3 May. The fact that the TUC presented the strike in terms of a routine industrial dispute displayed a ludicrous contrast to the government's insistence that it was a highly political event with potentially revolutionary significance. The strikers' newspaper, published by the TUC, the *British Worker* was at great pains to argue that workers 'must not be misled by Mr. Baldwin's attempt to represent the present struggle as a political one'.

The greater the government scaremongering, the more the TUC sought to limit the scope of the dispute and to work for its speedy end. From the very beginning negotiations continued between J.H. Thomas and Herbert Samuel at first secretly and then more openly. It resulted in the Samuel Memorandum – the so-called formula that was used to end the strike. This process was given a spurious legitimacy by the fact that the miners handed over their dispute to the TUC once the General Strike had been called. Had the government not adopted such a belligerent line it is quite likely that the General Council would have fought shy of entering the conflict in the first place, but they were left with no choice after workers on the *Daily Mail* refused to print a leading article denouncing the strike under the banner headline 'For King and Country'. Baldwin chose to treat this as an act of war and the bluff of the TUC moderates was called.

It is only against the background of the TUC's reluctance to act, its readiness to negotiate at all times and its ideological unwillingness to recognise the political nature of the strike that the decision to call it off after nine days can be understood. However it is less easy to understand why such a decision was made given the overwhelming support for the strike and its effectiveness despite the carefully laid plans of the OMS. This success was due in large measure to the work of trades councils and councils of action up and down the country. Because of their unique position as the local link between trade unionists and the community these were able to perform all manner of detailed work on picket lines, in soup kitchens and in terms of general propaganda through leaflets and meetings which brought the message of the strike to masses of ordinary people who might otherwise have remained uninterested or uninvolved. All such activities were accomplished in the teeth of police harassment and mass arrests, with the armed forces strategically positioned close to suspected 'trouble spots'. Paradoxical though it may seem it was the very success of the mobilisation of the movement which frightened the TUC leadership and hastened their resolution to end the strike as quickly as possible. Rather than seeing such self-organisation as a great achievement it was viewed instead by the TUC as a potential pole of rival authority in which communists and other militants were playing a leading role. It was vital, therefore, that the TUC maintain its grip before it lost control of the mass movement and this could only be done while it still controlled the situation. J.H. Thomas openly admitted this to the House of Commons:

What I dreaded about this strike more than anything else was this: If by any chance it should have got out of the hands of those who would be able to exercise some control, every sane man knows what would have happened ... that fear was always in our minds ... we wanted ... even in this struggle to direct a disciplined army. (Quoted in Hutt, *The Post War History of the British Working Class*, 1937)

Underlying this fear was the even greater fear that loss of control would also mean an acknowledgment of the political dimension of the struggle, and now with the forces of the state ranged against them and spoiling for a fight this could lead to an overt class struggle for power – to revolution. (The *British Gazette*, the government's anti-strike paper pointed this out on more than one occasion by characterising the strike as a challenge to parliament and asserting that if it was victorious the General Council would become the rulers of the nation.) The TUC, aptly described by Kingsley Martin (later editor of the *New Statesman*) as 'a combatant in a war which had been forced upon it and which it feared to win', certainly was not ready for this. As for labours' parliamentary leaders, it is doubtful which side some of them would have chosen!

Hence much to the surprise of the participants and to the shock of the miners the acceptance by the TUC of the Samuel Memorandum was used as the formula for a 'settlement'. In fact the memorandum settled absolutely nothing. It was merely a re-jigging of the proposals of the 1925 Royal Commission with the difference that it made vague the commission's more explicit demands for wage reductions. No promises were exacted from the government on the continuation of the subsidy to the coal industry, the withdrawal of lockout notices or the resumption of negotiations. Nor was there any pledge to ensure that all the workers who had participated in the General Strike would not be victimised by their employers.

This was nothing short of abject surrender on the part of the TUC. Despite the achievements of the left in building support for the strike even in areas like the more prosperous south where it seemed less likely, they were not strong enough to sustain it once the TUC had called it off. The miners, upon whose behalf the TUC had ostensibly been acting, rejected the 'settlement' entirely and were left, for six gruelling months, to fight on alone until they were starved back to work. During this time a breakaway right-wing association of miners in Nottinghamshire under the leadership of G.A. Spencer (a right-wing Labour MP who had opposed the strike), split away from the Miners' Federation.

The Aftermath

In spite of the TUC's surrender, the General Strike was a remarkable achievement demonstrating the innate, and for its opponents frightening, strength of working-class solidarity. There is no denying the fact, however, that the wake of the strike witnessed a crushing defeat for the mass movement from which it took at least a decade to recover. Apart from the crushing blow to the miners there was widespread victimisation in many industries, especially printing and railways. Trade union funds had dropped by £4 million by the end of 1926, and trade union membership fell by over half a million in 1927 alone.

Capitalising on its victory, government reaction was punitive. It rushed through parliament the Trades Disputes Act in 1927 by which general strikes and most sympathy strikes became illegal. The Act also outlawed the automatic political levy from members whose trade union was affiliated to the Labour Party, and instead introduced the requirement to 'contract in'. But as if this was not punishment enough the embattled right-wing trade union leadership embarked on a 'new' course the main aim of which was to punish the left, in particular the communists, and to ensure that by co-operating with capitalism they would never again have to be faced with fighting battles which relied for their success on the uncertain outcome of mass mobilisation. Prompted by the TUC and following the example of the Labour Party, many unions now invoked bans and proscriptions against communists holding office and showed open hostility to the Minority Movement. This followed a series of articles by Citrine attacking the movement. The persecution reached new depths in 1929 when the General Council published its 'Inquiry into Disruption' which alleged that disruptive activities in the trade union movement were the work of communists under orders from Moscow.

Mondism

The new direction taken by the TUC was but a re-hash of old class collaborationist ideas wrapped in new packaging. The lesson it learned from the General Strike was simply that such class warfare was never to be repeated and that capitalism was here to stay. Citrine argued that 'trade unionism has reached the end of a defensive stage in its evolution' and that its new aim should be to:

> actively participate in a concerted effort to raise industry to its highest efficiency by developing the most scientific methods of production,

eliminating waste and harmful restrictions, removing the causes of
friction and unavoidable conflict. (Citrine in *Manchester Guardian*,
Industrial Relations Supplement, 30 November 1927)

The TUC wrote to employers' organisations suggesting joint discus-
sions along these lines. Alfred Mond and 21 other employers mainly in
the newer industries responded favourably and hence in 1928 the
Mond–Turner talks began. (Ben Turner was Chair of the TUC General
Council in 1928.) A set of proposals were agreed which the TUC
regarded as the foundation of the industrial relations of the future in
contrast to the 'outdated' conflictual model of the militants. In return
for trade union recognition and promises of no victimisation, joint conciliation boards would be established to head off industrial disputes.
Conciliation was hardly a new invention but the proposal to create a
National Industrial Council consisting of equal numbers of employers
and trade unionists to engage in 'general consultations on the widest
questions' was hailed as a wonderfully innovative departure. However,
unlike similar efforts to reconcile both sides of the industrial divide in
France and Germany after great post-war displays of workers' power,
this British initiative was only moderately successful and even then only
in the newer industries. The main employers' organisations representing the older industries overwhelmingly rejected the Mond–Turner
proposals. These industries were all labour intensive and, as we have
seen, sought to maintain their profit by reducing labour costs through
sackings or wage cuts. The niceties of conciliation and consultation were
lost on them. Whether the TUC liked it or not the only way they could
operate was through the 'old-fashioned' class war method, and now that
the TUC had decided to drop its 'defensive' stance so much the better
for the profits of these employers.

The fight against this decisive turn to the right was not as strong as
might have been expected from the militant tradition against which it
was directed. This was in part due to the psychology of defeat, but more
importantly to the fact that the left, influenced by the Comintern's abandonment of the 'united front' strategy in 1929, entered its sectarian phase.
The left adopted a bunker mentality, concentrating its attention on
building rival organisations and strengthening the Communist Party,
thereby, at a critical moment leaving the right a free hand to impose
its ideological domination over the movement as a whole. A powerful
weapon in its ideological armour was handed to the TUC in 1929 when
it took editorial control of the *Daily Herald*.

Trade Unions and the Labour Party

Although the outcome of the second Labour government proved something of a shock to the trade unions, the policy of that government was in all essentials the political counterpart of Mondism. Given the closeness of the two wings of the movement, it would have been extremely difficult for Labour to have pursued the line it did had the TUC and its affiliates adopted a less collaborationist line after the General Strike. The link between the two wings was also a physical one when from 1928 the Labour Party and the TUC shared the same headquarters (Transport House) as that of the largest union, the Transport and General Workers. Following the Labour debacle in the general election of 1931 the TUC General Council held the party together through a re-vamped National Joint Council linking the two organisations and on which the TUC now had as many members as the Labour National Executive and the parliamentary party combined.

The Effect on Women

The effect of the General Strike's defeat was, as we have seen, severe indeed for the labour movement as a whole, but for women workers and women trade unionists it was disastrous. The peak of women's trade union membership reached in 1920 (nearly one and a half million, 25 per cent of the total female workforce), had dropped to a mere half a million by 1939 despite the fact that the percentage of women within the total workforce had risen.

This bleak statistic cannot be accounted for by suggesting that women somehow became 'anti-union' in the inter-war years. Obviously the decline in membership has to be placed in the context of the overall decline, but within this there were specific features which help to explain the factors affecting women. Chief among these were the attitudes of the unions themselves. In the general climate of unemployment, cost cutting and union reversion to narrow and sectionalist attitudes, women workers were perceived as a threat. Their employment was rising (from 27 per cent of the total workforce in 1923 to 30 per cent in 1939) at the expense, or so it was thought, of that of men. This provoked two contradictory attitudes on the part of the male leaders, both of which were motivated by self-interest. On the one hand many unions that organised in industries with a high percentage of women workers (e.g. USDAW, NUT, NALGO and the Post Office Workers (UPOW)) sought to restrict the employment of women by calling for a strict application of the marriage bar, or the introduction of one. Almost all of them refused to campaign or shelved demands for equal pay and instead pursued wage claims which increased the differentials between men and women. Others, like the UPOW in 1935, went even further and called on a halt to female employment altogether. In these ways many of the unions contributed massively to the problem they thought they were addressing, namely the use of women as cheap labour in a time of recession and high unemployment.

On the other hand, the drop in trade union membership was a problem that might be redressed if only women could be persuaded to swell the declining ranks and boost the depleted coffers. Thus at the same time as pursuing negative policies on the employment of women, individual unions and the TUC were actively involved in recruitment campaigns. To its credit the TUC did at least recognise that women were less likely to be used as a source of cheap labour if they were unionised. It established, in 1925, its own Women's Conference and later, in 1930, a Women Workers' Group (later known as the Women's Advisory Committee), to assist the General Council to tackle the 'problem' of women. The Women's Committee was left to launch a series of recruitment campaigns which proposed, sensibly, to increase the involvement of women by establishing local women's committees. Such committees would themselves campaign around the issues of most concern to women workers and would, thereby, assist in recruitment. These attempts were greeted with solid indifference. In the wake of their failure, the General Council itself intervened in 1937 and again in 1939 with its own remedy. It launched two campaigns both based on the assumption that trade unionism would attract women if it appealed to them on the basis of such 'womanly' issues as personal health and beauty. Trade unionism, according to a special leaflet adorned with a radiant looking female clad in a swimming costume, was the 'ticket' to health and beauty presumably because it would ensure that improved wages secured by unions could be used to buy cosmetics and other adornments. Apart from the fact that such male-designed campaigns were grossly insulting to women's intelligence, they were an abject failure anyway, as the membership figures showed. Then, as now, women workers needed to be convinced of the tangible benefits of trade unions on the issues of most concern to them as workers rather than as putative beauty queens. In the defeatist, defensive and sectional attitudes of the trade union leaderships of the inter-war period precisely the opposite message was conveyed.

Further Reading

Cole, G.D.H., *The Common People* (Methuen, 1972, first published 1938).

Farman, C., *The General Strike* (Rupert Hart-Davis, 1972).

Hannington, Wal, *Unemployed Struggles 1919–1936* (Lawrence & Wishart, 1979, first published 1936).

Hutt, A., *The Post War HIstory of the British Working Class* (Victor Gollancz, 1937).

Klugmann, J., *History of the Communist Party of Great Britain*, vol. 2 (Lawrence & Wishart, 1969).

Miliband, R., *Parliamentary Socialism* (Allen & Unwin, 1961).

National Minority Movement, *What the Minority Movement Stands For* (Miners' Support Group, 1984, first published NMM, 1924).

Skelley, J. (ed.), *The General Strike 1926* (Lawrence & Wishart, 1976).

13 The Labour Movement, Fascism, Anti-fascism and War

The collapse of the Labour government in 1931 created a political hiatus, temporarily filled by the TUC. The general election of that year in which MacDonald and his supporters stood as national government candidates had a disastrous effect on the parliamentary Labour Party, reducing it to just 46 MPs. Many of the big names who had forged the labourist consensus were swept up with or away on the tide of MacDonaldism. This left, for the first time, a distinctly socialist rump in parliament, almost half of which was made up of MPs sponsored by the Miners' Federation. Men with outspoken left-wing convictions like Lansbury, Stafford Cripps and Clement Attlee now came to the fore as Labour's political leaders, and until 1934 were responsible for the production of some of the most radical policies that the Labour Party has known either before or since.

The TUC's Political Influence

Although such men held office in the years following the 1931 collapse, they did not hold power, and hence their effectiveness was limited. Real power as we have seen, was in the hands of the TUC through the National Joint Council. Given the vehemently anti-left stance taken by the TUC and affiliated unions in the years following the General Strike, it welcomed with alacrity the opportunity to use its increased influence in the Labour Party for similar anti-left purposes. Thus it was that when for the first time the opportunity arose to build unity between the now apparently dominant labour left and the hitherto shunned extra-parliamentary movement, the TUC rose as a Colossus to champion the old-style labourist politics which had arguably been responsible for the mess the party was now in. The left was not strong enough to insist on the discussion and analysis of Labour's failings. It was far more convenient and certainly less embarrassing for those (i.e. the majority) who had gone along with the policies to blame the whole debacle on MacDonald. His somewhat meaningless punishment (considering he was Prime Minister of the national government) was, along with his supporters, expulsion from the Labour Party.

The undoubted influence of the left as shown in Labour Party conference decisions between 1932 and 1934 amounted more to a triumph of words over deeds, and as such represented a missed opportunity for those who sought to alter the fundamental course of the party away from labourism and towards socialism. This is not to minimise the achievements of those years in which a genuine commitment was made to put the party on a socialist course. 'For Socialism and Peace', the party programme adopted in 1934 outspokenly proclaimed 'that what the nation now requires is not merely social reform, but Socialism' and pledged a future Labour government to 'establish public ownership and control of the primary industries and services as a foundation step' with employees in them having 'an effective share in direction and control'.

However, aside from conference decisions and policy statements the force of the left's advance in practical terms was considerably weakened by the untimely and ill-judged decision of the ILP in 1932 to disaffiliate from the Labour Party. Its place as the socialist conscience of the party was inadequately filled by the newly formed Socialist League (1932) which, although presenting a much sharper ideological challenge to reformism than had the ILP, lacked the mass base that its predecessor had formerly achieved. Its membership never exceeded 3,000 and was primarily London based. The stranglehold of the TUC did not quash the popularity of socialist ideas in the Labour Party in the 1930s, but was sufficient to reduce their practical effectiveness and decisive enough to impose its dominance over two major policy areas, notably relations with the Communist Party and foreign affairs. As it turned out, these issues became decisively linked and prevented the Labour Party from playing as important a role as it might otherwise have done in the anti-fascist struggle at home and abroad because to have done so would have meant working alongside communists.

Anti-communism

By 1931 the Communist Party had jettisoned its sectarian 'class against class' line and sought to reconstruct alliances with the mainstream of the labour movement. The ground for unity was infertile even though the 1930s produced a rich crop of intellectual converts to Marxism. Both the TUC and the Labour Party leaderships had already displayed a hostilty to communism in the years following the General Strike before the Communist Party's sectarianism had provided them with a more legitimate excuse.

In 1933 the Communist Party formally proposed that the Labour Party join with them in creating a 'united front' against fascism and war. Not only was this met with a flat refusal from the Labour Party, but its National Joint Council issued a manifesto a few days later entitled 'Democracy and Dictatorship' which equated communism and fascism as twin evils from which the world could be saved only by asserting the supremacy of constitutional principles of which the Labour Party stood as a champion. The Labour left never succeeded in defeating this line which persisted throughout the 1930s and which led the Labour Party to reply to every proposal for joint action against fascism with the repeated refrain that voting Labour was the only way forward. The fact that there was no general election after 1935 until World War Two was over did not induce its proponents to change the refrain! This TUC-inspired manifesto was followed in 1934 by the General Council's own circular in which unions were advised to exclude communists from posts of responsibility and Trades Councils, over which it had more direct jurisdiction, were *instructed* that it was obligatory for them to operate such bans. Individual trade unions similarly caught the anti-communist disease, with consequent effects on their attitudes to militants within their own ranks.

Trade Unionism

Trade union membership grew once again from 1933 when the worst effects of the depression were over. Although the tameness of the trade union leaders ensured that there were very few official strikes, this did not mean that the six years before World War Two were marked by industrial harmony. The mutiny of the navy at Invergordon in 1931, whilst it did not signal a more general rising, set the pattern for later self-organised rank-and-file disputes which became the hallmark of militant activity in the 1930s. The Communist Party had been and remained in the forefront of the rank-and-file movement (RFM). The active and well-supported organisation of London busworkers, the bane of Bevin's TGWU, had its origins during the period of the party's sectarianism when it was attempting to form alternative 'red button' unions. Although the busworkers' RFM remained an unofficial movement, with communists like Bert Papworth in the leadership, by 1932 its journal *Busman's Punch* stated unequivocally that:

Nothing could be more against the interests of Busmen at the present time than a breakaway from the TGWU, and nothing could suit the combine better. (Quoted in Ken Fuller, *Radical Aristocrats*, 1985)

In railways, engineering and mining, where similar forms of organisation had been initiated by communists great gains were made in expanding trade union membership, often to hitherto unorganised areas like the aircraft industry. Despite the chronic weakness of trade unionism in the mining industry, militants managed to eliminate Spencerism (the company unions formed after the General Strike) by utilising the novel tactic of the stay-down strike.

More could have been achieved had not the paranoid anti-communism of the trade union leaders got in the way. The more successful were the militants the more determined was the leadership to smash them, even if this meant colluding with the employers against their own members. The starkest example of this was the TGWU's handling of the bus strike of 1937. The strength of the busworkers' organisation, which had its own status as a trade group with a seat on the union's executive, had succeeded in making the 1937 'coronation' strike (a bus strike which coincided both with the coronation of King George VI and cup final day) official. However, Bevin ensured that the busworkers were left isolated and hence unable to win their demand for a seven-hour day. His purpose in facilitating the strike's defeat was to destroy the busworkers' RFM. Bill Jones, one of the RFM leaders, later wrote that Bevin:

> knew that we were going to be beaten and he worked that way ... he wasn't averse to the timing of the strike because he thought that the popular feeling (was) against us – being on strike while the Coronation was on – plus the fact that ... sewing up all the other sections would sink us. (Quoted in K. Fuller, 1985)

The aftermath provided Bevin with the long-awaited opportunity to dismantle the London busworkers' section and to expel its leaders, Papworth, Jones and others, from the union.

Anti-facism

The Labour Party's rejection of the call to form a united front with others on the left meant that it was isolated from the increasingly broad-based movement in Britain which sought to expose the evils of fascism internationally and to fight its home-grown variety in the form of Oswald

Mosley's British Union of Fascists (BUF). Outside the Labour Party and TUC leaderships most progressive people did not equate communism and fascism and readily supported communist initiatives to combat facism.

Mosley tried first to tap what he thought were the latent fascist prejudices of the Tory voting middle and upper classes. There were good grounds for this given the fairly widespread admiration for Mussolini and Hitler in such circles. However, the economic dislocation in Germany and Italy which had pauperised the middle-class in particular and made it a fertile fascist recruiting ground did not exist to such a degree in Britain where economic recovery after 1932 had ensured greater political stability.

The Conservative Party, with its tough stand in defence of capital at home and its anti-Soviet and later appeasement foreign policy, ensured that it remained a suitable vehicle for the expression of right-wing opinion. However, anti-fascists had managed to gain entry to the big BUF rally at Olympia in June 1934 to which thousands of influential people had been invited on a ticket-only basis, provoking awful violence from Mosley's black-shirted henchmen. This served to alarm and alienate respectable opinion and as a result induced Mosley to change his tactics. From 1935 onwards his overtly anti-semitic propaganda was directed more specifically to the working-class in an effort to encourage them to blame the Jews for the all too obvious economic hardship. This approach led the BUF to concentrate its activity in working-class areas. In the case of the East End of London this involved an area that accommodated 90 per cent of Britain's 330,000 Jewish population. (Jews accounted for a tiny 0.8 per cent of the total population of Britain.)

With police protection the BUF attempted to stage a number of marches and rallies, the most provocative and infamous being the attempt to march through the East End in October 1936. Anti-fascist groups led by the Communist Party prevented or stopped many of these marches, but in the case of the East End this was accomplished only by barricades and pitched battles, particularly in Cable Street. Similar tactics were used by anti-fascists in Bermondsey. Despite the broad unity achieved in mobilising thousands of anti-fascists, the official Labour Party and trade union leadership took no part in, and indeed discouraged, such activities on the grounds that scenes of violence which would of necessity be provoked by counter demonstrations would only serve to play into Mosley's hands.

The official leadership of Anglo-Jewry, the Board of Deputies of British Jews, supported by the community's weekly paper the *Jewish Chronicle* took a similar line. However, such caution did not reflect the views of the majority of Jews in the East End and elsewhere who were subjected to frequent abuse and attack by fascist thugs. The Jewish People's Council Against Fascism and Anti-Semitism was formed to offer determined resistance to the BUF. It worked closely with other organisations, especially the Communist Party which counted many Jews among its London membership and reflected the progressive wing of Anglo-Jewry which had deep links with the labour movement through trade unions and 'workers' circles'. Its first conference in 1936 showed that its appeal went beyond the many Jews who were socialists. Delegates attended from synagogues, Zionist groups, Jewish youth groups and ex-servicemen's organisations.

The tactics of the Communist Party, agreed after much internal debate, were two-fold. First, the aim was to expose the fascist danger nationally and internationally and to ensure that it never gained a foothold in Britain. Since this was to be achieved by mobilising entire communities to fight it on the streets it meant fighting the police, too, who saw their role as protectors of the fascists' right to conduct their propaganda openly. The second aim was, as Phil Piratin (one of the communist leaders in the East End prominent in the anti-fascist struggle, and later Communist MP for Mile End) put it, 'to cut the ground from under the fascists' feet' (P. Piratin, *Our Flag Stays Red*, 1948, 1978). He and others argued that a distinction had to be made between the hard core of the BUF and the ordinary working-class people who were attracted to it. Having first dismissed such people as enemies, the party eventually drew the conclusion that:

> there were certain latent anti-semitic prejudices ... but above all these people, like most in East London, were living miserable, squalid lives. Their homes were slums, many were unemployed ... therefore the Communist Party should help the people to improve their conditions of life, in the course of which we could show them who was really responsible ... and get them organised to fight against their real exploiters. (P. Piratin, 1948, 1978).

This meant meticulous, slogging attention to local issues, particularly the grievances of tenants against rack-renting landlords and slum conditions, and slowly but surely building effective tenants' organisations, in Stepney in particular. (The Stepney Tenants' Defence League employed three full-time paid organisers.) It is impossible to assess the extent to which this kind of activity fulfilled the aim of winning away potential fascist sympathisers from the BUF. It is certain, though, that the prestige of the Communist Party was greatly enhanced. Piratin was elected to Stepney Council in 1937, and by 1945 there were twelve communist councillors as well as a communist MP.

Spain

In 1936 Franco and his fascist collaborators, aided by arms and ammunition from Nazi Germany and fascist Italy, staged an insurrection against the elected Popular Front government of the Spanish Republic, unleashing a civil war which by 1939 resulted in the military defeat of the elected government. It is hard to explain why the cause of Republican Spain attracted such widespread international support given that the fascist coups in Germany and Italy had passed without such worldwide democratic mobilisation. Perhaps it was due in part to the fact that the victory of fascism in those two countries had been achieved by the prior defeat of internal democratic opposition, and that such opposition had been rendered less effective in the case of Germany by the great hostility between communists and social democrats. Certainly by 1936 the real horror of fascism, now well established in those two countries, was evident for all to see, and the popular and broad-based opposition to it in Spain provided an opportunity for democrats of all political shades to show practical solidarity. Such work was now greatly assisted by the commitment of communists to the strategy of the united front, a strategy that had come too late for the survival of democracy in Germany.

Whatever the reasons, a huge wave of support for the Spanish Republic quickly developed within weeks of the military assault upon it. This was unlike an ordinary solidarity movement, although those characteristics were in evidence in Britain in the form of The National Joint Committee for Spanish Relief chaired by a Conservative MP, the Duchess of Atholl. The committee was supplemented by local 'Aid Spain' committees which mushroomed in almost every town. However, the uniqueness of the solidarity movement lay in the fact that it inspired men and women actually to go to Spain in the service of the Spanish Republic. From many countries, Britain included, volunteers were recruited (privately by communists) to the International Brigade to fight alongside their Spanish comrades-in-arms, risking death and injury from the superior military strength of the fascists.

Two thousand British volunteers went, attached first to different units but later forming the British Battalion under the command of Bill Alexander. Five hundred and twenty six of them were killed and many more were injured. Alexander's estimate of the total number of international volunteers was 42,000, of whom 20,000 were killed, reported missing or totally disabled. In January 1937 the British government made it illegal to volunteer to fight in Spain; however this did not stop the flow, it just made the process more difficult. Although the British Battalion included Labour Party members, the official line of that organisation and of the TUC was strongly hostile to the volunteer movement and was even opposed, despite the broad political base of the Relief Committee, to giving any support at all to the republican cause other than eventually agreeing, having first supported the government's non-intervention line, that Spain had the right to buy arms. Indeed Citrine (TUC General Secretary) even attempted to find a way of stopping unions from giving funds to the Dependents' Aid Committee. This attitude was doubtless influenced by the Tory press which insisted on seeing the republicans as crypto-communists, and hence viewed a fascist victory as a timely defeat for a Moscow-backed communist revolution.

Apart from the Soviet Union, the countries affiliated to the League of Nations resolutely adopted a non-interventionist policy in Spain although it was quite clear that Germany and Italy were breaching the League's covenant in their active support for Franco. The British government was the most stalwart in its refusal to aid Spain, and hence colluded tacitly in Hitler's vision of a fascist victory in Spain as a dress-rehearsal in the coming bid for world domination. Spain also provided a convenient opportunity to test the sophisticated weaponry to which so much of Germany's industrial production had been turned. In this sense, therefore, 'non-intervention' was plainly a euphemism for banning the supply of arms and volunteers to the republican side while doing nothing to prevent similar support for Franco.

The Approach to World War Two

Popular awareness of and opposition to the fascist threat at home and abroad contrasted sharply with the benign approach of the government, which remained until 1939 far more committed to anti-communism than to anti-fascism. In practice this meant ditching Britain's responsibility as a member of the League of Nations (forerunner of the United Nations) to retain peace through collective security by failing to take action when peace was threatened by Hitler and Mussolini's agressive and expansionist policies.

The TUC and Labour Party leadership accepted in broad principle the Foreign Office line. Anti-sovietism was entirely consistent with their domestic anti-communism. A statement agreed by both wings of the labour movement's leadership, 'War and Peace', published in 1934, rejected the policies of pacifism and the international general strike to prevent war, and instead proclaimed the movement's duty 'unflinchingly to support our Government in all the risks and consequences of fulfilling its duty to take part in collective action against a peace breaker'. The only problem with this was that it was increasingly obvious that the government had no intention of pursuing such a policy, and the labour leaders were so preoccupied with the 'red scare' that they hardly noticed.

In the early 1930s, before the fascist threat to world peace had shown itself, the by then well-publicised horror of the last war inspired mass support for the League of Nations as the only organisation likely to prevent a recurrence. The League of Nations Union organised what came to be known as the peace ballot, which turned out to be the largest poll (apart from general elections) ever to be conducted in Britain. In all, eleven and a half million people voted in response to five quite detailed questions relating to international arms reduction, attitudes to the league itself, the possibility of collective military security and/or economic sanctions and the banning of private arms sales. This was not simply a pacifist ballot but a clear statement of opinion on the way in which peace could be maintained. The overwhelming view was in favour of peace through collective security mediated by the league. The Tories were quick to seize upon the convincing message of the peace ballot which came before the 1935 General election. Baldwin used this to jump on the bandwagon and declare support for the league and collective security. The hypocrisy of this was to be revealed weeks later when the Baldwin government signed the Anglo-German Naval Treaty by which the Nazis were given the go-ahead to build 35 per cent of the naval tonnage of the British empire. By a strange quirk of fate the ballot results were announced in 1935, the year in which Mussolini invaded Abyssinia. It was soon discovered that the league was only as strong as its member states permitted it to be. Collective security was hardly put to the test other than in the form of pious phrases.

The United Front and the Popular Front
Apart from solidarity action with Spain, the years between 1936 and 1938 witnessed the emergence of a popular mass movement against fascism and war the like of which had not been in evidence for almost a century. Clearly the mass movement owed much to the decisions made at the Seventh Congress of the Comintern held in 1935. There Georgi

Dimitrov, the Bulgarian communist who had attracted worldwide attention when he stood trial by the Nazis for allegedly starting the Reichstag fire, presented a report 'For the Unity of the Working Class Against Fascism'. This called for an end *in practice* to 'self satisfied sectarianism ... which professes to know all and considers it superfluous to learn from the masses'. By implication this was a criticism of the fact that although communists had officially renounced the 'class against class' three years previously the commitment to unity remained a theoretical one. The victory of the Nazis injected a note of urgency into the debate. Dimitrov called for the building of united fronts in each country, but the distinction between this and the previous use of the term was that now such a front was not for the purpose of establishing socialism but a 'mighty weapon which renders the working-class capable not only of successful defence but also of successful counter-attack against fascism, the class enemy'.

The section of the report that dealt with Great Britain illustrated the changed approach. Whereas hitherto the line would have been to campaign for a 'Soviet' government 'as the only form of government capable of emancipating the workers from the yoke of capital' the most urgent task now was to defeat the national government and elect Labour despite their poor record. Such a government would not carry out socialist measures, but at a minimum it must 'defend the most essential economic and political interests of the working-class'.

Other countries, like France (1934) and later Spain, had already attempted such a strategy and elected Popular Front governments. Critics, especially Trotsky and his followers, then and now thought that such a strategy amounted to the submerging of socialism in the interest of mass unity. To some extent they were correct, in the sense that because bourgeois democracy was perceived as preferable to fascism, the advocates of united and popular fronts saw the necessity of defending the former. This did not transform them into bourgeois democrats, but rather because they were socialists it meant a realisation that whatever the limitations of bourgeois democracy it presented opportunities for socialist advance which would be totally nullified in conditions of fascist terror the very existence of which was predicated on the annihilation of the labour movement. Harry Pollitt, general secretary of the CPGB, endorsed Dimitrov's line and took it a stage further. In his speech at the Seventh Congress he argued that the united front should be broadened out in such a way 'that it can win to its support, not only organised workers, but every democrat and lover of peace, all sections of the petty bourgeoisie'.

This kind of thinking was readily translated into the broad movement to save Spain described earlier. It was evident in a great variety of other campaigns on international issues, some of which had unexpected dimensions. In 1936 the Olympic Games, much to the delight of the Nazis, was held in Berlin. The Socialist Workers' Sports International which had been in existence and organising international competitions between teams of 'worker athletes' since 1913, decided to bring forward plans for a People's Games and stage them in Barcelona in 1936 as an anti-fascist opposition to the official games. Four thousand athletes from most European countries thus gathered in Berlin, including 200 from Britain some of whom subsequently withdrew in protest against fascism. However, on the day the People's Games were due to start Franco unleashed his attack on the republic and the civil war began. Although the athletes did not stay to fight, they celebrated the first fascist defeat in Barcelona by parading through the streets dressed in their blazers and waving their team banners in a gesture of anti-fascist solidarity.[2]

By 1937, apart from their large-scale involvement in the Spanish Civil War, Italy had conquered Abyssinia, while Germany, fully rearmed, had recovered the Saarland and remilitarised the Rhineland (both territories denied to her by the Treaty of Versailles). A new note of urgency was now given to opposition to the appeasement policy of Neville Chamberlain, the new Prime Minister. Although the 1936 Labour Party conference gave a huge majority to the opposition of the national executive to the United Front, this did not end the issue. In 1937 the Socialist League agreed to launch a unity campaign together with the ILP and the Communist Party. A Unity Manifesto was issued, signed by leading members of all three organisations calling for 'unity of all sections of the working-class movement ... in the struggle against fascism, reaction and war and against the National Government'. Even though the manifesto called for the return of a Labour government as an integral part of this strategy, the response of the leadership of the party was hostile in the extreme. Aware of the preparations for this new venture, the NEC had already issued an 'Appeal for Party Loyalty'. It now not only vigorously denounced the campaign but expelled the Socialist League from the Labour Party. Having anticipated this, the

2 Most of the information on the Barcelona Games has been taken from an article by Matthew Sturgis (based on an interview with a member of the British team, Reg (now Lord) Underhill) published in a special supplement on the 1992 Barcelona Olympics in the *Independent on Sunday*, 26 July 1992.

Socialist League had dissolved itself, leaving its former members free to involve themselves in the unity campaign as individuals.

At a meeting of the Left Book Club in 1938,[3] the campaign went a stage further, rather more along the lines of what was already known elsewhere as a 'Popular Front'. Harry Pollitt called for a people's front 'of all peace and progressive forces with no prior condition' although it did not preclude independent socialist activity being undertaken at the same time. The theory behind such a strategy has already been noted. Whereas the original pre-1935 conception of the united front limited itself to a call for the unity of the working-class, the campaign now transcended class boundaries and party divisions. It was addressed to all anti-fascists regardless of party, and would now include a section of the Conservative Party led by Churchill which was increasingly critical of appeasement. Whilst these Tories did not share the socialists' ideological hostility to fascism, they were, for their own reasons, openly opposed to Hitler's plans for world domination and in favour of firm military action to stop him. The Popular Front was, therefore, not simply a means of a mass mobilisation of public opinion around the simple and immediate slogan 'Chamberlain Must Go', it was also a mechanism for splitting the Tories.

Despite the opposition of small groups on the left influenced by Trotsky who shrank from any association for whatever purpose with 'the class enemy', the Popular Front campaign attracted mass support from all shades of opinion. Although it did not succeed in its desired effect of removing Chamberlain before he had effectively colluded with Hitler in the annexation of Austria (the Anschluss) and, by the infamous Munich Agreement, the occupation of the Sudetenland (part of Czechoslovakia), it had a powerful impact. Some 100 local Peoples' Front Committees were formed in 1938 and a Popular Front candidate

3 The Left Book Club was established in 1936, shortly before the outbreak of the Spanish war, by the publisher Victor Gollancz in association with Harry Pollitt and John Strachey. It was closely associated with and provided imaginative propaganda for the campaign for united and popular fronts, and thereby with the Communist Party. For 2s 6d members received a Left Book of the Month. The books helped to educate their readers about the horror of fascism and war, but there was also a practical and mobilising side to LBC activity in the form of the 'Groups Department' which employed full-time workers to organise left groups throughout the country - over 730 of them by the end of 1937. These not only discussed the monthly choice but raised money for Spain and other causes, and organised meetings, rallies and demonstrations. By March 1938 the LBC had around 58,000 members, countless thousands of whom, irrespective of political affiliation, attended or participated in group activity.

(Vernon Bartlett) was returned at a by-election in Bridgwater in that year, defeating the government candidate.

Given the extent of support for the Popular Front campaign, which was clearly on the increase after the Munich fiasco, it is all the more surprising that Labour Party leadership persisted in dogged and sectarian opposition to it. This resulted in 1939 in the Labour NEC's decision to expel from membership of the party all those who continued to support the campaign – Stafford Cripps, Aneurin Bevan, Charles Trevelyan and others were among the victims. Cripps was a special target since he had defied the leadership by publishing, widely circulating and refusing to retract the Cripps Memorandum which urged support for the principle of collective security and the union of all anti-government parties 'to act together and at once for the sake of peace and civilisation'.

The 'Phoney War'

The German invasion of Poland in 1939 finally forced Chamberlain's government to recognise the failure of appeasement and to declare war on Germany in September 1939. However, this declaration proved to be purely formal. Emboldened by the non-aggression pact struck with the Soviet Union in August and confident that the British were unprepared for war, the German military machine struck. In a matter of months the German army had overrun eastern Europe, including the Baltic states, had occupied Norway and Denmark in the north, and Belgium and Holland in the west and had defeated France. Apart from the ignominious defeat and retreat from Dunkirk, from September 1939 until May 1940 Britain was hardly involved in the conflict that now engulfed all of continental Europe. The term 'phoney war', used critically to describe the government's inaction, was an accurate description of its lack of involvement and lack of serious military preparation. Dunkirk had shown, despite the bombast, Britain's military weakness. The LBC publication in 1940 of *Guilty Men* written by a group of Labour MPs under the pseudonym 'Cato', was a savage indictment of appeasement and characterised the Dunkirk debacle as a defeat of 'flesh against steel'. The British army was, it said, 'doomed *before* they took the field'.

The pressure on the government to pursue a more active opposition to Hitler was maintained although the Popular Front strategy suffered a setback as a result of the changed line of the Comintern which by the end of September 1939 proclaimed that 'in this war blame falls on all the capitalist governments and primarily the ruling classes of the belligerent states' (quoted in R. Palme Dutt, *The Internationale*, 1964). Having been at the forefront of the alliance to confront fascist aggression, the British Communist Party accordingly changed its line too. This was a dramatic and short-sighted reversal of policy that two leading members, including Harry Pollitt, could not support. It was one thing to understand and view with some sympathy the difficult situation of the Soviet Union which had been forced to abandon its frequent attempts to form an alliance with Britain and France against Hitler. The appeasement policies of both countries had precluded such a possibility, ultimately forcing the USSR to buy time to prepare itself for the coming struggle which she might have to face alone. However, it was quite another matter for the Comintern to instruct European Communist Parties who had long advocated a war against facism to change their position now that at last war had been declared. The Comintern line, misguidedly cobbled together in the interests of Soviet foreign policy, argued that the war was nothing more than a squabble between rival imperialisms and that Chamberlain and Churchill were as bad as Hitler and Mussolini. It thus ordered affiliates to accept a complete volte-face. The pamphlet written by Pollitt, *How to Win the War*, issued shortly after war was declared, was withdrawn and owing to the fact that he stuck by the original party line he resigned as General Secretary and was replaced by R. Palme Dutt.

Labour's record during the period of the phoney war was not much better. Although the Labour Party rejected an invitation to be represented in Chamberlain's cabinet, it accepted the Tory call for an electoral truce and was deflected from a more strenuous criticism of governmental inaction by joining the furore occasioned by the Soviet invasion of Finland. The government, in contrast to its accustomed lethargy in dealing with Hitler, sent 50 bombers to help the Finns, and for a while it seemed that Britain and its allies had forgotten on whose side they were fighting. The Germans decided the issue for them by the invasion of France and the Low Countries – an act that sealed the fate of Chamberlain who was now unable to resist the Tory revolt that finally overthrew him in May 1940. Labour played little part in these developments but reaped the reward of office in the new coalition government headed by Churchill.

Further Reading

Branson, N. and Heinemann, M., *Britain in the Nineteen Thirties* (Panther, 1973).
Cato, *Guilty Men* (Victor Gollancz, 1940).

Fuller, K., *Radical Aristocrats: London Busworkers from the 1880s to the 1980s* (Lawrence & Wishart, 1985).

Fyrth, J. (ed.), *Britain, Fascism and the Popular Front* (Lawrence & Wishart, 1985).

Green, N. and Elliott, A.M., *Spain Against Fascism 1936–9* ('Our History' pamphlet no. 67).

Palme Dutt, R., *The Internationale* (Lawrence & Wishart, 1964).

Piratin, P., *Our Flag Stays Red* (Lawrence & Wishart, 1978, first published, 1948).

Pollitt, H., *Selected Articles and Speeches*, vol. 1 (Lawrence & Wishart, 1953).

Rosenberg, D., *Facing Up to Anti-Semitism* (JCARP Publications, 1985).

14   War and Peace 1940–51

The roots of the first majority Labour government 1945–51 are to be found during World War Two during which, from 1940, Labour participated as a full partner in Churchill's coalition government. During the war, after twenty years in the wilderness, Labour leaders not only acquired invaluable experience of ministerial responsibility but also helped to construct the collectivist practices of wartime which laid the foundations of the welfare state. Whatever the failings of the Labour Party in the 1930s its domestic policy had advanced steadily along the lines of nationalisation and the redistribution of wealth, projecting the claims of the party as the natural successor in peacetime to the successful experiments at state control and 'equality of sacrifice' demanded by wartime conditions. The mass participation in the war effort and the popular radical spirit inspiring it was strong enough to exact its reward. This reward, whilst falling short of socialism, ensured a consensus to retain the state controls which had been grudgingly conceded during World War One and hastily dismantled after it.

Whereas the 1914–18 war was unpopular as a mismanaged fight between rival imperialisms, the war of 1939–45 was not perceived in the same way. Whilst it undoubtedly retained the features of a capitalist power struggle, the mass mobilisation of opposition to the Axis powers (Germany, Italy and Japan) was motivated by a higher ideal – the determination to rid the world of fascism. Of course, not every participant in the struggle was a conscious anti-fascist, but as news of the horrors perpetrated by fascism and the heroic resistance movements of nations under its control gradually filtered through, so the war itself took on something of the character of a 'people's war'. The wartime alliance with the Soviet Union whose decisive contribution to the defeat of fascism was widely acknowledged lessened for a while the anti-sovietism and anti-communism that had pervaded the inter-war years. In these conditions the post-war domestic policies of the Allied powers were forced to pay regard to the needs of the masses to a greater extent than ever before. For Britain the political wartime consensus extended beyond state controls to social reform, enabling parliamentary labourism in the form of the first majority Labour government to reach its 'finest hour'.

The post-war Labour government represented the triumph and the limit of social change through the mechanism of reform within the framework of the capitalist system. The peaceful transition to a mixed economy and welfare state capitalism, the proud boast of labour's leaders, could only have been accomplished under these special conditions of consensus, but even by the end of the 1940s this was threatened once capital and its Tory political voice had a chance to realign itself under the aegis of the cold war politics which dominated post-war international relations. As Labour was to find to its cost, its naive reliance on the parliamentary system and what it regarded as the neutral state machine were no substitute for the mass movement outside parliament to defend the reforms it championed.

The Labour Movement and World War Two

Of the the five members of Churchill's war cabinet formed in May 1940 two, Clement Attlee and Arthur Greenwood, were Labour MPs. Other Labour members held ministerial positions and the most important of these in terms of labour relations was Ernest Bevin, Minister of Labour and National Service. Clearly Bevin's standing as leader of Britain's biggest trade union (the TGWU) was intended to deflect the kind of opposition to the control of labour which had been such a feature of World War One. The measures introduced during this later war were similarly draconian. The Emergency Powers Act and Defence Regulations provided the government with all the power it needed to direct and control labour. Strikes and lockouts were banned under Order 1305 and the 1941 Essential Work (General Provisions) Order allowed for the dilution of labour and the direction of skilled workers to wherever they were most needed. Bevin established a Joint Consultative Committee of seven employers' representatives and seven trade unionists to advise in the conduct of the war effort on the home front. Hence labour was incorporated into the state machine more fully, and apparently with a greater degree of acceptance, than in 1914–18.

Until 1941 when the Soviet Union entered the war communists in Britain, having little commitment to the war effort, refused to be bound by the national unity consensus, and in particular the ban on strike action. In fact during the period of the 'phoney war' there was a general resentment against government attempts to control labour given that it was doing very little to mobilise for the war effort. The 'phoney war' cannot be held responsible for the Communist Party's continued opposition to the war. In a pamphlet published in 1940, after Chamberlain had been ousted, Harry Pollitt proclaimed 'it is time to organise against every encroachment on the living conditions and the rights of the worker'. He condemned Labour's coalition with the Tories as a device, reminiscent of ruling-class tactics during World War One, 'to save capitalism and enable attacks to be made on the workers' and said very little about the war against fascism. Given the party's record pre-1939 and post-1941 on fighting fascism, it is perhaps understandable that the collective communist conscience has chosen to regard this Comintern-inspired line as, at best, a woeful interruption.

During the first few months of the war there were over 900 strikes, almost all of them very short but illegal nonetheless. Despite the provisions of Order 1305 there were very few prosecutions until 1941 since Bevin, anxious to avoid the labour unrest of World War One, sought to promote conciliation rather than conflict. The number of strikes increased each year until 1944, almost half of them in support of wage demands and the remainder being defensive actions against deteriorations in workplace conditions. Coal and engineering were particularly affected. In fact it was a strike in the Betteshanger colliery in Kent in 1942 that prompted the first mass prosecutions under Order 1305. Three officials of the Betteshanger branch were imprisoned and over 1,000 strikers were fined. However, such repression and the general 'shoulders to the wheel' approach to industrial production in support of the war effort (strongly backed by the Communist Party after 1941) did not stop strikes. In 1943 there were two major stoppages; one was a strike of 12,000 bus drivers and conductors, and the other was of dockers in Liverpool and Birkenhead. Both were a considerable embarrassment to Bevin since they involved mainly TGWU members. The year of 1944 marked the peak of wartime strike action with over 2,000 stoppages involving the loss of 3,714,000 days' production. This led to the imposition of Defence Regulation 1AA, supported by the TUC, which now made *incitement* to strike unlawful. Although not used, Regulation 1AA was in fact the most powerful anti-strike weapon possessed by any government since the 1799 Combination Acts, and despite the fact that it aroused considerable opposition within the parliamentary Labour Party it was astonishingly, supported by the trade unions.

These figures of wartime strike activity surpass those of the 1914–18 war and yet parallel conclusions cannot be drawn from them. Although backed by a growing shop stewards' movement it is clear that unofficial action in this period did not have the kind of political inspiration that motivated the workers' committees of the previous war. This is partly due to the fact that the war itself, especially after the Soviet Union's entry, was a popular one. Similarly the coalition government did much more than Lloyd George's administration to spread the burden of sacrifice (although it did not equalise it) through state controls and important measures of social reform. Such reforms included the provision of cheap school meals and day nurseries, improved pre-natal and infant welfare facilities, and the abolition in 1941 of the hated means test. Due to the sustained German bombing of urban areas (the 'blitz') the government also provided emergency housing, and in 1943 the main provisions of the Beveridge report which laid the foundations of the welfare state were accepted by the cabinet, although not acted upon until the war was over. Hence there was much less ground for sustained political opposition to the government than had been the case in the 1914–18 war. The strikes that took place had thus much more of a purely trade union character in defence of immediate interests and reflected the growing strength of organised labour. The fact that so many of them took place in the mining industry was due in the main to the fact that the designation of coal mining as essential war work entailed the direction of selected conscripts to work in the mines ('Bevin boys'). This was very unpopular among regular miners.

Trade unions (TUC affiliates) increased their membership by about three million during the war – from roughly four and a half million in 1938 to around seven and a half million in 1946, and this was accompanied by the spread of recognition agreements to industries in which unions had only a toe-hold before the war. To some extent this extension of trade union rights was underwritten by the government which denied war contracts to firms (under the Essential Works Order) who failed to conform to minimum standards demanded by the unions.

The Third Labour Government

No one was more surprised than the Labour leaders themselves at the scale of the Labour victory in the general election of 1945. Indeed Attlee was so convinced of Churchill's popularity that he had initially wanted to fight the election as part of the wartime coalition. There appeared to be little on which the party leaders had disagreed during the war, although there was an ominous portent of the gap between the Labour leadership and backbench Labour MPs over the government's controversial handling of the situation in Greece.

The Greek resistance, ELAS, having accomplished the miraculous defeat of the Nazi occupation forces in 1944, was set to establish its own government in which the communist backbone of the resistance movement would have a major part. The first signs of the anti-communism which was to dominate post-war British foreign policy, temporarily put on the back-burner in the interests of Allied unity during the war, now rose to the surface. The Allied troops which had belatedly assisted the Greek resistance now turned on their former friends and used force to crush ELAS in order to back those Greeks who had collaborated with Hitler and in their interests force the reintroduction of the monarchy and a right-wing government. (The fact that the Soviet Union gave no tangible aid to ELAS undoubtedly strengthened the hand of the western allies.) The significance of this episode lies in the fact that it was an early indication that Labour, despite its domestic radicalism, intended to allow its foreign policy to be dictated by the traditional conservatism of the Foreign Office.

The size of the Labour majority in the 1945 election gave it a mandate for the first time to carry out its election manifesto 'Let Us Face the Future'. Labour won 393 seats, the Tories 213. The Liberals were reduced to twelve seats and the Communist Party won two. Overall, Labour's absolute majority was 146, although the vagaries of Britain's 'first past the post' electoral system in fact gave Labour a minority (47.8 per cent) of the popular vote. The explanation of this victory lies as much in the political maturity and radicalism of British voters as in the undoubted popularity of Labour's programme which caught the mood of an electorate who now wanted their wartime sacrifices to be rewarded by the creation of a fairer and more equitable society. The memory of the depression and the harshness of the many years of Conservative domination of the political scene were not forgotten in the heady peace celebrations. An appreciation of the role of Churchill as a wartime leader was not allowed to obscure the fact that before the war he had acted consistently against the interests of workers and trade unionists, the employed and the unemployed.

The undoubted radicalism of Labour's programme must also be set in the context of the post-war policies of the governments of the former Allied powers. In Europe the communist role in the resistance movements was now reflected in their participation in, and in eastern Europe their domination of, many peacetime administrations which pursued radical social change and redistribution of wealth. The 'new deal' policies of the Roosevelt government in America, now continued by Truman, were a similar indication of the pervasive popular radical climate immediately after 1945. Hence the British experience was not unique, although for Labour its ability to use the parliamentary system to achieve a better society was the ultimate test of its 45 years of existence. Labour's method thus showed a continuity with the past, but the course it now charted was far more decisive than previous efforts.

The sum total of the achievements of the 1945–51 Labour administration are perhaps best appreciated now that they have been systematically dismantled by four successive Tory governments in the 1980s and 1990s. Labour proclaimed itself a socialist party 'and proud of it'. However, its 1945 programme did not promise socialism on the grounds that, desirable though socialism was, it 'cannot come overnight as the product of a weekend revolution' – a somewhat spurious argument given Labour's six years in office! 'Practical minded men and women' would understand this, and instead the appeal was to undo the damage that the 'hard faced men' had inflicted on the economy in the inter-war years which had seen the 'concentration of too much economic power in the hands of too few men' ('Let Us Face the Future' manifesto).

Although the analysis of the past was made in class terms the vision of the future was one in which narrow class considerations melted into the 'national interest'. The programme was based on 'a genuine workmanlike plan conceived without regard to sectional vested interest'. It envisaged through state planning, nationalisation, state welfare, and improved housing and education a more equitable system of taxation and price control to create a better society 'free from the horrors of unemployment and insecurity'. The proposals for nationalisation came as no surprise since they were based on policies developed with the aid of the Fabian Research Bureau in the 1930s. The only difference in 1945 was that a plan to nationalise the land and the joint stock banks was now omitted.

Labour's Record in Office

In its essentials the Labour government fulfilled its election pledges, but it did so inheriting the severe economic problems of the pre-war period with the added burden of the economic destabilisation of war. British exports in 1945 stood at one-third of their already low 1939 level. The flurry of legislation covered three main areas, nationalisation and economic planning, social welfare and trade union law.

The immediate reward for trade union compliance in the war effort was one that could have been expected from a Labour government in any circumstances. The 1927 Trades Disputes Act (passed by a vindictive

Tory government after the General Strike) was repealed in 1946. Welcome though this was, it marked merely a return to the pre-1927 position which still left the question of picketing and 'sympathy' strikes in some confusion.

Nationalisation and Planning

On the face of it, despite its watering down, Labour's programme of nationalisation was extensive and bold. Energy supplies, coal, gas and electricity were taken into state control in 1947. Similarly, the transport infrastructure, railways, most wharves and docks, London's buses and tubes, and later road haulage were nationalised. The major but ailing iron and steel industry was nationalised in 1950, as was the Bank of England in 1946. Several smaller industries and services like cables and telecommunications and parts of the hotel and catering trade were also in state hands by 1951. By that year roughly 20 per cent of the national economy was controlled by the state, employing a workforce of over two million people.

However, in practice Labour's nationalisation programme, far from being a step on the road to socialism, was the means by which capitalism was strengthened. This was because only decaying and unprofitable sectors were taken into state control in order, as Morrison put it, to 'make possible the organisation of a more efficient industry' in the interests of the nation as a whole. The ailing industries comprised the industrial infrastructure, and by relieving private capital of the responsibility of financing them the government was in fact subsidising the private sector by providing it with cheaper and more efficient sources of power and transport. This and the fact that astronomical sums in compensation payments were given to the former owners help explain why there was so little opposition to nationalisation (except in the case of iron and steel) even from the Tories. (£164 million was paid in compensation to the mine-owners alone).

The transition was made even smoother in that many of the former owners became leading figures on the boards of their respective public corporations. Hence for the workforce of such industries there was very little of the change for which they had hoped from the nationalised industries. They had little say in their running – this was left to government appointed 'expert' managers and boards of directors. The fact that Labour's programme had paid so little attention to the *mechanism* of nationalisation permitted badly run private corporations to transform themselves into slightly better run but huge and remote public bureaucracies, tolerated in the short term, but inspiring little affection or support when they were later attacked.

Similar deficiencies can be seen in the mechanisms established to achieve the laudable aim of state planning and control. Much of this had already been set up during the war so it was simple enough to allow it to continue. The object was to promote a healthy economy by increasing Britain's gross domestic production and export potential. The means, via four civil service committees (manpower, materials, balance of payments and capital investment), fell far short of the aim, given the irreconcilable clash of interests between the profit motive of private capital and that of the so-called 'national interest' which Labour claimed to represent. This unacknowledged conflict was compounded by the fact that the very people appointed to police the planning mechanisms were themselves drawn from private industry. As one example among many – no less than 90 employees of Unilever occupied posts in the Ministry of Food. Although the government maintained a naive belief in the impartiality of such appointees, the ultimate failure of their endeavours is a personal and political reflection of the impossibility of harmonising public and private economic interests. Put simply, the Labour experiment indicated that their concept of the 'national interest', while quite different from the Tory sham, was an illusory Fabian ideal impossible to implement in a class-divided society. Labour's political opponents constantly appealed (and still do) to the needs of the nation, but they make no secret of the fact that they identify this as synonymous with the needs of capital.

The fact that Labour, both in theory and in practice, regarded itself as the neutral arbiter in promoting the economic and social well being of the nation meant that by default, and in spite of its good intentions, its plan for a mixed economy slid into one of helping ailing British capitalism to cope better with its profound problems. The enthusiasm for change in the early years of the government gradually waned as Britain's economic problems proved more intractable. By 1947, the crisis year, it was clear that the middle course between socialism and capitalism, so earnestly championed by Labour's leaders in an effort to avoid Soviet-style state planning, was not working. As the problems mounted even the limited attempts were ditched and political principle came to be sacrificed for more orthodox capitalist solutions. Labour, trapped by the logic of market forces, was forced to abandon even its weak attempts at control which anyway had never extended to profits, exports or personal incomes. Within three years Harold Wilson at the Board of Trade was ignominiously presiding over periodic 'bonfires' of licences and quotas. The clamour for de-control of the economy became the rallying cry of private industry, backed by the Tory Party and the Tory press. Labour's economic plan, such as it was, was in tatters.

The extent of the reversal was to be seen in the budgets of 1948 and 1949 which were based on Stafford Cripps's (the new Chancellor of the Exchequer) statement that 'the redistribution of wealth could go no further until new wealth had been created – and in the meantime there must be a ceiling on the social services' (quoted in D. Coates, *The Labour Party and the Struggle for Socialism*, 1975). The impetus for retrenchment and a return to economic orthodoxy was also inspired by the government's reliance on American aid in the form of the Marshall plan. The price for such aid was clearly stated by the Americans – Britain had to cut back on spending on welfare and had to de-control the economy in order to make the entire European market more favourable for American exports. He who pays the piper calls the tune.

The Welfare State

Labour's detractors often point to the fact that the main principles of the Beveridge Report were laid down before the Labour government's existence and were not opposed by the Tories then or subsequently. (Although whether the Tories would have implemented Beveridge in full is highly unlikely; as it was, the fact that the report appeared during the war gave them an excuse for inaction.) Indeed, the basic principle of using the resources of the state to provide and finance social need (collectivism) was pioneered by the Liberal Party under Gladstone in the nineteenth century and further developed by the reforming Liberal government of 1906 with universal schemes for national insurance and old-age pensions. However, Labour from the 1930s onwards was the only party that made the extension of social benefits for all from 'the cradle to the grave' a top campaigning priority, and its achievement in government gave concrete expression to this via two major chunks of legislation in 1946 – the Social Security Act and the National Health Service Act. The former provided for sickness and unemployment benefit for all, so long as they had paid the required national insurance contributions. The National Health Service aimed, according to the Act's preamble, 'to promote the establishment ... of a comprehensive health service designed to secure improvement in the physical and mental health of the people' and, weathering the storm of protest from the doctors' organisation the BMA, ensured that it would be free at the point of need.

Although Labour cannot claim the credit for the content of this legislation other than the fact that it had the political commitment to act on Beveridge's findings, its own unique contribution was expressed in its insistence on the principle of universality. The Tories, whilst not attacking the legislation as such, advocated that it should be targeted at those most in need. This would have meant instituting some kind of means test. Labour resolutely opposed this not only because the means test with its association with the hard-faced parsimony of the 1930s was so hated, but also because it took the view that the welfare state would be a non-starter unless its benefits were genuinely open to all. This principle of universality remained the cornerstone of Labour's social policy for the next five decades and is in danger of reversal only now, in the 1990s, after the Tories' sustained attack on the entire collectivist edifice.

Apart from universality, Labour's policy at the time was criticised by the left who wanted the health service to be nationalised and private medicine to be abolished. Aneurin Bevan, Minister of Health, instead pursued a course which attempted to placate the doctors' anger which was chiefly fuelled by the fear that they might become salaried state employees. So, private medicine remained and the doctors were allowed to retain their semi self-employed professional status by opting for a fees-plus-salary system or fees alone.

Women and the Welfare State

Aside from the health service, a huge deficiency of Labour's social insurance scheme unremarked at the time (and hardly commented upon by male historians since) was the effect it had on women. The benefit system was firmly based on the notion that the whole of civil society was organised into family units with a male breadwinner at the head of each. Married women, therefore, were not entitled to benefits on the assumption that they were, like children, dependants of the male head of the household. Even if they opted to pay their own contributions they could receive only reduced rate benefit on the spurious argument that their expenses were lower. Wittingly or not, Labour fell for the capitalist ideological construct of the family wage developed in the nineteenth century, which as we have seen bore no relation to women's reality then much less in the inter- and post-war periods when the economy was just as dependent on the employment of female labour regardless of marital status. Such state myopia in relation to women had a practical motivation in that the welfare system was far cheaper to administer if its benefits were fully accorded only to adult males, but it was also based on deep-seated suppositions that the place of women was in the home and that their entry into social production was secondary to their domestic responsibilities. The Beveridge Report was thoroughly impregnated with overtly sexist and indeed racist ideas on the 'place' of women and the role of motherhood:

> That attitude of the housewife to gainful employment outside the home should not be the same as that of the single woman. She has other duties ... Taken as a whole the Plan for Social Security puts a premium on marriage in place of penalising it ... In the next thirty years housewives as mothers have vital work to do in ensuring the adequate continuance of the British Race and of British ideals in the world. (from the 'Social Insurance and Allied Services Report by Sir William Beveridge presented to Parliament 1942', quoted in Elizabeth Wilson, *Women and the Welfare State*, 1977)

Such assumptions were given a further ideological boost in the post-war era by the 'scientific' findings of the psychologist John Bowlby who popularised the theory of 'maternal deprivation'. He issued dire warnings about the harmful long-term effect on children and adolescents who received anything less than 100 per cent of their mothers' attention during their first five years of life. Apart from the impact that this had on female work patterns, the unchallenged acceptance of such views fed the truly reactionary Labour policy of closing the state day nurseries which had been opened to meet the need of women workers during the war. This was a useful cost-cutting exercise, but there is no doubt that it was motivated by anti-feminist considerations. A Ministry of Health and Education joint circular sent to local authorities in 1945 expressed it thus:

> The proper place for a child under two is at home with his [sic] mother ... the right policy to pursue would be to positively discourage the mothers of children under two from going out to work. (Quoted in Sarah Boston, *Women Workers and the Trade Unions*, 1980)

Hence, despite the undoubted merits of the welfare state in general, its benefits for women left much to be desired and indeed its family-centred orthodoxy did much to keep women locked into traditional subservience. In practice the principle of universitality was to apply only to the male half of Britain's population.

1947: The Turning Point

The Labour government cannot be blamed for the extraordinarily harsh winter of 1947 which exacerbated the fuel shortage, neither can it be held responsible for the deep-seated economic problems the war had temporarily masked, nor for the financial crisis of August 1947, the gravest since 1931. However it was responsible for the policies it adopted to deal with the crisis, and it is on those grounds that it can be judged. Hugh Dalton (who dubbed 1947 as the 'annus horrendus') and Cripps, his successor as Chancellor, embarked upon a series of 'austerity' measures which effectively transformed Labour from a party of reforming zeal into one of retrenchment and economic orthodoxy. An attempt was made to reduce the balance of payments deficit by cutting down on imports. This affected imported foodstuffs especially and meant a cut in the already meagre rationing still extant from the war. The 'black' market provided extra rations for those who could afford it. Domestic spending on social services was cut drastically and in 1948 the government introduced a wage freeze. Such policies presaged a growing convergence between austerity-minded Labour and the less hard-faced element within the Conservative party. The term 'Butskellism', coined by the *Economist* in the 1950s (an amalgam of the names of the reform-minded Tory, R.A. Butler and Hugh Gaitskell, Labour's successor to Attlee), caught on as an expression of this trend.

Labour's manifesto for the 1950 general election, 'Let us Win Through Together', displayed the caution already evident in its post-1947 policies. Nationalisation was barely mentioned, and the planning and control of industry was dropped altogether. Instead, under a subheading, 'Encouragement for Enterprise', the manifesto stated that 'private enterprise must be set free from the stranglehold of restrictive monopolies'. Labour's somewhat pedestrian promise was to maintain full employment, to raise domestic production and to increase exports. The gains of the welfare state were proclaimed, the assumption being that they were complete in themselves, further improvements being unnecessary.

Labour's pledges were so minimalist that by 1951 Morrison complained that the chief whip 'was having difficulty in finding enough legislative business to occupy the available Parliamentary time' (quoted in K.O. Morgan, *Labour in Power 1945–1951*, 1985). The election campaign was lack-lustre, a fact not reflected by the extraordinarily high turn out, which at 84 per cent was and remains a record. Although Labour's overall majority dwindled to five, its share of the popular vote remained high at 46 per cent , but since parliamentary votes count for more than popular votes it was just a matter of time before a fresh election was held to give Labour a more workable majority. But by 1951, when the election was held, the tide had turned. Labour actually won more votes than the Tories but the result of boundary changes gave the latter an undeserved slim majority and secured their position as the party of government for the next 13 years.

Labour's Foreign Policy

Long-term judgements of the extent of Labour's radicalism in its domestic policy start from the assumption that in this sphere, initially at any rate, it was genuinely attempting something different. The same cannot be said of Labour's conduct of colonial, defence and foreign policy which from the start was hardly distinguishable in essentials from that of the Conservatives. None of Labour's three election manifestos between 1945 and 1951 paid much attention to foreign affairs. On colonial issues the party had been silent for decades. Although some left-wing individual members like Fenner Brockway were active in support of the anti-colonial cause, the Labour Party itself had never taken a public anti-imperialist stance despite the growth of independence movements in many British colonies. Now, as a government, Labour was forced to accept the fact that it ruled a vast colonial empire and the absence of an anti-imperialist policy inevitably implied its opposite. The Fabians filled the breach. In 1940 the Fabian Colonial Research Bureau was established. Its leading figures, Arthur Creech Jones (later colonial secretary) and Rita Hinden, argued against negative anti-imperialism and in favour of a 'positive' colonial policy. This was grist to the mill of Attlee, Bevin (Foreign Secretary) and Herbert Morrison (Lord President) who warmed as to the manor born as guardians of Britain's imperial role. Indeed Bevin fully acknowleged the social imperialist argument as justification for labour imperialism. In 1946 he proclaimed to an unshocked House of Commons:

> I am not prepared to sacrifice the British Empire [because] I know that if the British Empire fell ... it would mean that the standard of life of our constituents would fall considerably. (Quoted in Ron Ramdin, *The Making of the Black Working Class in Britain*, 1987)

On this argument it is possible to view the great achievements of the welfare state as the ultimate expression of the social imperialist ideal. The racist attitudes informing it were never far from the surface. Hugh Dalton referred to the colonies as 'pullulating poverty stricken, diseased nigger communities', but echoing the theme of the 'white man's burden' he did not advocate relinquishing them. In the case of South Africa, a prized part of the 'white' commonwealth, Labour, perceiving its strategic and economic importance, was content to condone the vicious racism in the form of the apartheid system established by the Nationalist government under Malan after its election victory in 1948. The fact that Malan was an open supporter of the Nazis during the war did nothing to deflect Labour support. The argument that the 'granting' of independence to the Indian subcontinent in 1947 indicates that Labour's colonial policy was progressive is not only specious but smacks of white supremacism. It fails to recognise the massive struggle of the Indian people over decades which, by 1947, threatened to erupt in open revolution.

It was generally acknowledged, even by the Tories, that in these circumstances British rule was impossible to maintain and a 'damage limitation' exercise was the only feasible alternative. This took the form of exploiting ethnic and religious differences which resulted in the drawing of artificial boundaries to create two states, India and Pakistan. In fact this solution, in ensuring that British investments were safeguarded post-independence, provided the model for neo-colonialist policies of the 1950s and beyond when Britain was forced to bow to the inevitable change in her traditional relationship with her colonies.

For the time being, however, Labour did everything possible to maintain Britain's colonial empire. In true social imperialist fashion, the super-expoitation of the colonies was used to offset the full cost of Britain's post-war reconstruction. Although the sterling area, which bound Britain, her empire and commonwealth in a system of imperial preference, was anathema to the economic interests of America who saw herself (as Britain had done in the previous century) as the workshop of a free trade world, she was nevertheless prepared to tolerate the British empire for political reasons. To the US, the British empire was seen as a useful bulwark against communism.

In foreign affairs generally Britain still swaggered as a great world power but in reality played second fiddle to America, the new super-power standing as the protector of the entire 'free world' against communist encroachment. The Truman doctrine and Churchill's concept of the 'iron curtain' ushered a new phase of anti-communism in the form of the cold war. The pursuance of Nazi war criminals took second place to the preoccupation with the new enemy – the Soviet Union. The somewhat ineffective opposition of the parliamentary 'Keep Left' group of Labour MPs which advocated a vague 'socialist foreign policy' was no match for the determination of the Labour leadership actively to support the cold war line. Bevin, the Foreign Secretary, took every opportunity to stress that British foreign policy would not be altered by Labour. Britain's dependence on Marshall Aid provided a material reason for Labour support of the 'special relationship' with America, whilst its own home grown anti-communism provided it with such ideological fervour that even the left, the 'Tribune' Group and 'Keep Left', lamely succumbed, confining their criticism to mere detail rather than root and branch opposition to the general direction of foreign affairs.

Britain's defence policy was formed to meet the needs of her colonial and foreign policy. All three were bound by the timeless web of protecting the interests of capital, mediated now by pervasive anti-communism and subservience to America. An empire the size of Britain's demanded considerable military expenditure to police it which explains why even in conditions of labour shortage her military establishment after the war accounted for 18.7 per cent of available manpower and why military spending amounted to 18.8 per cent of her national income. This was almost double the corresponding figure for the USA. In total the Labour government spent more on defence than any other non-communist country, and in 1946 Attlee earned the unenviable distinction of being the first British Prime Minister to introduce conscription in peacetime. Even more remarkable was the fact that in 1945, in conditions of absolute secrecy, hidden even from the cabinet, Attlee embarked on a programme of nuclear armaments. In fact it was not until 1952, when it was first tested, that Britain's possession of the ultimate and most deadly weapon of mass destruction – the nuclear bomb – became public knowledge.

The Labour Government and the Trade Unions

Two factors led to an almost supine compliance by the TUC with every whim of Labour policy during its period in government. Of overriding importance was the very fact of the existence of a Labour government which, even when it pursued unpopular measures after 1947, drew the familiar 'don't rock the boat' response from the TUC. The trade union leaders compromised their independence by accepting Labour's wage freeze and anti-strike policies under its austerity programme in the belief that maintaining Labour in power was worth any sacrifice the working-class was called upon to make. The other factor inducing an uncritical attitude was founded on the continuance of the anti-communism that the trade union leaders had already displayed before the war and now found little difficulty in sharing with the government. The rank-and-file opposition to the government's austerity programme after 1947, identified as the work of communist militants, was interpreted as an attack not only on the government, but on the trade union leaders who tamely supported it, and hence fuelled their latent anti-communism.

A new wave of 'red baiting' was inaugurated with the publication by the General Council of two pamphlets, *Defend Democracy* and *The Tactics of Disruption*. Communists were labelled as 'abject and slavish agents of forces working incessantly to intensify social misery', and calls were made to ban them from holding office in trade unions and trades councils. Several trades councils were de-registered for failing to toe this line, but the only trade union which obeyed it to the hilt was the TGWU under its new general secretary, Arthur Deakin. Nine communist full-time officials were sacked from the T&G including, yet again, Bert Papworth the busworkers' leader, who also lost his seat on the TUC General Council. The fact that other unions did not follow suit (with the exception of the National Union of General and Municipal Workers whose rules already excluded communists from holding office), is a reflection of the undoubted strength and influence of the Communist Party within individual unions and as leaders of the opposition to the wage freeze. In this sense the TUC paranoia about communist influence was justified and they looked on helplessly as their own lack of leadership was thwarted by a succession of strikes in a variety of industries – railways, docks, engineering and mining – defying Order 1305 which remained in operation until 1951. This and the invocation of the Emergency Powers Act marked the unprecedented use in peacetime of the legal and repressive apparatus of the state, all the more remarkable emanating as it did from a Labour government loyally supported by the TUC at every turn. Seven London dockers were prosecuted under Order 1305 in 1951.

World diplomacy was not the only setting for the clash of rival ideologies. Anti-communist paranoia found a place as well within the international trade union movement, shattering the unity which had been achieved in 1945 when the World Federation of Trade Unions was established. The only national trade union centre which had held aloof from this body from its inception was the American Federation of Labor (AFL), although its then rival the Congress of Industrial Organisations (CIO) did participate along with delegations from 46 other countries. The British TUC hosted the founding conference in London and was enthusiastic about the meeting itself, although more cautious on the prospects for a permanent organisation. The dictates of American foreign policy and its Marshall Aid programme sought busily to divide east and west in every sphere of activity. The European Recovery Programme Trade Union Advisory Committee was the US mechanism for achieving the split in the WFTU which remained as the last symbol of the unsectarian wartime alliance.

The British TUC was a key and receptive pawn in this strategy, as was noted by the AFL leader David Dubinsky: 'Once the British TUC frees itself from its paralysing ties with the World Federation the ERP Trade Union Advisory Committee will be able to go forward' (quoted in Allen Hutt, *British Trade Unionism*, 1941, 1975). By 1949 his hopes were realised. Deakin, who was the WFTU president at the time, told the TUC in a remarkable about-face that the World Federation was 'nothing more than another platform and instrument for the further-ance of Soviet foreign policy' and led a walk-out to join the AFL in establishing a new anti-communist international, the International Con-federation of Free Trade Unions, founded in London in December 1949.

Further Reading

Barnes, D. and Reid, E., 'A new relationship: trade unions in the Second World War' in B. Pimlott and C. Cook (eds.), *Trade Unions and British Politics* (Longman, 1991).

Boston, Sarah, *Women Workers and the Trade Unions* (Davis–Poynter, 1980).

Coates, D., *The Labour Party and the Struggle for Socialism* (Cambridge University Press, 1975).

Cook, C. and Sked, A., *Post War Britain: a Political History* (Penguin, 1990).

Hutt, Allen, *British Trade Unionism – A Short History* (Lawrence & Wishart, 1975, first published 1941).

Labour Party, *Let us Face the Future – 1945 Election Manifesto*.

Morgan, K., *Labour in Power 1945–1951* (OUP, 1985).

Pollitt, H., *The War and the Labour Movement* (CPGB, 1940).

Pritt, D.N., *The Labour Government* (Lawrence & Wishart, 1963).

Ramdin, Ron, *The Making of the Black Working Class in Britain* (Gower, 1987).

TUC, *General Council and Congress Reports*, 1945–1951.

Wilson, Elizabeth, *Women and the Welfare State* (Tavistock Publications, 1977).

15 The Workers the Labour Movement Forgot – Women and Black People 1926–51

The experience of a majority Labour government in office represented the zenith of parliamentary labourism. The socialist experiment had never been tried, and if it had it may well have been found wanting. Before World War One its syndicalist variant had shown its limitations in its failure to comprehend the needs of women workers, and leading Marxists like Hyndman had succumbed to the racist ideology inherent in their support for imperialism. Thereafter the left in general, trapped by the succession of capitalist crises at home and abroad, reacted defensively and thereby never fully developed its socialist vision.

Socialist theory based on an understanding of the inner workings of capitalism and imperialism was able to show the link between class exploitation and oppression, and hence displayed, in theoretical terms at least, the possibility of comprehending the specifics of the super-exploitation of women and black people mediated by the unspoken ideologies of racism and sexism. Practice, however, usually fell far short of theory. Within the labourist tradition there was not even the theoretical base for addressing the issue of class exploitation, much less for understanding or acting upon the deeply divisive ways in which capitalism has used the issues of sex and race to maintain its ascendancy.

The question as to whether a movement can be judged for what it failed to do is one that does not seem to trouble historians or commentators when their own particular hobby-horse is at stake. There is a strange silence when we use the yardstick of the experiences of half the human race to weigh up the balance sheet. And when the balance sheet is the labour movement itself, the silence gives way to cries of teleological unfairness bordering on treachery. And yet women comprise half the population in Britain and a large (usually underestimated) part of its working population. Numerically the same cannot be said of black people, although it is often forgotten that there was a black population settled in Britain for a considerable period before the first major wave of migrants arrived (at the behest of the government) after World War Two. However, taking the British empire as a whole, black people far outnumbered their white rulers.

The Black Presence

Black scholars and historians have taught us much in recent years about the presence since Roman times (before the English even arrived) of a black community in the British Isles. That such a fact has been hidden for so long is not attributable simply to the small size of the community; after all, women have accounted for around half the population and they too, until recently, have been similarly obscured by and from history. Reconstructing the role of black people within the labour movement is fraught with even more difficulties, but again, in common with women, their position has been and still is marked by their exclusion rather than their presence.

The permeation of the ideology of white supremacism associated with Britain's imperial role and its (often unconscious) effect on the labour movement has already been discussed (see Chapters 5 and 7). After so many decades of the seepage of racist ideas, the conditions which fostered the possibilities for black leaders like William Cuffay and Robert Wedderburn to rise to prominence in the radical and Chartist movement had, by the twentieth century, been eclipsed. Despite the fact that World War One had increased the black population living in Britain, particularly in the port towns of Cardiff and Liverpool, the black community was more isolated than ever. The incidence of race riots in Cardiff in 1919, with its repercussions in other cities, provides evidence of the deep racist attitudes of British workers, supported at the time by the labour movement. Demobilised sailors helped to swell the ranks of unemployed seamen in the declining shipping industry, and since this was one of the very few areas in which black people had found employment, the bitterness of white seamen was turned against the right to work of black Britons. The call to oust black seamen from their jobs in preference to their British (i.e. white) counterparts was supported by a resolution of the TUC in 1919 which supported the seamen's union campaign for preference to be given to first British white and then British black labour. This racist divisiveness quickly developed in the ensuing physical attacks on black families into a more generalised campaign to discredit the black presence by pointing out its moral undesirability and, to clinch the argument, its cost to the taxpayer. With the support of Labour, the government, in time-honoured fashion, blamed the 'alien' presence as the cause of the problem and passed two overtly racist laws, the Alien's Order of 1920 and the Special Restriction (Coloured Alien Seamen) Order of 1925. Both were concerned to restrict immigration but the latter introduced a form of pass law specifically aimed at black seamen irrespective of nationality. Whether or not they held British passports they were required on demand to produce evidence of registration on pain of arrest, imprisonment or even deportation.

In view of such overt racial prejudice which fuelled the colour bar in the labour market it is not surprising that black Britons suffered disproportionately from the generally prevalent high rates of unemployment in the inter-war years. In Cardiff, for example, it was estimated that roughly 80 per cent of black men were unemployed between 1934 and 1935. The outbreak of World War Two changed the employment situation for black people, although the underlying racism that confined their job opportunities and life chances in general remained unaltered. The labour shortage caused by conscription and the increased demand of wartime production eliminated domestic unemployment and led to a government-sponsored scheme for colonial immigration which provided a free passage to Britain and back! Some of the workers who came were, to the surprise of their white counterparts, highly skilled, thus upsetting the traditional prejudices which ascribed underdevelopment to black people. Many, having had considerable labour movement experience in their own countries, joined trade unions here, although only two unions, the AEU and the electricians' union, the ETU, were welcoming. Additionally around 8,000 West Indian soldiers in the British army were stationed in the UK during the war, most of them working as flight engineers.

After the war immigration was again officially encouraged due to a continued labour shortage in Britain and high rates of unemployment in the colonies. The 492 Jamaicans who arrived at Tilbury in 1948 on the *Empire Windrush* were greeted with banner headlines in the London *Evening Standard* – 'Welcome Home'. This was followed by a steady trickle from the West Indies during the following ten years, which by 1958 amounted to 125,000.

Black Resistance

Given the generally unwelcoming attitude of the labour movement to black people and the issue of racism in the post-1850 period, the black community relied upon its own resources to tackle the problems that beset it. The self-organisation of black people has thus a long pedigree born of the hostility or indifference of white society. The organisations so formed had a dual function. They attempted to give some support to black Britons at the sharp end of racial prejudice and in addition they were at the forefront of the anti-colonial struggle. This latter function could hardly be avoided, especially in the twentieth century when the legacy of the imperial expoitation of the black colonies in Asia, Africa and the West Indies forced fresh waves of black migrants to flee the hardships of their own countries and settle in Britain.

It is beyond the scope of this book to look at the patterns of immi-gratation to Britain. Not all who came were poor. Many came to study. The British colonialists had done little to establish an all-through education system in most of the countries they dominated, though what they had set up was thoroughly English in character. It was from those who came to finish their education in Britain at the turn of the century that the main (although not necessarily the first) intellectual and practical challenges were launched at the insidious pseudo-scientific racism peddled by white academics and intellectuals. J.A. Thorne, a Barbadian doctor who had studied and qualified in Britain, Celestine Edwards (a Dominican) and Henry Sylvester Williams, among others, advocated and popularised (pre-dating Marcus Garvey) the idea of Pan Africanism. For some this meant finding a settled homeland for all those of African descent, for others it meant campaigning to secure civil and political rights for black people, but for all it meant inspiring a sense of pride in the black race. This was no easy task given the white predominant notion of black subhumanism and the jingoistic expansion of the European empires from the 1880s and beyond.

Williams was the main force behind the establishment in 1897 (the year of Victoria's diamond jubilee) of the African Association, one of the aims of which was 'to promote and protect the interests of all subjects claiming African descent'. The first Pan African Conference was held in London in 1900 under the slogan 'Light and Liberty'. It drew black delegates from around the world and established the short-lived Pan African Association. The conference attracted financial support from the Asian community resident in Britain.

Williams, the main driving force behind Pan Africanism in Britain, attempted to set up branches of the Pan African Association in Jamaica, Trinidad and the US. He was also involved in Labour politics in Britain, becoming one of the first black men to be elected in 1906 as a local councillor (Marylebone). In this he had the support of the most pro-gressive trade union, the Workers' Union. The other black pioneer in British municipal politics was John Richard Archer. As a member of the Labour Party he held office in Battersea variously as councillor, alderman, mayor, election agent and leader of the council. As election agent he skilfully piloted the successful candidature of Saklatvala, the communist, as the first black MP (and the first communist) to be elected in Britain. Archer was also involved in Pan Africanism, becoming in 1918 President of the African Progress Union formed in that year. This organisation, led by John Alcindor, was the largest of the black organisations active in the 1920s – the others being student bodies.

In 1931 in the wake of the race riots in Cardiff and Liverpool a Jamaican, Dr Harold Moody, founded the League of Coloured Peoples. This was a 'respectable' organisation of well-educated blacks which acted as a kind of pressure group, intervening on behalf of black people among whose moderate aims was 'to improve relations between the races', but it contained within its ranks a variety of political views. In contrast to Moody himself who was a committed Christian and definitely not a socialist, the league counted among its active members Ras Makonnen and George Padmore, both Marxists and sometime members of the Communist Party, and Desmond Buckle, a communist activist. The Marxist intellectual C.L.R. James also served on the league's executive for a while and contributed articles to its quarterly magazine, the *Keys*. These four, together with Jomo Kenyatta, later the President of Kenya, provided the intellectual driving force behind Pan Africanism in the 1930s and 1940s. Britain, the heart of the biggest colonial empire, was their base.

Socialism, and especially communism, provided a point of contact between black activists and the British labour movement especially in the anti-colonial struggles of the pre and post World War Two era, by which time communist or workers' parties affiliated to the Comintern had been established in almost every country in the world. Nonetheless such contact was beset by differences in both theory and practice. These differences sometimes mirrored those within the socialist movement revolving around the role of the Soviet Union, particularly during the Stalin period, but there was an added dimension in the black movement because of differing trends within Pan Africanism. Although there was no split or breech so characteristic of white left politics, there was nonetheless a difference in outlook between the two major black American Pan Africanist leaders, the communist W.E.B. DuBois and Marcus Garvey. Put very simply and somewhat crudely, the former campaigned for the rights of black people to self-determination in the colonies linked to their full civil and economic rights in the white colonial heartlands while the latter's position can best be summed up by the slogan of the Universal Negro Improvement Association (UNIA, the organisation he founded for black people) – 'Back to Africa'.

Until 1928 the Comintern supported Garveyism. It had paid detailed attention to the 'Negro Question' as a key aspect of the anti-imperialist struggle. The fourth Congress of the Comintern (1922) recognised 'the necessity of supporting every form of the Negro Movement which undermines or weakens capitalism' (quoted in R. Lewis, *Marcus Garvey*, 1987).

It saw the UNIA as integral to this. This and other decisions favouring black self-organisation undoubtedly aided the many black organisations internationally and cemented the appeal of socialism. However, the Comintern line changed in 1928, and although the anti-imperialist content remained, many of the national and liberation movements were condemned if they were not avowedly socialist. The UNIA fell foul of this sectarianism.

Within Britain the as yet small black community was reinforced by a powerful stream of intellectuals and labour movement activists from the colonies, many of whom, like Krishna Menon (India), Kwame Nkrumah (Ghana) and Kenyatta, were later to become leaders in their own countries post-independence. They played an important role in maintaining black consciousness through Pan Africanism as well as fighting the anti-colonial battle against Britain.

Apart from support given by some internationalist organisations like the Communist Party and assorted individuals on the left of the Labour Party, the predominantly white labour movement took little interest in such matters and thereby turned its back on a rich stream of ideas and experience. Such colour blindness was of course fuelled by the invasive racist ideology which if it did not lead to outright collusion with imperialism at best led to a superior kind of paternalism. This reaction sometimes showed pity for the poor downtrodden blacks in the colonies and even occasionally in the 'mother' country but it failed to recognise, let alone listen to, the highly articulate black voices that had raised questions and posed solutions long before the white liberals had even identified the problem.

It was not only on the question of race that the labour movement failed to benefit from the years of work in the black community in Britain. No regard was paid to the fact that this small community also had within it trade union and labour movement activists of a very high calibre, some of whom had actually founded unions in their own country under conditions of illegality and who had considerable organising experience. Whilst black people maintained this commitment in Britain, joining unions even when they were not made particularly welcome, there was no similar effort on the part of most white activists to learn from their black brothers and sisters. Thus it was that a kind of separate development between the two communities was unofficially institutionalised and survives to the detriment of the labour movement to the present day.

Women and the Labour Movement

The inter-war and post-war period was a bleak one for women. The ideology of home and hearth fitted comfortably with the divisiveness caused by mass unemployment when women were frequently accused of taking men's jobs. Sexist ideas and practices had long been internalised into the labour movement, certainly at leadership level, but their presence was all the more marked after the General Strike for three reasons. First, the presence of women in the workforce was less hidden than it had been hitherto. Secondly, female recruitment was consciously sought to stem declining union membership. But this contrasted sharply with the third factor – the class collaborationist orientation of the trade union leadership which in itself engendered an uncritical assumption of capitalist values as an antidote to the shared anti-communist paranoia. For women workers this meant that, as has been shown (Chapter 12), the unions and TUC gave with one hand and took with another.

For a while World War Two swung the pendulum in women's favour. The massive size of the war effort entailed a correspondingly huge call on the labour of women, one that was far greater than in 1914–18. This was not peculiar to Britain. Throughout Europe and America women's work was no longer seen as peripheral to social production; it was now at the very centre of it. This entailed a major, albeit temporary shift in social attitudes, the practical expression of which was the provision of state measures like nurseries and free school meals to enable women to combine more easily their dual roles. Did the attitude of the trade unions change? In a purely pragmatic and opportunist sense they did, although not nearly as fully as might have been expected given the changed climate towards women.

The TUC in 1940 passed motions calling for equal pay for women who took over men's jobs and for an end to the marriage bar. In 1942 the AEU at last opened its doors to women members and broke new ground the following year when it established a separate women's conference. Women's trade union membership more than doubled during the war years – it stood at 552,000 in 1939 and rose to 1,341,000 by 1945. But despite these advances the warning signs were there. The TUC hardly mentioned women after 1940 on the assumption that their wartime position in the workforce was but temporary and that after the war, if they worked at all, they would return to their traditional sphere as domestic servants; indeed, in 1943 the TUC's Women's Advisory Committee drew up a memorandum outlining how they could be persuaded so to do. This pre-dated, and possibly even influenced, government thinking on the matter. In 1944 the Ministry of Labour issued a pamphlet which proclaimed that 'domestic service is a priority job'.

It is thus hardly surprising that gains women made during the war were so quickly jettisoned in peacetime. We know how swiftly the government moved to restore women's traditional role and the underlying assumptions about this role. Without a labour movement fighting to maintain such gains as nurseries and other wartime 'benefits' the Labour government's task of pushing women back was made infinitely easier. As the tame lap-dog of the government it might be expected that the TUC would do all in its power to support everything that Labour did, and on the 'problem' of women it did not need much persuading since its attitudes were quite as reactionary on this issue as those of its political masters. This was clearly demonstrated by its policy on two issues in particular – equal pay and day nurseries.

Equal pay was hotly debated in the post-war period. The 1944 Royal Commission established to inquire into the subject, reported in 1946 that it accepted equal pay in principle but advised against its implementation on the grounds that to do so would be inflationary. The TUC, mindful of its long-standing commitment to equal pay since 1888 but at the same time not wishing to 'embarrass' the Labour government, now advocated a compromise. In a pamphlet published in 1948, *Questions and Answers on Equal Pay*, it urged the government to implement equal pay in the public sector whilst accepting that it was a lost cause in the private sector. (Interestingly, one of the largest private sector unions, the AEU, did not share this view and boldly launched a campaign for pay equity in the engineering industry.) However, even this compromise was meaningless, for in the same year, despite the urging of the Women's Committee, the General Council statement at the Margate conference declared that the introduction of equal pay:

> would have to be considered in the light of the White Paper 'Statement on Personal Income, Costs and Prices' ... [and thus] it would be

impractical for the TUC ... to extend its activities to include the holding of a series of large public meetings throughout the country.

Having decided against this minimalist effort it was but a short step the following year, 1949, at Bridlington for the General Council to ditch the issue altogether:

In the light of ... the continuing need for counter-inflationary policies, the committee decided that a further approach by the TUC to the government on equal pay would be inappropriate at the present time.

If any progress at all was to be made on equal pay it would be up to individual unions to press for it – a somewhat forlorn hope at least until the 1950s when white-collar unions in the public sector, under pressure from their women members, engaged in an intensive campaign which resulted in 1955 in a government announcement that it would attempt to equalise pay in the public sector by 1961 in seven stages for some women workers. (Women manual workers, government typists and nurses were to be excluded.) Women civil servants had been to the forefront in the campaign for equal pay since the 1930s. (This may not be unconnected with the fact that they were organised in their own union, the Federation of Women Civil Servants, and then from 1932 in the National Association of Women Civil Servants.) Apart from the abolition of the marriage bar in the Home Civil Service, however, during the period of the Labour government no progress was made, and the gap between men's and women's earnings was, on average, 50 per cent.

A similarly depressing tale unfolded in relation to nursery schools. Their fate and the consequences for women was all the more grim since this was a cause which had apparently been won during the war and was lost thereafter. It was all the worse given that the reasons for closing the day nurseries were motivated as much by ideological as economic considerations and hence revealed once more, after an all too brief semi-respite, the deeply sexist seam running through all layers of British society including its trade unions. The TUC offered no resistance to the government plan to cut the grant to local authority day nurseries; indeed its report for 1947, presented to the 1948 Margate conference, expressed its ideological approval. It prefaced its comments on day nurseries by '... welcoming the Minister of Labour's statement that mothers of young children should not be encouraged to go into industry', and went on to state:

The General Council are therefore of the opinion that the case for Day Nurseries must be proved in each locality after an examination of all the circumstances, and that they should not press for a general extension of them.

Worse was to come. In a rare statement of its underlying philosophy the 1948 Annual Report of the TUC contained the following gem of unenlightenment:

There is little doubt in the minds of the General Council that the home is one of the most important spheres for a woman worker and that it would be doing a great injury to the life of the nation if women were persuaded or forced to neglect their domestic duties in order to enter industry particularly where there are young children to cater for.

The message for women was clear, but it was also contradictory in the light of the post-war labour shortage and the clear demand for female labour. How could the necessity for women's presence in social production be reconciled with its perceived ideological undesirability? The solution was the same as ever – to marginalise women workers in an attempt to hide the fact of their vital role in the labour force. This was accomplished in two ways, one of them traditional and the other new. Job segregation was the age-old lot of women. They were removed as far as was possible from those areas of social production in which they could compete with men, and were consigned to the jobs that could more properly be viewed as offshoots of their feminine domestic responsibilites. The war had been but a temporary interruption to this pattern. The post-war period restored 'normality' (see Chapter 5). But where such total segregation proved impossible the new device of part-time work presented itself as a neat way of ensuring that women fitted themselves into the ideological stereotype of wife and mother while at the same time avoiding any claim for additional state expenditure on such costly items as day nurseries. Such a construct fitted nicely with the ideological presuppositions about the role of the family as enshrined in the state benefit system introduced after the war, as we have seen in the previous chapter. So successful was the use of part-time work that it spread to almost all branches of female employment, and despite the lower wages offered was even welcomed by women workers who saw it as the only way, in the absence of real practical help, to combine their dual roles.

Having colluded in the marginalisation of women workers, with the new problem of an atypical employment pattern, the trade unions now viewed them as a weak link in organisational terms. It was far easier, in view of the notorious difficulties in organising part-time workers to view women themselves as the problem, a problem that could be safely ignored when in the post-war period of full employment and the welfare state it could be comfortably imagined that the family was secure under the care of its male breadwinner and that women who worked did so from choice to earn a bit of 'pin money'. Such was the ideology; reality, as ever, was very different.

Further Reading

Lewis, R., *Marcus Garvey: Anti-Colonial Champion* (Karia Press, 1987).
Rich, P., *Race and Empire in British Politics* (CUP, 1990).
Ramdin, Ron, *The Making of the Black Working Class in Britain* (Gower, 1987).

Conclusion

The story of a movement still alive and kicking can hardly be concluded, even though some would have us believe that today, in the 1990s, the labour movement is a spent force and that its history is no more relevent than that of the lost tribes of ancient Judaea.

Although this survey stops in 1951 the 40 years since then have witnessed great changes as the structure of the working-class has altered to reflect the new technology of the microchip and the (mis) fortunes of the British economy, which by now has sunk permanently into the doldrums of deindustrialisation. The basic industries upon which Britain's industrial pre-eminence was based have now become extinct, save for the fight to retain an already decimated coal industry. But a working-class still exists, and so does the labour movement. The evidence is before our eyes in the daily battle between capital and labour that continues to be waged in altered forms and circumstances despite the current legal restrictions to curtail it. The fact that we are in an era of declining trade union membership and high unemployment during which we have witnessed more defeats than victories should not lead us to question the movement's viability now any more than in the nineteenth century when its trade union wing was pitifully small, or in the late 1920s and early 1930s when defeat and decline were also the order of the day. The history of the labour movement has always been halting and problematic.

This is not the place to examine the labour movement's current form and prospects, nor is it appropriate to wax lyrical about its 'glorious past' or to be cynically downcast about its lost opportunities. The past is there; it cannot be altered, it can only be studied, discussed and better understood.

So, what can be concluded from the first 200 years? The most obvious point is that the labour movement has an uncanny ability to re-build and renew itself with the consequence that its detractors, keen as they always are to write the movement's premature obituary, continue to be wrong-footed. Working-class organisations do not proceed in a linear onward and upward fashion. They are always marked by peaks and troughs in activity, effectiveness and membership. These ups and downs are not always crudely determined by economic circumstances but have a great deal to do with the prevailing level of political class consciousness. The fact that this elusive construct escapes causal explanation does not invalidate its existence. At key moments its presence determines the defiant rather than the defensive aspect of the movement when it consciously seeks to break the ideological yoke chaining it to capitalist society, its norms, practices and values. The development of the British labour movement throughout its history is a product of the tension between rival ideologies – between the vision of harmonious accommodation within the capitalist system and the vision of a different system altogether. Variously the ideologies inspiring these visions and the practices they inspired could be called, in their pure and most polarised forms, left or right, radical or reactionary, socialist or capitalist, revolutionary or reformist. Rarely are the complex battles which shape a movement played out in their starkest forms, but nonetheless the underlying tension is there.

In Britain the infinite capacity of the first industrial nation to accommodate dissent led ultimately to a dominant labourist consensus which, while offering at times the possibility of hope and change, accepted the parameters of the existing social order and sought defence of its interests within it. On the other hand those whose consciousness of class led them to challenge consensus and collaboration bequeathed to us the legacy of defiance, and this legacy because of its hostility to and rejection of the settled values of capitalist society began to encompass, albeit in halting measure, the wider cause of the struggle to end oppression as an integral part of the fight to eradicate class exploitation.

But this is all very general and theoretical. No one would deny a left and a right trend within the labour movement today, and likewise it would not take a genius to notice that the forces of the traditional left are in disarray. Defiance is in short measure and a defensive form of labourism reigns supreme. Explanations are far harder than observations. Why political class consciousness (socialist consciousness) emerges more strongly at certain times defies any clear-cut explanation. It is far easier to explain the existence of class collaboration and the fact that the forces of the left, even at the time of their greatest strength, were never powerful enough to shift the reformist labourist consensus. The struggle between the rival ideologies within the labour movement is one of the themes of this book. The fact that the reformist consensus in its various forms dominated from the 1850s onwards has, I hope, been explained. The great unanswered question remains particularly relevant for the class-conscious activists of today – namely, under what circumstances and by what means can the consensus be broken in order to end class exploitation once and for all?

Throughout these 200 years support for such a project has assumed a much greater significance than those who today ridicule the socialist cause would have us believe. Splits and divisions often marred the effectiveness of the cause, but the reason why it had more of a mass appeal in the 1880s than in the 1870s, or more in the 1940s than the 1950s, for example, cannot be explained solely by analysing internal weaknesses. This begs the question the answer to which, if we knew it, would have yielded a magic formula; and the magic formula, if applied could have led us to a socialist paradise long ago.

Perhaps one clue revealed in this book is the one that prompted its writing in the first place. For socialism to have a genuine and lasting mass appeal its vision must address the needs of the entire working-class and must practise the politics generated by its theories – those of democratic collective involvement. This means consciously extending its appeal, as some of the early socialists attempted, to *all* workers and in particular those most vulnerable to super-exploitation because of their race or gender. This in turn entails an understanding that working-class unity is not just a desirable but an essential goal, and that its achievement is only possible if differences born of life experiences of centuries of disunity founded on oppression are recognised and respected. It also means that forms of organisation must not only reflect those differences but must actively seek to overcome them.

Such a perspective has proved to be far harder to accept in Britain where the political objectives of the labour movement, after 1850, were sacrificed to a defensive and somewhat narrow trade union movement founded on the experiences of the skilled and better-off section of male workers. The unions formed in the mid-Victorian period, which laid the basis for what exists now, pre-dated the formation of the political wing of the movement and became its servant. In other words, initially at least, politics followed economics. But in creating its political wing the accumulated sectional interests of the trade unions founded a Labour Party which turned tail and ultimately mastered its creators. If that political creation had held to the socialist vision that from time to time emerged within it this history might have had a different conclusion. The fact that it was not to be cannot be ascribed to a capitalist conspiracy in which trade unions are viewed as the organs of pure class struggle whose interests were sacrificed to the power-hungry ambitions of a collection of besuited white men who had forgotten the movement's origins. Rather, as this book has attempted to show, no single branch of the movement was the repository of political correctness, and the resulting mish-mash was the product of the interplay between often conflicting forces mediated in the last instance by the seductive ideological, political and economic power of capital.

Even to pose the question as to whether things might have been different is profoundly unhistorical. The fact is that it wasn't, and the real test of historical understanding is better examined by asking another question – namely why it was that faced with options in any given situation one particular course was followed rather than another? Real choice was quite rare, or at any rate very limited, circumscribed as it always was by the unequal balance of power between capital and labour, but if we deny absolutely the possibility of choice, then we deny too the possibility of change and must therefore conclude that the labour movement's course and development was predestined. Clearly, events like the 1926 General Strike and the experience of the third Labour government show that within the welter of debate a conscious decision was made to pursue one line rather than another, and that at such moments the consequences of such decisions displayed continuities with one kind of ideological tradition and had far-reaching repercussions for the future.

The defensive labourist tradition which usually prevailed was itself forced to change and adapt under pressure from its opponents. At its best this tradition delivered a powerful solidarity of predominantly male workers to defend hard-won gains against the encroachments of capital – the sentiment of fraternity or brotherhood expresses its essence in language and in fact. The defiant, radical and socialist tradition glimpsed both in its theory and in its practice something wider – comradeship. Comrades are brothers and sisters in struggle, black and white. Comradeship builds on fraternity but transcends it. The use of such terms – comrade or brother – is at one level simply linguistic, and would thus seem to have more significance today with our greater consciousness of the sexist and racist implications of language. There was little reflection on such semantic implications for the greater part of the period covered in this book. At a deeper level, however, the fact that such terms were used at all did indicate, consciously or unconsciously, a distinction between the defensive and the defiant traditions within the labour movement, and there is little doubt, as this book has tried to show, that the latter tradition was less afraid to include within it the 'outsiders' within the working-class – women and black people. The distinction was not rigid, merely indicative of a trend or tradition. It is for the labour movement activists of today, the products and the inheritors of the dual traditions, to interpet this, their history, as they will, and to fashion the future as they must.

Bibliography – General Works

Bellamy, J. and Saville, J. (eds.), *Dictionary of Labour Biography* (Macmillan, 7 vols., 1972–84).

Boston, Sarah, *Women Workers and the Trade Unions* (Davis-Poynter, 1980)

Cole, G.D.H. and Postgate, R. *The Common People* (Methuen University Paperbacks, 1971, first published.1938).

Fryer, P., *Staying Power – the History of Black People in Britain* (Pluto Press, 1985).

Harrison, J.F.C., *The Common People* (Croom Helm, 1984).

Hobsbawm, E.J., *Labouring Men* (Weidenfeld & Nicolson, 1968).

Hobsbawm, E.J., *Industry and Empire* (Penguin, 1969).

Hunt, E.J.H., *British Labour History 1815–1914* (Weidenfeld & Nicolson, 1981).

Lane, T., *The Union Makes Us Strong* (Arrow Books, 1974).

Lawton, R. (ed.), *The Census and Social Structure* (Cass, 1978).

Lewenhak, Sheila, *Women and Trade Unions* (Benn, 1977).

Mitchell, Juliet and Oakley, Ann, *The Rights & Wrongs of Women* (Penguin, 1977).

Mitchell, B.R., *Abstract of British Historical Statistics* (CUP, 1962).

Morton, A.L. and Tate, G., *The British Labour Movement* (Lawrence & Wishart, 1956).

Neff, Wanda, *Victorian Working Women* (Cass, 1929).

Pelling, H., *A History of British Trade Unionism* (Penguin, 1963).

Price, R., *Labour in British Society* (Routledge, 1990).

Rendall, Jane (ed.), *Equal or Different – Women's Politics 1800–1914* (Blackwell, 1987).

Roberts, Elizabeth, *Women's Work 1840–1940* (Macmillan, 1988).

Rothstein, A., *British Foreign Policy and its Critics 1830-1950* (Lawrence & Wishart, 1969).

Webb, Beatrice and Sidney, *The History of Trade Unionism* (Chiswick Press, 1898).

Williams, G. and Ramsden, R., *Ruling Britannia: A Political History of Britain 1688-1988* (Longman, 1990).

Index